EXPLORING
CATHOLIC
THEOLOGY

EXPLORING
CATHOLIC
THEOLOGY

Essays on God, Liturgy, and Evangelization

ROBERT BARRON

Baker Academic

a division of Baker Publishing Group
Grand Rapids, Michigan

Published by Baker Academic
a division of Baker Publishing Group
P.O. Box 6287, Grand Rapids, MI 49516-6287
www.bakeracademic.com

Printed in the United States of America

Library of Congress Cataloging-in-Publication Data
Barron, Robert, 1959–
   [Essays. Selections]
   Exploring Catholic theology : essays on God, liturgy, and evangelization / Robert Barron.
     pages cm
   Includes bibliographical references and index.
   ISBN 978-0-8010-9750-8 (pbk.)
   1. Catholic Church—Doctrines. I. Title.
  BX1751.3.B364 2015
  230′.2—dc23

2015007898

The following chapters were previously published and are used with permission:

"Augustine's Questions" first appeared in LOGOS: A Journal of Catholic Thought and Culture (Fall 2007), 35–54.

"The Metaphysics of Co-Inherence" first appeared in Handing on the Faith: The Church's Mission and Challenge, ed. Robert P. Imbelli (New York: Crossroad, 2006), 77–90.

"A Tale of Two Cardinals" first appeared in Chicago Studies (Summer 2008), 190–208.

"John Henry Newman Among the Postmoderns" first appeared in Newman Studies Journal (Spring 2005), 20–31.

"Biblical Interpretation and Theology" first appeared in Letter and Spirit (Spring 2009), Vol. 7, 2:173–92.

"The Liturgical Self" first appeared in The Liturgical Subject: Subject, Subjectivity, and the Human Person in Contemporary Liturgical Discussion and Critique, ed. James G. Leachman, OSB (South Bend, IN: University of Notre Dame Press, 2009), 17–31.

"From Correlation to Assimilation" first appeared in Nova et Vetera (2009), Vol. 7, 2:389–403.

"To Evangelize the Culture" first appeared in Chicago Studies (Spring 2013), 7–27.

15   16   17   18   19   20   21   7   6   5   4   3

To Monsignor Robert Sokolowski,
teacher par excellence

Contents

Foreword by Charles J. Chaput, OFM Cap.   ix

Preface   xiii

Part 1 Doctrine of God

1. Augustine's Questions: Why the Augustinian Theology of God Matters Today   3

2. Thomas Aquinas and Why the Atheists Are Right   17

3. The Metaphysics of Coinherence: A Meditation on the Essence of the Christian Message   31

4. The Trinity on Display in the Economy of Salvation: An Irenaean Meditation   45

Part 2 Theology and Philosophy

5. To See according to the Icon of Jesus Christ: Reflections on the Catholic Intellectual Tradition   63

6. A Tale of Two Cardinals: Avery Dulles's Creative Engagement with the Thought of John Henry Newman   79

7. John Henry Newman among the Postmoderns   95

8. Biblical Interpretation and Theology: A Meditation on Irenaeus, Modernity, and Vatican II   109

Part 3 Liturgy and Eucharist

9. The Eucharist as the *Telos* of the Law in the Writings of Thomas Aquinas   131

10. The Liturgical Self: An Exploration of Christian Anthropology in Light of the Liturgy   145

11. The Eucharist: Sacred Banquet, Sacrifice, Real Presence   159

Part 4 A New Evangelization

12. Why Bernard Lonergan Matters for Pastoral People   175

13. Announcing the Lordship of Jesus Christ: The Evangelical Task within Contemporary Culture   185

14. From Correlation to Assimilation: A New Model for the Church-Culture Dialogue   203

15. To Evangelize the Culture   217

Notes   233

Index   243

Foreword

Life as a bishop doesn't leave much time to spend on poetry. But a few years ago a friend loaned me a volume of Rainer Maria Rilke, and, of course, Rilke's work can be quite beautiful. In it I found some lines from his poem *Evening* that speak to the same urgent longing that drives all great theology and worship:

> Slowly now the evening changes his garments
> held for him by a rim of ancient trees;
> you gaze: and the landscape divides and leaves you
> one sinking and one rising toward the stars.
>
> And you are left, to none belonging wholly,
> not so dark as a silent house, nor quite
> so surely pledged unto eternity
> as that which grows to star and climbs the night.
>
> To you is left (unspeakably confused)
> your life, gigantic, ripening, full of fears,
> so that it, now hemmed in, now grasping all,
> is changed in you by turns to stone and stars.[1]

Philosophers and psychologists have offered many different theories about the nature of the human person. But few have captured the human condition better than Rilke does in those twelve lines. We are creatures made for heaven; but we are born of this earth. We love the beauty of this world; but we sense there is something more behind that beauty. Our longing for that "something" pulls us outside ourselves.

Striving for "something more" is part of the greatness of the human spirit, even when it involves failure and suffering. In the words of St. John Paul II, something in the artist, and by extension in all human beings, "mirrors the image of God as Creator." We have an instinct to create beauty and new life that comes from our own Creator. Yet we live in a time when, despite all our achievements, the brutality and indifference of the world have never been greater. The truth is that cruelty is *also* the work of human hands. So if we are troubled by the spirit of our age, if we really want to change the current course of our culture and challenge its guiding ideas, then we need to start with the author of that culture. That means examining man himself.

Culture exists because man exists. Men and women think, imagine, believe, and act. The mark they leave on the world is what we call culture. In a sense, that includes everything from work habits and cuisine to social manners and politics. But I want to focus in a special way on those elements of culture that we consciously choose to create—things such as art, literature, technology, music, and architecture. These things are what most people think of when they first hear the word *culture*. And that makes sense, because all of them have to do with communicating knowledge that is both useful and beautiful. The task of an architect, for example, is to translate abstract engineering problems into a visible, pleasing form; in other words, to turn disorder into order, and mathematical complexity into a public expression of strength and elegance. We are social animals. Culture is the framework within which we locate ourselves in relationship to other people, find meaning in the world, and then transmit meaning to others.

In his 1999 *Letter to Artists*, John Paul II wrote that "beauty is the visible form of the good, just as the good is the metaphysical condition of beauty." There is "an ethic, even a 'spirituality' of artistic service which contributes [to] the life and renewal of a people," because "every genuine art form, in its own way, is a path to the inmost reality of man and of the world."

He went on to say that "true art has a close affinity with the world of faith, so that even in situations where culture and the Church are far apart, art remains a kind of bridge to religious experience. . . . Art by its nature is a kind of appeal to the mystery. Even when they explore the darkest depths of the soul or the most unsettling aspects of evil, artists give voice [to] the universal desire for redemption."

Christianity is an *incarnational* religion. We believe that God became man. This has huge implications for how we live and how we think about culture. God creates the world in Genesis. He judges it as "very good" (Gen. 1:31). Later he enters the world to redeem it in the flesh and blood of his Son (John 1:14). In effect, God licenses us to know, love, and ennoble the world through the work of human genius. Our creativity as creatures is an echo of God's own creative glory. When God tells our first parents, "Be fruitful and multiply, and fill the earth and subdue it" (Gen. 1:28), he invites us to take part, in a small but powerful way, in the life of God himself.

The results of that fertility surround us. We see it in the great Christian heritage that still underpins the modern world. Anyone with an honest heart will grant that the Christian faith has inspired much of the greatest painting, music, architecture, and scholarship in human experience. For Christians, the work of the mind and the heart is a holy vocation with the power to elevate the human spirit and lead men and women toward God.

Having said all this, we still face a problem. And here it is: God has never been more absent from the Western mind than he is today. Additionally, we live in an age when almost every scientific advance seems to be matched by some increase of cruelty in our entertainment, cynicism in our politics, ignorance of the past, consumer greed, little genocides posing as "rights" such as the cult of abortion, and a basic confusion about what—if anything at all—it means to be human.

Science and technology give us power. Philosophers such as Feuerbach and Nietzsche give us the language to deny God. The result, in the words of Henri de Lubac, is not atheism but an *anti-theism* built on resentment. In seeking to destroy God, man sees himself as "overthrowing an obstacle in order to gain his freedom."[2] In contrast, the Christian understanding of human dignity claims that we are made in the image and likeness of God. Aquinas said, "In this [likeness to God] is man's greatness, in this is man's worth, and in this he excels every creature." But this grounding in God is *exactly* what the modern spirit rejects.

Of course, most people have never read Nietzsche. Nor will they. Few have even heard of Feuerbach. But they do experience the benefits of science and technology every day. And they do live inside a cocoon of marketing that constantly strokes their appetites, makes death seem remote, and pushes the really important questions—questions about meaning and morality—down into matters of private opinion.

The result is this: While many people in the developed world still claim to be religious, their faith, in the words of the Pontifical Council for Culture, is "often more a question of religious feeling than a demanding commitment to God." Religion becomes a kind of insurance policy for eternity. Too often it's little more than a convenient moral language for daily life or a form of self-medicating. And what's worse is that many people no longer have the skills, or even the desire, to understand their circumstances or to think their way out of the cocoon.

So where am I going with this brief reflection?

You have in your hands a collection of essays by one of the finest Catholic scholars working today in English. Father Robert Barron's gifts go well beyond a faithful and sophisticated intellect. They include extraordinary talents as an evangelist, teacher, writer, and master of an immense range of material from theology, to science, to liturgy, to culture and history. The church in the new millennium is blessed with many good women and men of intelligence, but very few have Father Barron's ability to shift almost effortlessly from rigorous scholarly inquiry to appealing popular explanations of Christian truth. He is a man equally at ease with Augustine, Newman, Irenaeus, and Avery Dulles, along with all the human foibles and challenges of contemporary everyday life.

Truth is beautiful, and real beauty lifts us outside of ourselves and points us toward God. One of my privileges in life is to call Father Barron a friend and to benefit, as so many of us do, from his service to the truth. These essays are the evidence of a rich mind in love with God—and by that love, enriching to us all.

+Charles J. Chaput, OFM Cap.
Archbishop of Philadelphia

Preface

When I was a philosophy student at the Catholic University of America many years ago, I had the privilege of studying under Msgr. Robert Sokolowski, one of the great contemporary interpreters of Husserl's phenomenology. Sokolowski's master idea, grounded in the two-natures doctrine of the Council of Chalcedon, is that God is noncompetitively transcendent to the world—that is to say, that God is so radically other than creation that he can enter into what he has made in a nonintrusive manner. Sokolowski construed this insight as foundational for understanding a wide variety of Catholic doctrines, including creation, divine agency, providence, the sacramental economy, the Eucharist, and so on.

As I have undertaken my own philosophical, theological, and evangelical projects, I have come back again and again to this seminal notion. I trust the essays in this collection on God make clear that the correct understanding of the nature of God is essential for both engagement with the "new" atheism and dialogue with the culture. As far as I can tell, every one of the spokespeople of the new atheism is busy swatting down the idolatrous notion that God is one important being among many, a denizen of the universe, "the biggest thing around," competing with creatures on the same ontological playing field. If they had bothered to read Thomas Aquinas with even a modicum of attention, they would have seen that the mainstream of the serious theist tradition agrees with them in rejecting such a fantastic entity. The true God, who is the sheer energy of to-be itself, is not a threat to human flourishing but precisely the ground of human flourishing. St. Irenaeus's adage "*Gloria Dei homo vivens*" expresses this notion admirably, and the image of the burning bush—a creature rendered radiant by the presence of God but not consumed—provides the scriptural foundation for it. The Sokolowski clarification also illumines the faith-culture dialogue, for it allows us to see the unconditioned reality of God not as a fussy intruder into cultural endeavors but rather as the ground and lure of those various attempts to seek the good, the true, and the beautiful. Paul Tillich commented that the Christian ought to go out to meet the culture *mit klingindem Spiel* (with fife and drum). A correct understanding of God allows for such joyful confidence.

A number of essays in this collection suggest, however, that the faith-culture conversation within Catholicism had become skewed in the years following the Second Vatican Council. A correlational method had come to dominate Catholic reflection on fundamental theology, apologetics, and evangelization, and this in turn had allowed the questions surging up from human experience to dictate Christ's position. But such a move is repugnant to the structuring logic of the New Testament, according to which Jesus, as the very Logos of God, is the *norma normans sed non normata*. Consequently, I have argued for an understanding of the faith-culture relationship along the lines suggested by John Henry Newman's theory of assimilation. The church, the body of Christ, takes to itself what it can from the cultural environment, even as it resists what it must. When Thomas Aquinas was critiqued for "diluting the wine of the Gospel with the water of Aristotle," Thomas responded, "No, rather I am turning water into wine."

Another major theme in this collection is liturgy, which is only natural for a Catholic theologian writing under the influence of the documents of Vatican II. In the magnificent text on the liturgy, *Sacrosanctum concilium*, the council fathers said that the liturgy is the "source and summit of the Christian life," implying that the Mass is the place where the "Catholic thing" is most thoroughly displayed and realized. If we want to understand who God is, who Christ is, who we are in relation to God, and what our mission and purpose might be, we look to the Eucharistic liturgy. This is, furthermore, precisely why the liturgy is so crucial in regard to the conversation with the culture. Peter Maurin and Dorothy Day, the cofounders of the Catholic Worker Movement, formulated the adage "cult cultivates the culture," implying that the central prayer of the church radiates outward and shapes the worlds of art, politics, economics, and so on. Both the rabbis of the intertestamental period and the fathers of the church interpreted Adam before the fall as the prototypical priest and the Garden of Eden as a kind of primordial temple. The right praise offered by Adam was meant to infiltrate every aspect of life, coming in time to "Edenize" the world. This is the central idea that shapes the essays on liturgy.

From the very beginning of my career as a theologian and evangelist, I have staked out a position against what I have termed "beige Catholicism," a Catholicism drained of its distinctive coloration and texture, a Catholicism concerned, above all, with accommodating itself to the surrounding culture. Similarly, I have defended the paradox that the more we emphasize the church's uniqueness and doctrinal integrity, the more effectively the church will engage and transform the culture. I have long stood against Schleiermacher's apologetic strategy in his *Speeches* of attempting to convince skeptical critics that the faith, properly understood, is perfectly congruent with their own convictions and assumptions. I believe that classical Christianity, which holds to the divinity of Jesus, the facticity of the resurrection, and the efficacy of the sacraments, actually constitutes the greatest humanism ever proposed. The church fathers summed up this idea with admirable laconicism: *Deus fit homo ut homo fieret Deus* ("God became human so that humans might become God"—sharers in the divine life). No philosophy or ideology—ancient or modern—has ever proposed a more noble and thrilling vision of what human beings might attain.

I hope that the essays in this book, most of which were either published in academic journals or delivered as public lectures, might, when read together, provide a framework to help Christians think through some of the most pressing issues of our time.

PART 1

DOCTRINE
OF GOD

1

✠

Augustine's Questions

Why the Augustinian Theology of God Matters Today

In the end, it all comes down to a correct description of God. Everything else—culture, politics, nature, human relationships—is properly understood only in the measure that ultimate reality is grasped with at least a relative adequacy. Like all the other great theologians of the tradition, St. Augustine struggled with this central question his entire life. Though his restless mind ranged over innumerable issues, from human psychology, to Roman history, to Christology and eschatology, his primary preoccupation was determining the meaning of the word *God*. And he found answers. Though he was one of the greatest searchers in the Western tradition, Augustine did not have a romantic attitude regarding the search as an end in itself. Here I think John Caputo, reading Augustine through the lens of Derridean undecidabilty, has misconstrued his subject.[1] At the end of his questioning, Augustine found a truth in which he could rest, a truth that, he was convinced, had set him free. And this was none other than the conviction that ultimate reality is the Trinitarian God revealed in the life, death, and resurrection of Jesus Christ. I believe that Augustine's questions and answers are remarkably relevant to

our time, and that finding for ourselves the truth that he found is important
not only for our personal spiritual fulfillment but also for the health of our
church and culture.

What I would like to do in this chapter is to follow, in a necessarily sketchy
way, the Augustinian path toward the understanding of God, thinking with him
and after him. And I would like to demonstrate throughout the analysis how
Augustine's questions and solutions matter for us, especially for those committed to carrying on and making effective the intellectual heritage of Catholicism.
I will undertake this task by looking at three key arguments that Augustine
had at different points in his intellectual journey, the first with the Manichees
and the Platonists when he was a comparatively young man, the second with
the Arians when he was in mid-career, and the third with the Romans as he
approached the end of his life. What emerges, as Augustine wrestles with these
various opponents, is that very distinctive understanding of ultimate reality
that we Christians call belief in the God who is Father, Son, and Holy Spirit.

Augustine's Argument with the Manichees and the Platonists

The work of St. Augustine that has exercised most fascination and given rise
to most commentary over the ages is, of course, his great autobiography, *The
Confessions*. Relying implicitly on the double sense of the Latin term *confessio*,
Augustine uses this text as a means both to confess his sins and to profess his
praise of God. In fact, those two moves are, in his mind, inextricably linked:
the more he becomes aware of his sins, both intellectual and moral, the more
he is able to acknowledge and thank the true God—and vice versa. Nowhere
is this link between contrition and praise more clearly on display than in the
seventh book of *The Confessions*. In this densely textured section of his autobiography, Augustine recounts the tortuous process by which he wriggled
free from the influence of Manichaeism, the dualist, quasi-Gnostic system
of which he had been, for nine years, a faithful adept. The principal allure of
Manichaeism—both in Augustine's day and in ours—is the simple and elegant
way that it handles the problem of evil. If the world is, at the most basic level,
a struggle between a force of good and a force of evil, then we are not obliged
to blame God for suffering. Instead, we should simply side with him in his
just and worthwhile enterprise, even as we hate the principle responsible for
evil. Manichaeism solves the problem of theodicy by dissolving it.

Now what is the conception of God associated with this Manichaean philosophy? It would not be quite right to say, as most popular accounts have it,
that God is, on the Manichaean reading, purely spiritual, set radically apart

from the realm of matter. Here is how Augustine expresses the theory: "I thought of you as a vast reality spread throughout space in every direction: I thought that you penetrated the whole mass of the earth and immense, unbounded spaces beyond it on all sides, that earth, sky, and all things were full of you."[2] What is being described here is a kind of materialistic panentheism, God as a force or power running through and uniting all material creation. This view of God is extremely old and remarkably enduring. We can find versions of it in ancient Stoicism, in the peculiarly modern metaphysics of Spinoza, as well as in the mystical religious philosophy of Friedrich Schleiermacher.

And we can very clearly discern it in contemporary conceptions of God, mediated to us by the popular culture. In his many books and especially in his series of interviews with the journalist Bill Moyers, the comparative mythologist Joseph Campbell expressed a notion of God remarkably similar to the one outlined at the beginning of book seven of *The Confessions*. When asked by Moyers whether he believed in a personal God, Campbell replied "No," and when pressed to elaborate, he said, "I think that God is the 'transcendent ground or energy in itself.'"[3] He explained, furthermore, that the Hindu meditative exercise of pronouncing the syllable "Om" is nothing other than an attempt to harmonize with this fundamental power.[4] Needless to say, this conception of God has had a massive influence on the development of various "New Age" philosophies and spiritualities. Joseph Campbell exercised perhaps his most pervasive influence through the efforts of his disciple, the filmmaker George Lucas. In many ways, the *Star Wars* movies are, by Lucas's own admission, an elaborate narrative and pictorial representation of the worldview espoused by Campbell. And nowhere is this clearer than in the master idea of the *Star Wars* religion, namely, the Force. Borrowing consciously from the Catholic liturgy, Lucas's *Star Wars* characters regularly greet one another with the phrase "May the Force be with you." It becomes eminently clear in the course of the narrative that the Force is a sort of energy field that runs through and unites all material things and that it can be exploited in either a positive or negative direction, appearing thereby as either dark or light. Here the connection to Manichaeism is quite clear. The young Augustine was devoted to roughly the same idea of God that adepts of the New Age find amenable today: a notion of God as impersonal, intimately tied to the material world, and manipulable through the human will.

Now this idea might delight *Star Wars* aficionados, but the more he considered it, the more it puzzled and bothered Augustine, for it seemed sorely inadequate to the perfection of God. If God were a kind of quintessential physical energy, then it would appear that he is divisible and measurable. Here is the way Augustine expressed his puzzlement: "A larger part of the earth would contain a larger portion of you, and a smaller a lesser portion, and all things would be full of you in such a way that an elephant's body would contain a larger amount of you than a sparrow's."[5] Anything as quantifiable and worldly as that, he concluded, couldn't possibly be the perfect One. But when he tried to think of God as utterly perfect, thoroughly good, he faced the dilemma of explaining the provenance of evil. If God is the creator of all things and God is infinitely good, there should be no evil. And blaming evil on the free will of angels and men doesn't solve the problem; it only postpones it, for God is himself the author of the will. Similarly, claiming that corruption flows from a flaw in nature only leads us to wonder how the utterly good Creator could have given rise to a flawed nature.

And so he found himself stuck. "Such thoughts as these was I turning over in my miserable soul, weighed down as it was by the gnawing anxieties that flowed from my fear that death might overtake me before I had found the truth."[6] And then God showed him a way out. "You provided me with some books by the Platonists, translated from Greek into Latin."[7] These pivotal texts were most likely treatises by Plotinus and his secretary Porphyry wherein was exposed the great middle Platonic theory of the One and its emanations. According to this philosophy, the immense, unknowable, unsurpassable power of the One gave rise by an automatic emanation to a second hypostasis, Intellect, in which are found all the forms that Plato spoke of. Then, by a further emanation, Soul separated itself from Intellect, and from Soul came the lower regions of mutable materiality. The goal of the spiritual life, on this reading, was the gradual escape from the material and ascension through the levels of the spiritual emanations until reaching the point of union with the One, becoming, in Plotinus's famous phrase, "alone with the Alone." This peculiar theory seemed so attractive to the young Augustine precisely because it extricated him from the horns of the dilemma on which he had been stuck. By articulating God as the distant and perfect One, it allowed Augustine to think of ultimate reality apart from materialistic and this-worldly categories. Further, by removing God from this obviously ambiguous realm through a series of ontological buffers, it allowed Augustine to see how God is not directly implicated in evil. He could breathe easy again.

Just as the quasi-Gnostic Manichaean notion of God finds a contemporary resonance, so this Plotinian doctrine remains, *mutatis mutandis*, as an intellectual option on the table today. In the early modern period, just after the Reformation, a view of God emerged that was neither classical theism nor pantheism nor panentheism but rather Deism, that is to say, the construal of God as the creator and designer of the world, who exists at a remove, both spatial and chronological, from the world that he has ordered. Serious

intellectual players—from Locke and Leibniz to Newton and Benjamin Franklin—entertained some version of Deism, and many religious people today,
especially in the West, hold to it in one form or another. It still exercises the
charm that beguiled the youthful Augustine, the capacity to account for the
godliness of God and, at the same time, to keep God free from too much
involvement with the messiness and ambiguity of the world. An extremely
important side effect of Deism—and another reason for its attractiveness—is
the opening up of a properly secular realm, that is to say, a dimension of being
that remains essentially untouched by God. This secular space permits people
to be vaguely religious, even as they keep God far away from the arena where
they actually live, work, and make moral decisions.

Though it has, in its various forms, intrigued people over the ages, this
Plotinian doctrine convinced Augustine only for a short time. He certainly
tried to follow the Platonic exercises designed to liberate him from matter
and facilitate the ascent through the emanations to the One, but he never
succeeded in affecting closeness with Plotinus's God. Though the intellectual
idea proposed by Plotinus was clearer and truer than that entertained by the
Manichees, it didn't seem to move Augustine appreciably closer to God. "I
knew myself to be far away from you in a region of unlikeness."[8] Augustine
realized that to solve the problem of evil by distancing God from the world is
to create a far greater problem: the alienation of the seeker from the God that
he desires. And he knew that to preserve the godliness of God by sequestering
him in a zone of pure transcendence is to strand the religious person in the
disenchanted space of secularity, the "region of unlikeness." So Plotinianism,
that proto-Deism, would not do.

What rescued Augustine at this anxious stage of his quest was not something
that he read in the books of the Platonists but rather something that he found
in a letter written by the first-century rabbi Saul, who had become, through
an extraordinary experience of conversion, the Christian apostle Paul. In his
letter to the tiny Christian community at Philippi, Paul wrote this concerning
Jesus: "Though he was in the form of God, [Jesus] did not count equality
with God a thing to be grasped, but emptied himself, taking the form of a
servant, being born in the likeness of men" (Phil. 2:6–7). While remaining in
the form of God, which is to say, utterly unlike any worldly thing, the Logos,
Paul maintained, emptied himself out of love and entered radically into the
world. In the wake of reading Paul, a question grew in Augustine's mind—
namely, who precisely is the God capable of such a feat, a God who retains
his transcendence and perfection (the form of God) even as he displays, in
the most dramatic way possible, his immanence? He cannot be the imperfect
God of the Manichees, and he cannot be the distant God of the Platonists.

He must be a God who can become a creature without compromising his own divinity or the integrity of the creature he becomes, and this means he must be the creator of all things. If God were a being in or alongside the universe, he would be, necessarily, in competition with other worldly objects. There is a mutual exclusivity about worldly natures, one thing maintaining its onto-logical integrity only in the measure that it is *not* anything else.[9] Therefore, if God is capable of true incarnation—becoming a creature without ceasing to be himself—then God cannot be a worldly nature, a thing, one being among many, even the supreme being. God must be other but, if I can put it this way, *otherly* other, enjoying a transcendence that is not contrastive to the world. Nicholas of Cusa would express this notion many centuries after Augustine by saying that God, while absolutely other, is the *non-aliud*, the "non-other."

What Augustine found, through Paul, was a way of combining and over-coming the tension between the Manichees and the Platonists. He found the creator God who, in his perfection and godliness, is *not* the world and who, in his love, becomes one with the world. He found, in a word, the God of Jesus Christ.

Augustine's Argument with the Arians

We now turn to from *The Confessions* to the *De Trinitate*, a doctrinal tour de force that preoccupied Augustine for nearly twenty years. Here, as always, the central concern is a correct description of God. Augustine wants to make plain that the God of creation and incarnation, whom he described in book seven of *The Confessions*, is also the Trinitarian God, the God whose very unity is constituted by a set of relations. The best-known sections of the *De Trinitate* are undoubtedly the eighth and ninth books, wherein Augustine lays out his psychological analogies for the Trinitarian persons: mind, self-knowledge, and self-love. But I would like to concentrate on an earlier section of the great opus, specifically the fifth book, where Augustine takes on what he considers a very serious challenge to the orthodox teaching concerning the Trinity. The Arian heresy, which arose in the early fourth century, was debated at a number of local synods in Egypt and then definitively addressed and condemned at the Council of Nicaea in 325. Nevertheless, it continued to exert a strong influence in both the East and the West, drawing under its sway any number of bishops and theologians. Accordingly, by Augustine's time, there had arisen a sophisti-cated intellectual tradition surrounding the central claim of Arian Christology that the Logos present in Jesus was not fully divine but rather the highest of creatures. And Augustine feels that, before he enters into a detailed account of the Trinity, he must wrestle with a pointed argument that emerges from that tradition. This debate is the centerpiece of book five of the *De Trinitate*.

The book begins with an extraordinary observation: "From now on I will be attempting to say things that cannot altogether be said as they are thought by a man—at least as they are thought by me."[10] Augustine knows that he is entering that paradoxical space where there is a sharp distinction between—to use Aquinas's terms—the *res significata* and the *modus significandi*, between the thing to be signified and the manner in which it is signified. He will say what he takes to be accurate things about God, but he won't know quite what he means when he says them. When responding to the Arians, Augustine will be compelled to move outside ordinary modes of discourse to modulate into a new metaphysical key precisely because he will be speaking of the God who is not a being in the world, not one thing among many.

The argument proper begins with the observation that God is a substance or essence, indeed the fullness of being, since he says of himself in Exodus 3:14, "I AM WHO I AM." Now, according to classical philosophy, substances admit of accidents, that is, modifications and nonessential attributes, through which and because of which they are capable of change. But God, who is absolute, simple, and unchanging in his reality, cannot admit of such features. With this basic principle, Platonists, orthodox Christians, and Arians would be in agreement. But on the basis of the divine simplicity, the Arians forwarded an objection to Trinitarian language that Augustine himself qualified as "cunning and ingenious."[11] Orthodoxy, they said, speaks incoherently, for it characterizes the Father as unbegotten and the Son as begotten, even as it confirms that the Father and Son are of the same substance. But this kind of attribution of mutually exclusive qualities—continues the argument—is possible only if one is referring to accidental modifications of a substance. Thus I can coherently say that I am wearing a black shirt and wearing a white shirt, if I am referring to time-conditioned accidents: a black shirt on Monday, a white shirt on Tuesday. But I cannot say, without contradiction, that I am a human being and an angel, since those terms describe not accidents but substance. But, as both the Arians and the orthodox agree, there are no accidents in God. Therefore, it seems to follow that these terms—"begotten" and "unbegotten," "Father" and "Son"—must refer to different substances, and this is precisely the Arian position. The Son, begotten of the Father, they maintained, is a creature, a being separate from the Creator. Thus it appears as though the Arian position is logically coherent, whereas orthodox theology is again caught on the horns of a dilemma.

What does Augustine do? Compelled by the exigencies of revelation and the pointedness of this objection, he searches for a metaphysical category beyond the pair of substance and accident. The Arians have convinced him not that Trinitarian language is incoherent but that whatever these terms *Father* and *Son* refer to must be something other than substance and other than accident. Here's the way that Augustine states it: "The negation of accidental predication of God does not mean that everything said of him is said substance-wise."[12] At this point he is speaking, in terms of classical metaphysics, so much nonsense, and he knows it. What he implies is that the terms that properly describe worldly things cannot adequately describe the one who is the creator of the world and therefore outside of the nexus of conditioned things. From the data of revelation, Augustine knows that the Father is spoken of only in relation to the Son (he is the one from whom the Son comes forth and the one who sent the Son) and the Son is described only in relation to the Father (as the recipient of that begetting and that sending). Both Father and Son are constituted, as it were, *ad aliquid*, in relation to one another. It would be quite impossible to speak of the Father in abstraction from the Son and vice versa. At the same time, the revealed Scriptures also teach that neither Father nor Son can be described as subject to accidental modification, since both are clearly described as divine. "In the beginning was the Word, and the Word was with God, and the Word was God" (John 1:1). Therefore, both are *ad aliquid*, yet without change, modification, or evolution. "Since the Father is only called so because he has a Son, and the Son is only called so because he has a Father, these things are not said substance-wise, as neither is said with reference to itself. . . . Nor are they said modification-wise, because what is signified by calling them Father and Son belongs to them eternally and unchangeably."[13]

So what precisely are these strange things, these relational substances, these substantial relations, unlike anything in creation? Following the lead of the tradition, Augustine chooses to call them "persons," but he is well aware of the problem inherent in this kind of appellation. To call the Father, Son, and Holy Spirit *persons* is to run the risk of giving the false impression that they are three separate beings, three substances standing over against one another, like three human persons meeting one another across a table. So why use this highly ambiguous term? Augustine's answer constitutes, I think, one of the great moments in the history of negative theology: "We call them 'persons' not in order to say precisely what they are, but in order not to be reduced to silence."[14] In other words, we give them this name so that we have something to say when we are asked what they are. Centuries after Augustine, St. Anselm would memorably call the Trinitarian persons *nescio quid*, "I don't know what." And Thomas Aquinas would use Zen-like language, describing them as "subsistent relations."

Now to be fair, a critic might wonder at this point how all of this is anything but logic-chopping, special pleading, and obfuscation. The language that Augustine formulates to hold off the Arian criticism is a gesture in the direction of something quite revolutionary, namely, that to be God is to be a community of relationality. This peculiar set of terms indicates that the ground of existence, the Creator of all things, is a coinherent *communio* of three persons, each one constituted by its relation to the other two. In his *Introduction to Christianity*, Joseph Ratzinger, later Pope Benedict XVI, commented that the Trinitarian formula implies that the relative has been absolutized, thereby turning both ancient and modern philosophy on their heads.[15] In most forms of metaphysics, both ancient and modern, and in accord with common sense, substance is privileged over relationship, the latter viewed as a modification of the former. On Aristotle's reading, for example, substance comes first, since substance coincides with the basic category of being, and relationships, derivative of substance, come definitively second. But in light of the Trinitarian formula, we see something completely different: at the most fundamental level of existence, substance and relationship utterly coincide. To be is to be in rapport with another, for the Father is the Father only in relation to the Son, the Son is the Son only in relation to the Father, and the Holy Spirit is nothing but the relation between the Father and the Son. Through and through, the divine reality *is* a communion of love. God is like a harmony or a musical chord. Though it is impossible to think three things or objects together as one, without falling into contradiction, it is altogether possible to think three notes together as one, perhaps the note A played in three different octaves. This we find to be not contradictory but delightful and congruent. And so the three "persons" of the Trinity, the three subsistent relations, might be construed as a musical pattern.

Now even if we have followed Augustine's argument to this point and find it convincing as an answer to the Arian objection, we might perhaps still wonder why this clarification matters for us today. As I've already hinted, the modern world is very much under the sway of a substantialist notion of reality, the conviction that individual things are the basic constituents of being. We can find this individualist and antagonistic ontology in Leibniz's monadology, Kant's account of the moral life, and Nietzsche's doctrine that plays of power are metaphysically basic. We can also discern it in the assumptions that undergird the political life in most of Western culture, including and especially in the United States. The principal philosophical figure among the founding fathers of this nation was Thomas Jefferson, and the opening paragraphs of the Declaration of Independence are the clearest articulation of Jefferson's perspective. Society, we hear, is not natural but artificial, a

construct of individuals whose pursuit of happiness lands them in the untenable position of violating one another's rights. Government is instituted,
we are further instructed, so as to secure and protect these threatened rights.
The chief influence on Jefferson's political philosophy was, of course, John
Locke, but behind Locke stood the pivotal figure of Thomas Hobbes, the first
great philosopher to dissent from the classical position that human beings are,
by nature, social animals. Hobbes taught that we are, by nature, not social
but antagonistic, since we are all striving as fully as possible to achieve our
self-interested ends. This condition results in the war of all against all, the
terrible state of nature that Hobbes famously described as "nasty, brutish,
and short." The fear of violent death is what compels individuals, very much
against their wills, to enter into a social contract and institute government.
Though somewhat softened and nuanced, this same basic form is easily dis-
cernible in the ruminations of Jefferson.

My point is this: the Hobbesian account of politics rests upon the assumption of the primacy—both chronological and ontological—of the individual
person over the community. Modern politics, like classical metaphysics, is
thus rooted in the conviction that substance trumps relationship. What would
political philosophy look like were the Trinitarian assumption that relationship is ontologically basic to hold sway? Would social contract theories not
have to give way to accounts of society that are far more communitarian and
mystical? And would the sovereign individual not have to cede to the self
constituted precisely by a set of relationships with others? Would not society,
in a word, have to be rethought precisely as an *imago Trinitatis*?

Augustine's Argument with the Romans

The two arguments that we have been considering led to a third, one that
preoccupied Augustine toward the end of his life and that found expression in
the third of his masterpieces, *The City of God*. As is well known, Augustine
composed this work in order to counter the charges made after the sack of
Rome in 410 that the empire had collapsed because of the nefarious influence
of Christianity. His answer was, in a nutshell, that Rome fell not because
of its adoption of Christian thought and practice but because of decidedly
un-Christian vices buried deep within its own body politic. What strikes the
modern reader of *The City of God* most immediately perhaps is Augustine's
adamant refusal to dialogue with representatives of the polity of Rome. In so
many of the theological engagements with culture today, a correlationist model
holds sway, that is to say, the establishment of a correspondence between the

concerns and questions of the secular society on the one hand and the data contained in revelation and tradition on the other. But Augustine's style is not the least correlationist or accommodationist. He is not looking for a way to make the social theory of Rome compatible with an interiorized Christian piety; rather, he is attempting to show that what passes for justice and right social order in Rome is in fact fraudulent and that the church alone represents the right political vision.[16]

Though it was seen by its own apologists as the paragon of law and justice, Rome is in fact nothing but a collectivity of thieves. The reason is that Roman order is based upon self-love, the fundamental principle of what Augustine calls the *civitas terrena*, the earthly city or the city of man. His argument for this extraordinary—and at the time deeply counterintuitive—claim has a theological phase and a political phase. Let us consider first the theological dimension. Many contemporary readers of *The City of God* find puzzling the amount of time and space that Augustine devotes to the critique of the Roman gods and goddesses and of Roman practices of worship. In point of fact this critical analysis is decisive to his overall argument, for Augustine is convinced that political rectitude follows as a direct consequence of right religion. Rome is an ersatz political order precisely because it indulges in the worship of false deities. Even the most casual survey of Roman mythology and literature reveals that the gods whom Rome reverenced were, from a moral standpoint, highly questionable. According to the accounts of their own devotees, they engaged in every sort of immoral activity from rivalry, pettiness, and jealousy to backstabbing and outright warfare. They seemed hardly gods at all but projections of the worst elements of human beings. Augustine in fact does not hesitate to characterize them as the demons spoken of in the Scriptures.[17] But the point is this: to discover what a society worships is to discover what it values most highly, seeks to imitate, and considers ontologically basic. Rome's worship of violent and antagonistic gods thus gives away the game. Romans must believe that proper social order is a declension of the morally disreputable social order of the Olympian deities, and this means that their justice is, despite its sterling reputation, phony.

And from this theological analysis flows the properly political phase of Augustine's anti-Roman argument. Rome is a social order based upon the *libido dominandi*, the lust to dominate, which is so characteristic of the gods that Rome honors.[18] This particular determination of Roman society can be easily discerned in the founding myth of Romulus and Remus. The twin boys, who were tellingly nursed by a wolf, came into conflict soon after establishing the new city, and Romulus killed his brother, thus establishing his dominance. The political lesson implied in this story is that order is a function of violence and conquest. And this lesson, on Augustine's reading, provided the leitmotif for all of Roman history. He remarks that the door to the temple of Mars—the god of war—has been open throughout the Roman centuries, proving that the "justice" of Rome is not the *tranquillitas ordinis* but a certain quietude born of fear. The *libido dominandi* of the gods and goddesses became the *libido dominandi* of the Roman political authorities, bad worship conducing to bad government. It was due, Augustine argues, to the fundamental injustice of this Roman pseudo-order that the empire dissolved and was overrun.

What Augustine proposes over against the Roman *ordo* is a different form of worship and a different form of government. Christians believe not in the dysfunctional and demonic gods of paganism but rather in the one God of creation, the power who brings the whole of the universe into being *ex nihilo*. In the pagan myths, order comes through a primal act of violence and conquest: Saturn devouring his children, Jupiter conquering and killing his father and then parceling out earth, sea, and sky to his pliant siblings. But there is none of this in the Christian account, according to which God, who has no need of the world, brings the whole of creation into being from nothing.[19] This means that God does not wrestle anything outside of himself into submission or subject it to conquest, for there is, quite literally, nothing upon which God could impose himself. Rather, in a sheerly generous and nonviolent act, God brings the universe into existence, gifting it with a participation in his own act of existence. In a word, *ordo* comes through peace. Augustine insists that when such a God is worshiped, a fundamentally different form of social order comes into existence, one based upon connection, compassion, forgiveness, and nonviolence. This other city, this alternative form of political arrangement, is the *civitas Dei* that figures in the title of Augustine's great work. It is an earthly community that mirrors the heavenly *communio* of the angels and saints, gathered in worship around the throne of God.

Augustine affects a brilliant correlation between the founding myth of Romulus and Remus and the biblical story of Cain and Abel. In the scriptural account, Cain in his jealousy slays his own brother and becomes, in a fascinating detail, the founder of cities, thus a blood brother of Romulus. But whereas Romulus is the hero of the Roman story, Cain is cursed in the biblical account. Both Romulus and Cain are, through their violence, progenitors of the earthly city, but the Bible is under no illusion that that way of arrangement is anything but criminal and unjust. In the Roman myths, the gods sanction the primal violence; in the biblical story, God sides with the murdered victim.[20] Just before commencing his public ministry, Jesus confronts the devil in the wilderness. In Matthew's version of this story, the climactic temptation has to do with power. In one glance, the devil shows Jesus all the kingdoms of the world in their splendor and offers them to him, specifying that they are his to give precisely because they belong to him. That frank biblical assessment of the nature of worldly power is perfectly in line with the story of Cain and utterly antipathetic to Rome's self-congratulatory conviction that it is the paragon of justice.

Now Augustine's metaphysical vision of creation and participation held sway in the Christian thought world through the high Middle Ages and was given especially convincing expression by Thomas Aquinas in the thirteenth century. Thomas saw creatures as intimately connected to one another through their common connection to the creator God. As the myriad elements in a Gothic rose window are linked to one another and to the center by the integrity of the design, so all creatures are united to one another by their shared provenance from the God who creates *ex nihilo*. This integrated vision begins to come apart through the metaphysical and epistemological adjustments proposed by Duns Scotus and William of Occam in the later Middle Ages. Turning from Aquinas's analogical conception (the epistemological correlate to a participation metaphysics), they opted for a univocal construal of the term *being*, thus placing God and creatures under the same ontological umbrella. And this move turned God into one being—however supreme—among many, thereby effectively severing the links between God and creatures and hence among creatures themselves. No longer joined ontologically by the most intimate bonds, creatures and God had to negotiate their relationship artificially and extrinsically, by means of law. That this theological move had a political counterpart in social contract theories of modernity should not, if we are careful Augustinians, surprise us in the least.

Does this final Augustinian argument have a resonance today? Many contemporary theologians—Stanley Hauerwas, John Milbank, Graham Ward, and Michael Baxter, to name just a few—hold that Augustine's disagreement with Rome remains extremely instructive in regard to our engagements, both theological and political. They think that we have largely lost sight of the properly subversive quality of the biblical revelation that God is love and that all creatures exist in the measure that they participate in the divine love. The modern nation-state, they tend to argue, resting as it does on fundamentally Hobbesian foundations, grows up out of a metaphysical vision at odds with that of authentic Christianity. And one of the principal tragedies of our time, they continue, is the co-opting and positioning of Christianity by the nation-state. Conforming to the banalities of a civil religion, the Christian churches lose their prophetic edge and ratify a fundamentally Deist conception of God and an antagonistic understanding of social relations.

And what the churches should be doing is following the program laid out in *The City of God*, namely, the identification of the contemporary political order as antithetical to the gospel. And, on a more practical level, they should be following the example of Martin Luther King Jr. in this country and John Paul II in Poland. Both of those prophetic figures refused the easy option of correlation and accommodation and, from a gospel perspective, named the false theologies that undergirded the unjust social practices against which they fought. John Paul II was consistently careful to root his critique of Communism in an alternative vision of reality, a metaphysics of love and coinherence. Precisely because God is who he is, the social practices of Communism are dehumanizing. How thoroughly Augustinian, by the way, was John Paul's practice of situating the celebration of the liturgy at the heart of the project of social critique. Both Augustine and John Paul knew that right politics follows from right worship.

Conclusion

Let me bring this essay to a close with just a couple simple remarks. First, as John Henry Newman knew, the theological principle is basic to a healthy Christianity.[21] This means that a properly functioning Catholicism is a thinking religion. Catholics are not fideists; instead, they stubbornly reflect upon the data of revelation, drawing out their implications and seeing their interrelationships. They take as their model the Virgin Mary, who did not simply observe the extraordinary events of revelation but rather "turned them over in her heart, treasuring them." Throughout his long life, Augustine thought about God, asking the hard questions, pursuing puzzles and conundrums that would not have occurred to the average believer. And in the process he produced a subtle, beautiful, and finally revolutionary theology of God. So those of us today who are committed to the propagation of the Catholic tradition in and for the wider society should take Augustine's restless intelligence as a model.

Second and related, ideas have consequences. Over the centuries, so-called pragmatists have opined that abstractions have little to do with the real world. To be sure, they have to find effective mediators, but abstract ideas are practically the engine of historical change. The most potent idea of all, of course, is that of God, and St. Augustine perceived that the correct articulation of that notion can and must have far-reaching practical implications. We, the present-day keepers of the compelling Catholic understanding of God, should share that Augustinian perception.

2

✠

Thomas Aquinas and Why the Atheists Are Right

The great English Dominican theologian Herbert McCabe engaged a number of atheists in the course of his career as a public intellectual. Typically, he would allow his interlocutors to make their opening statements, detailing why they didn't believe in God. McCabe would respond, "I completely agree with you." Similarly, the Anglican New Testament scholar N. T. Wright tells of an encounter he had with a young undergraduate when Wright was chaplain at Oxford. The freshman said, "Chaplain, don't expect to see a lot of me; I don't believe in God." Wright asked him what he meant by God, and upon hearing the young man's account, he responded, "Son, I can assure you that I don't believe in that God either."

Like McCabe and Wright, I have always found atheists of all stripes helpful, both spiritually and theologically, precisely in the measure that they clarify what the true God is not. They expose and implicitly undermine new forms of idolatry. One of the clearest in this regard is one of the fathers of modern atheism, Ludwig Feuerbach, who famously held that God is a projection of man's idealized self-understanding—which is to say, a simulacrum of God made in the image of man—precisely what the Bible would have called an idol.

The only thing particularly "new" about the new atheism is its nastiness. Christopher Hitchens and Richard Dawkins (who Terry Eagleton famously combined as "Ditchkins"), along with Sam Harris, Daniel Dennett, and their numerous disciples, have borrowed many of the intellectual insights of Feuerbach, Marx, Freud, Sartre, and Nietzsche, but what they've added is a dismissive contempt for religion and religious people. Whereas Nietzsche and Sartre gave the impression that they were in a battle with a pretty serious opponent, Ditchkins and company imply that they are exposing the delusions of an idiot child. Nevertheless they serve, for our generation, their essentially prophetic function of displaying idolatry. And this is continually needed, since, as St. John of the Cross suggested, the mind is an idol-making machine.

The Competitive God of the New Atheists

There is so much we could say about the ruminations of the new atheists, so many ways that we could engage them: their obsession with biblical literalism; their deep concern about religion in relation to violence; their conviction that religion is irreconcilable with modern science, precisely because it is a form of primitive, outmoded science; their conviction that faith poisons the minds of the young, and so on. But I want to draw attention to one theme that I take to be basic, one misunderstanding that conditions everything else that they discuss, namely, the view that God is a being among many, one cause amid the range of contingent causes, a reality in the world whose existence or nonexistence can be determined through rational (for them, scientific) investigation.

The late Christopher Hitchens delights in recounting the famous tale of the encounter between the emperor Napoleon and the French scientist Pierre-Simon Laplace, the author of *Celestial Mechanics*. Having heard Laplace's exposition on the movement of the planets within the solar system, Napoleon reportedly asked why the figure of God did not appear in Laplace's schema—to which the scientist laconically responded, "*Je n'ai pas besoin de cette hypothèse*" (I have no need of that hypothesis).[1] The assumption of both Napoleon and Laplace was, apparently, that God is rightly understood as one of the mechanical causes that contributes to the motion of the planets. Perhaps he was the largest and most important cause, but still one among many. Though Napoleon seemed to favor the existence of such a cause and Laplace to deny it, both thought of God as fundamentally like other worldly agents. We find something very similar in Richard Dawkins's *The God Delusion*. Dismissing Stephen Jay Gould's position that religion and science deal with qualitatively different dimensions of reality (i.e., NOMA: Non-Overlapping Magisteria), Dawkins opines that science can and must adjudicate the question of God's existence. Turning certain cosmological questions that seem to pass beyond the province of the sciences over to the chaplain makes as much sense as turning them over to "the chef or the gardener."[2]

Here is how Dawkins characterizes the religious position: "The God-Hypothesis suggests that the reality we inhabit also contains a supernatural agent who designed the universe and even intervenes in it with miracles."[3] And this is precisely why Dawkins can compare belief in God to belief in "the Flying Spaghetti Monster," a fantastical imaginary being for whom there is not a trace of physical evidence. Here he simply mimics his master Bertrand Russell, who famously speculated that it is as impossible to prove the nonexistence of God as to demonstrate the nonexistence of a china teapot orbiting the sun between earth and Mars. What is so telling about both analogies, again, is that God is being compared to some agent or entity within the universe and operating alongside other agents and entities. Dawkins concludes, on the basis of this understanding of the divine, that God's nonexistence can be demonstrated to a very high degree of probability. If Occam's great principle holds, then God is not required, since we can explain most if not all worldly phenomena by appealing to worldly causes. "*Je n'ai pas besoin de cette hypothèse.*"

This way of approaching God is on particularly clear display in the manner in which the new atheists assess the traditional arguments for God's existence. Both Hitchens and Dawkins dismiss Thomas Aquinas's arguments in favor of a first mover or uncaused cause with the cavalier question, "Well then, what caused God?" The observation proves, of course, that neither thinker has grasped the nettle of the argument, but for our present purposes, it shows that both persist in thinking of God as one more cause in a chain of contingent causes. We see it as well in their preoccupation with "the God of the gaps." All the new atheists revel in what they take to be religion's instinctive but pathetic retreat into the gaps in present-day scientific accounts of reality. With some justification, they characterize "intelligent design" theory as just this sort of illegitimate move. Because we can't discern a clear and uninterrupted path by which certain living forms today evolved from lower forms, we assert, "God did it." But what will happen to God so construed as the fossil gap closes or as our imaginations enable us to picture the evolutionary process more exactly?

Dawkins laments the fact that while scientists try to clear up mystification, theologians exult in it, playing temporarily in the darkness that science will eventually illumine. Once more, God is being thought of as a competing cause, ontologically at the same level as conventional, empirically verifiable causes. Now the new atheists are far from reluctant to extrapolate from this metaphysical conception of God to what they take to be deeply disturbing implications for human flourishing. Representing as they do a supreme being, competitive with other causes and brooding over the human project, the religions foster a "police state" in which "all aspects of the private and public life must be submitted to a permanent higher supervision."[4] "God" watches and governs the world from the outside and imposes his rules on a recalcitrant human freedom. Hitchens seems to accept Sartre's famous syllogism to the effect that if God exists, I cannot be free; but I am free, therefore God does not exist. This explains, Hitchens believes, why religion and political totalitarianism are usually closely allied.

Thomas Aquinas's Simple God

I maintain that the exertions of the new atheists in regard to God are, for the most part, an exercise in knocking down a not-very-impressive straw God. A God who dwells in or alongside the cosmos, whose existence or nonexistence could be determined through scientific investigation, who might himself be susceptible of causal influence, who bears even the slightest resemblance to a Flying Spaghetti Monster, and who presides over the human project in the manner of Kim Jong Il presiding over Korea, is an idol of the worst type.

And Thomas Aquinas can help us to see this. One of the most remarkable features of Thomas's doctrine of God is its agnosticism. In the prologue to question three in the first part of the *Summa theologiae*, which deals with the divine simplicity, Thomas famously comments, "Since we are not able to know what God is, only what God is not, we are not able to consider in regard to God how he is, but rather how he is not."[5] Though we say many things about God, we're not entirely sure what we mean when we say them. The Fourth Council of the Lateran taught that, in regard to our speech concerning God, "*in tanta similitudine, maior dissimilitude*" (in however great a similitude, there is an even greater dissimilitude). Thomas picked up on this in making his distinction between the *res significata* and the *modus significandi* (the thing signified and the manner of signifying).

This is why Thomas prefers the negative path when speaking of God, taking away from the concept of God whatever belongs to creatureliness. Though, for instance, we can speak positively enough of God's goodness, we don't really know what we mean when we use that term. And to say that God is eternal is tantamount to saying he is not in time; to say that he is a spirit is to say that he is not marked by matter. But what any of these terms signal positively remains quite mysterious. What precisely does it mean to be outside time? No one here below can possibly know. What precisely is it like not to be material? No one whose mind and senses are ordered to the realm of physical things can ever really grasp. The parables of Jesus can be read under this rubric. We say, quite correctly, that God is just, but in light of the parable of the vineyard owner who pays the same wage to those whom he hired at different times of the day, we find our conventional view of justice confounded. We say, quite correctly, that God is compassionate, but in the light of the parable of the prodigal son, we realize the inadequacy of even our most generous interpretation of compassion.

If we press the question, wondering precisely why the God of the Bible remains so mysterious, so resistant to description and nomination ("Truly, you are a God who hides yourself"), the answer lies in the opening line of the book of Genesis: "In the beginning, God created the heavens and the earth." Because God brought the whole of the finite universe into existence, God cannot be an ingredient within the universe; he must be other in a way that transcends any and all modes of otherness discoverable within creation. Spatial distance; modal diversity; differences in grade, degree, kind, species; variations in speed, temperature, or density—none of these can begin to in-dicate the radicality of the difference that obtains between God and anything that God has made. In Kathryn Tanner's language, God is not simply other; he is "otherly other."[6] To put it still another way, God's transcendence must be construed in such a manner that it precludes the possibility of contrast in the ordinary acceptance of the term. Nicholas of Cusa caught this when he commented that God, though radically not the world, still must be seen as the *non-aliud*, the "non-other."

This is why Thomas typically refers to God not as *ens summum* (highest being) but rather as *ipsum esse subsistens* (the sheer act of to-be itself). If God were the highest being, then he could, in principle, be categorized alongside other beings. *Ipsum esse*, however, is not the most powerful and impressive instance of the genus "being." In fact, Thomas specifies that God cannot be placed in any genus, even that of being! He is, but not in the manner that creatures are—just the contrary. Creatures are analogues of God's essentially mysterious modality of existence. The technical term that Aquinas typically uses to signal this unique quality of the divine manner of being is *simplicitas* (simplicity). By this he means that in God there is no distinction between essence and existence, a distinction that, perforce, obtains in anything that God has made. To be a desk is to be a kind of being, namely, that which is constrained by the essential properties of deskness; to be human is to be, precisely, a human being, an existent delimited by the form or essence of humanity. In both cases, the act of being (*actus essendi*) is, as it were, poured into the receptacle of a particularizing essence, and hence the things in question are, to that degree, metaphysically complex.

But in God, the source of existence itself, there is no such distinction. God is not this kind of being rather than that; he is not in this category rather than that; he is not great rather than small; he cannot be placed, positioned, or indicated. In the strictest sense of the term, he cannot be defined, since definition necessarily implies delimitation. As David Burrell put it, to be God is to be to-be. God certainly cannot fit into any of the "gaps" in a conventional scientific account of things. We see now why Aquinas so consistently correlated the divine simplicity to the self-designation of Yahweh in Exodus 3:14. Moses was asking a commonsensical question; he was assuming the mode of the scientist: Which God are you? What kind of being am I dealing with? God's answer—"I AM WHO I AM"—might be interpreted as off-putting: "Stop asking me such silly questions." But Thomas reads it as darkly illuminating: "My existence (who I am) is identical to my essence (what I am)." And this is precisely why Yahweh told Moses that he should take off his shoes, as he was standing on holy ground.

What becomes abundantly clear in this discussion is that the simple God is, *pace* Ditchkins, never reducible to the level of a creaturely nature. He could never, even in principle, become the object of an empirical or scientific investigation. He could never be defined or categorized by an inquiring mind. He is about as far from "a Flying Spaghetti Monster" as it is metaphysically possible to be. A passage in Thomas Merton's *Seven Storey Mountain* comes to mind in this context. Merton read, almost by accident, Etienne Gilson's book *The Spirit of Medieval Philosophy*, in which the subtle philosophical doctrine of the simple God is laid out. Merton was stunned, for he had always considered God "a noisy mythological being" and never imagined that the Christian understanding of God could be presented in a sophisticated way. It seems to me that the young Merton had a good deal in common with the new atheists.

Thomas's Creator God

It is only this simple God who can, in the proper sense of the term, create, since "creation" designates the act of giving rise to finite being *ex nihilo* (out of nothing). That creation is a pivotal idea for Thomas Aquinas is evident throughout his writings. Chesterton caught this when he commented that Aquinas should be known as "Thomas of the Creator." Getting right the absolutely unique way that the simple God relates to what he has made will go a long way toward clearing up the pseudo-problems raised by Hitchens, Dawkins, and company.

Thomas's most thorough and technical treatment of creation occurs in question three of the *Quaestiones disputatae, De potentia Dei*, composed in the mid-1260s while Thomas was stationed at Santa Sabina in Rome. In article one of question three, Thomas maintains that it must be firmly held (*tenendum est firmiter*) that God not only can but does create *ex nihilo*. His justification for this claim rests upon the intensity of God's actuality. Every agent, Thomas says, acts in the measure that it is in act, which is to say, in possession of some perfection of being. Thus a finite cause—fire, sunlight, a carpenter—produces a finite mode of existence, being *secundum quid*, determined in this way or that. Another way to state this is to say that a finite cause acts by moving, changing, or further specifying the being of another in some way. But God, who is totally actualized in his being, can affect things not simply through motion or change but through bringing forth the totality of their being, through creating them *ex nihilo*. In creating, God does not affect preexisting reality in some accidental way; rather, he brings the whole of that reality into being.

Thomas insists that creation does not take place in time, since time itself is a creature; further, it doesn't occur within the theatre provided by space, since space is a creature. There is no matter or energy upon which God acts, since both matter and energy are creatures. As such, creation never appears to the senses, nor can it be measured, nor can it be specified temporally. It is better to speak of it as a continual act (*creation continua*). As is true in the case of the divine nature, we know that creation is, but not really what it is. The anomalous, elusive quality of creation is reiterated in the third article of question three, which raises the issue of the "locale" of creation, that is to say, whether it is something really *in* the creature or perhaps between the creature and God. Thomas responds that creation, as an act, is in God, since whatever God does is identical to what God is, given the divine simplicity. But creation "in" the creature is harder to pin down, for we can't say that it is simply received by the creature as an outside influence, since that would presume there is a receptacle that is not, itself, created.

We can only say (and it puts us in mind of a Zen koan) that God creates that which is receiving the act of creation. Hence, creation is "a kind of relationship to the Creator with newness of being."[7] God is responsible, in short, for the entirety of a creature's being, yet his influence is not external to the creature. And this is why he speaks of it as a "kind" of relation. Thomas was well acquainted with the Aristotelian notion of relationship as an accidental qualification of two or more substances, but he knew that creation, which is responsible for the whole of a creature's being, cannot be imagined as "between" the creature and God. As he does when speaking of the Eucharist, Thomas here uses Aristotelian language but in a decidedly non-Aristotelian way, signaling that something else, metaphysically speaking, is the case. God is therefore properly discovered as the deepest ground of the creature's ontological identity. Thomas Merton was entirely in a Thomist frame of mind when he said that contemplative prayer is finding that place in you where you are here and now being created by God. This clarification is of enormous importance as a preliminary response to the atheists' contention that the human rapport with God can only be one of abject submission to a tyrant.

The Creator is certainly other than the creature, yet his otherness is congruent with his absolute closeness to the creature. Thomas holds that the transcendent God is "in all things by essence, presence, and power . . . and most intimately so."[8] His lordship over creation is, simultaneously, the most gentle letting-be of creation. Creatures don't so much *have* relationships to God; they *are* relationships to God. This is why Meister Eckhart, who sat in Aquinas's chair in theology for a time in Paris, said that the best way to find God is to "sink" into him.

John Milbank and others in recent years have drawn out a most important feature of this teaching, namely, that creation from nothing is an essentially nonviolent act. In most of the mythologies of the ancient world, creation takes place through a primordial act of violence, god or the gods wrestling some enemy into submission. The philosophical accounts of Plato and Aristotle represent a more sophisticated version of this myth in the measure that they picture a divine figure (the demiurgos, or the prime mover) shaping matter into form. But there is none of that in the doctrine of *creatio ex nihilo*. God cannot, even in principle, wrestle some alien and recalcitrant opponent into submission, or shape from the outside, in an intervening way, some substance that stands opposed to him. Rather, he brings the whole of finite reality into being nonviolently. The biblical narrative here is quite telling. God doesn't fight the world into existence; he speaks it into existence.

Another question that can be explored under the rubric of the divine creativity is this: why precisely does God create at all? If, as Thomas insists, God in his perfection is utterly self-sufficient, why would he feel obligated to give rise to finite being? One classical way to solve this problem is to dissolve it and say that God creates because he has to. The medieval Arabic philosopher Avicenna, for example, argued that creation is a kind of automatic emanation from God. In saying this, he anticipated by eight centuries the dialectical theology of Hegel and by nine centuries the process theology of Whitehead and his disciples. But with this sort of emanationism Aquinas has no truck.

While natural causes that act through necessity are determined toward the production of one kind of effect (think of a plant that gives rise predictably to seed after seed), causes that act through will and intelligence produce a wide variety of effects (think of Picasso or James Joyce). God's production, obviously, is wild in its fecundity and diversity, and thus it follows, for Thomas, that God's mode of creativity is not automatic but intelligent, purposive, and artistic.

Thus God chooses, with artistic intent, to give rise to the universe, but he does so in utter freedom from self-interest. And this implies, necessarily, that God's creative act is a gesture of love, for love is the willing of the good of the other as other. Since God has no ontological need, any and all of his actions *ad extra* are for the good of the other. Therefore, the world has been spoken into being nonviolently and lovingly. In response to certain Hegelianizing tendencies in the theology of the nineteenth century, the First Vatican Council reiterated this point, stating that God creates not out of any sort of need but out of a desire to share his goodness and glory.

Here again, we can see how far this Thomistic sense of God is from the caricature proposed by the new atheists. The creature's relation to the creator God is not crushing and oppressive; instead, it is the very act by which the creature subsists. More to it, this act is fundamentally nonviolent, nonintrusive, nonaggressive—and is done out of the sheerest love.

Thomas's Providential God

Having sketched Aquinas's treatment of the divine simplicity and creativity, I would like to examine, however inadequately, one more major motif in his doctrine of God, namely, his teaching concerning the relationship between divine causality and creaturely causality. The problem is a vexing one, and much hangs on its resolution. As we clearly see in the new atheists, the modern mind reacts against any claim that God interferes with the movements of nature or the movements of the human intellect and will. The objection is theoretical (for don't the natural sciences and psychology adequately account for these phenomena?) but also existential (a competing supernatural cause is an intolerable affront to finite freedom). What I've been exploring more abstractly now becomes focused and concrete: how exactly does the noncompetitiveness of God play itself out in terms of specific interior and exterior events?

I would first observe that Thomas speaks of God as both creator (the one who gives rise to the whole of the universe from nothing) and mover (the one who directs particular creatures and creation as a whole to their appointed ends), and he sees no contradiction or tension between the two characterizations. God affects creatures at the deepest possible level of their existence and in relatively secondary ways as well. Now when God moves or otherwise affects a creature, he is not, strictly speaking, creating, but he never ceases to be the Creator. And this means that the noncompetitiveness that obtains in regard to the unique act of creation holds, analogously, in regard to less dramatic instances of divine influence. Thomas explores this matter in detail in the seventh article of the famous question three of the *De potentia*. The topic for discussion is whether God operates in the operation of nature. The dilemma should be clear: if God is the creator of the entire universe in every detail, what room is left for the free exercise of creaturely agency? Wouldn't the presence of the Creator simply absorb any purposeful causality outside of himself?

The *sed contra* to this article could function as the leitmotif of my entire discussion of the God-world relationship. "O LORD, . . . it is you who have accomplished all we have done" (Isa. 26:12 NAB). There it is stated clearly and unapologetically, the dimensions of created and uncreated causality placed side by side. We have really done certain things, and yet they have been accomplished in us by God. This sort of juxtaposition is possible only on the assumption that God and creatures are not competing for space on the same metaphysical playing field. The high paradox, once more, is that the very strangeness and otherness of God is what allows for God's close cooperation with finite agency. In the course of his *respondeo*, Thomas lays out a number of models for understanding the synergy between divine and nondivine causality. I'll look here at only one. One thing, he says, can operate in another in the measure that the former provides the latter with its *virtus* or power, as, say, when the sun influences a solar heating device. Now God certainly acts in this way since, as Creator, he continually provides not only power but being to all his creatures. He is the condition for the possibility of their being and acting in the first place.

Then Thomas adds this: "The higher the cause, the more common and efficacious, and the more efficacious, the more profoundly it can penetrate into the effect." A finite cause can influence another finite cause, but the infinite Creator, who is the sheer act of to-be itself, can "penetrate" utterly the effect, acting thoroughly but nonobtrusively in the agency of that effect. With this clarification, we come to the heart of the matter. In our ordinary experience of instrumental causality, the "using" cause invades the being of that which it uses, but God, precisely as the creative cause of all that exists, can use finite causes instrumentally but noninvasively. Of course the most interesting instance of this dynamic (at least from our perspective) is the manner in which God works in and through the moves of the human free will. Aquinas is convinced that God moves human wills in such a way as to achieve his purpose and that this providential direction in no way compromises human freedom. This is the case precisely because God doesn't push or pull human wills from outside as much as he energizes them from the inside. Freedom is not unmitigated spontaneity but the ordered pursuit of the good in accord with the deepest desire of the free subject.

The otherly other God can operate at the level of the ground of the will, luring it in accord with its own-most nature and hence can enable the human subject to be itself precisely through surrender. It is fascinating how this non-competitive play is consistently displayed in the biblical narratives. Yahweh acts in human affairs, but not typically in an interruptive way. Rather, he accomplishes his purposes through the play of human freedom. The narratives concerning David are particularly instructive here. There is very little of the explicitly supernatural in those stories, yet Yahweh is clearly presented as achieving what he wants. That achievement takes place in the densely textured political and psychological drama involving Hannah, Eli, Samuel, Saul, Jonathan, and David. The story is, on one level, completely understandable in political and psychological terms; yet the author of the Samuel cycle wants us to penetrate to the deeper level of divine agency. Because the highest cause is not a being among many, it can operate in the realm of beings nonviolently, or as the book of Wisdom has it, "sweetly" (DRA). Once more, it is the very otherness and simplicity of God that permits God to act in this way.

We see again how the atheists' concerns about the god of the gaps who tyrannizes the human project from without are, at least from the perspective of Thomas Aquinas, completely misplaced.

The Genealogy of Atheism

One might be forgiven for wondering how things got so confused. How exactly did we get from Thomas's subtle metaphysics of divine simplicity and noncompetition to the overwrought and misplaced preoccupations of the new atheists? A good deal of the blame can be assigned to Duns Scotus and William of Occam and their option for a univocal over an analogical conception of being. Within the confines of this brief chapter, I can hardly do justice to the complexities of this shift in epistemology. Suffice it to say that once Scotus and Occam had posited *being* as a univocal term, God and creatures had to be categorized under the same general metaphysical heading as modalities of being. Though he was supreme, infinite, all-powerful, and so on, God, on the Scotist/Occamist reading, was one reality alongside others and hence competitive with them. On Aquinas's reading, all creaturely things were linked to one another through their shared centeredness in the creative ground of existence; but on Occam's interpretation, the totality of being is made up of mutually exclusive and unconnected individuals: *prateter illas partes absolutas nulla res.*

As the late medieval world gave way to the modern, this conception of the God-world relationship became solidified. Even as God was affirmed by modern philosophers from Descartes to Leibniz to Thomas Jefferson, he was more and more imagined as a distant being who had a mechanistic relationship to natural causes and an interruptive relationship to human freedom. But the ever more precise specification of the physical forces involved in cosmic movement conduced toward an ever more abstract and distant view of God. And the ever greater assertion of human freedom conduced first toward the marginalization of God and finally to his elimination. Commencing with Feuerbach, atheist philosophers began to say that the no to God is the yes to man. This trajectory reached finally toward Sartre's famous syllogism to which I alluded above (if God exists, I cannot be free; but I am free, therefore God does not exist).

It is only the competitive supreme being, the unhappy offspring of the univocal conception of being, that could possibly be the object of that kind of contempt. The God articulated by Thomas Aquinas is a competitor neither to the mechanistic causes named through the physical sciences nor to a robustly functioning human freedom. Rather, he is the one whose glory, in the words of St. Irenaeus, is a human being fully alive—and by extension, a cosmos operating according to its own principles, laws, and rhythms.

Conclusion

Through my wrestling with the new atheists in both academic and popular contexts, I've become convinced that the Catholic Church, in the years following Vatican II, has been rather inept at presenting its own textured and intellectually satisfying understanding of God. As I've tried to demonstrate in this chapter, the contemporary atheists are doing battle essentially with caricatures, and therefore it is altogether right to say to them, with Herbert McCabe, "You're absolutely right." But this is not enough. We have to get much better at giving a reason for the hope that is in us; we have to get much more adept at articulating our belief in the simple God whose otherness enhances rather than competes with the world. We have to formulate a new fundamental apologetics.

When I was coming of age in the years just after the Council, apologetics had a very bad name; it was defensive, rationalistic, unbiblical, and above all disrespectful of other religions. Furthermore, my postconciliar teachers and formators were enthusiastic advocates of a positive engagement with the environing secular culture—even going so far as to suggest, according to the slogan of the time, that the world sets the agenda for the church. But all of this was exaggerated and one-sided. Every culture, very much including our own, is evangelically ambiguous, that is to say, to some degree amenable to the proclamation of the gospel and to some degree quite inhospitable to it. Simply to pursue a culture and seek accommodation to it is, therefore, never a healthy evangelical strategy. My own conviction is that during these years when the church was running after the secular culture, that culture was not the least bit eager to reciprocate. Instead, it went about its business more or less indifferent to the church. And then, in the wake of September 11, a significant portion of the secular world—led by Ditchkins and company—turned rather aggressively against religion in general but Christianity in particular. When they did so, we found ourselves ill-equipped to defend ourselves, having long before jettisoned our evangelical and apologetic tools.

Ironically, it is the premodern doctrine of Thomas Aquinas that provides the surest foundation for this evangelical apologetics in the postmodern world.

3

✠

The Metaphysics of Coinherence

A Meditation on the
Essence of the Christian Message

Around the year 750, scribes, artists, and illustrators of the monastery of Iona, situated on an island just off the western coast of Scotland, produced a book of the Gospels. We know that, for a time, it rested at the shrine of St. Brigit in Kildare, where a visitor referred to it as "the High Relic of the Western World." A twelfth-century pilgrim to Ireland gave us a vivid description of its pages. "If you take the trouble to look very closely . . . you will notice such intricacies, so delicate, so subtle . . . so involved and bound together . . . that you will not hesitate to declare that all those things must have been the work not of men but of angels."[1] This remarkable sacred object is now known, from the last place that it rested, as the Book of Kells. One of the most famous of its pages is the "Chi-Rho page," the opening of the Gospel of Matthew. Sinuous lines cross one another, twisting, turning, overlapping, intertwining, forming tightly woven patterns. Often within an already densely textured design, a smaller and even more intricate pattern can be picked out. Animals abound (including two mice who tug at a consecrated host!), and they find their place alongside human figures, who in turn are implicated in the structure of the letters. The playful, colorful, interlacing style of the Book of Kells has been called typically Irish. This may be so, but at a much more basic level it is Catholic and Christian. Charles Williams, who (along with J. R. R. Tolkien and C. S. Lewis) was a member of the Oxford writers' group known as the Inklings, claimed that the master idea of Christianity is *coinherence*: the implication of the being of one in the being of the other, the intertwining and interlacing of reality. He saw it in the *circumincessio* of the Trinitarian persons, the coming together of divinity and humanity in Jesus, the dynamics of Christ's atoning death, and the corporate life of the church, the way the members of the body of Christ bear one another's burdens.[2] Like the lines and patterns of the Book of Kells, reality, seen through Christian eyes, has a stubbornly coinherent structure.

That coinherence is metaphysically basic is the content of our catechesis and teaching; it is one way of stating the core belief that we Catholic Christians want to communicate to the next generations. I stand with Hans Urs von Balthasar in claiming that the most effective starting point for our teaching and proclamation is the beauty of our message, a beauty very much like that of the Book of Kells—engrossing, fascinating, intricate, and deeply involving. When Charles Ryder, the narrator of Evelyn Waugh's great Catholic novel *Brideshead Revisited*, comes to Brideshead for the first time, he is overwhelmed and attracted by the mansion's beauty. It is only in time, as he interacts with the various people that inhabit the home, that he comes to appreciate that living there carries with it an intellectual and moral demand. Brideshead—much like Paul's Christ, who is head of his bride, the church—is symbolic of the mystical body of Jesus. Waugh seems to be teaching us that the optimal way to lure the nonbeliever into the communion of the church is through the attractive quality of Christianity's beauty, trusting that, once captured by beauty, he will be led to truth and goodness as well.[3] Thus, I will attempt to show the compelling doctrine of coinherence as it is displayed paradigmatically in the incarnation of the Lord and then to demonstrate the implications of this teaching for Christian metaphysics, epistemology, and ethics.

The Distinction and the Connection

G. K. Chesterton said that even those who reject the doctrine of the incarnation are different for having heard it.[4] The claim that God became one of us changes the imagination, compelling a reassessment of both God and the world. This odd assertion is made, implicitly or explicitly, on practically every page of the New Testament. When, in Mark's Gospel, Jesus says to the paralytic, "Child, your sins are forgiven," the onlookers respond, "Who but God alone can forgive sins?" thereby, despite themselves, stating the evangelical faith (see Mark 2:1–7 NABRE). In Luke's Gospel, Jesus says, "Unless you love me more than your mother and father, indeed your very life, you cannot be my followers" (AP, see Luke 14:26) implying that he is the Good that must be loved above even the highest created goods. In Matthew's Gospel, Jesus asserts, "Heaven and earth will pass away, but my words will not pass away" (see Matt. 24:35)—a claim that can consistently and sanely be made if and only if the speaker is himself the eternal Word. And that, of course, is precisely what the prologue to the Gospel of John explicitly affirms: "In the beginning was the Word, and the Word was with God, and the Word was God . . . and the Word became flesh and dwelt among us." John's magnificent confession is echoed in the hymn that found its way into Paul's letter to the Colossians: "In him [Christ] all things were created . . . in him all things hold together" (see Col. 1:16–17). As this unprecedented and intellectually provocative assertion made its way across the centuries, it proved both illuminating and deeply disconcerting, as is evident from the boisterous debate that it inspired among Christians. How, many wondered, is God capable of such an act of condescension?

The classic doctrinal statement of the church's faith in the incarnation is the formula hammered out at the Council of Chalcedon in 451. Battling both monophysitism and Nestorianism, the council fathers maintained that Jesus's two natures—human and divine—are grounded and instantiated in the person of the Logos, affecting thereby a hypostatic union of divinity and humanity. Though the natures are realized in the one person, they come together without "mixing, mingling, or confusion," that is to say, without losing their ontological integrity and distinctiveness. According to the logic of Chalcedon, it is decidedly not the case that God turns into a creature, ceasing to be God and transforming himself into a created nature; and it is assuredly not the case that a human being stops being human and turns into the Creator. Rather, divinity and humanity come together in the most intimate kind of union, yet noncompetitively. But such noncompetitiveness is possible only in the measure that God is not himself a creaturely or finite nature.[5] Due to their metaphysical structure, finite things, despite the numerous ways in which they can find communion with one another, remain, at the most fundamental level, mutually exclusive, so that one can "become" another only through ontological surrender or aggression. For example, a wildebeest becomes a lion only by being devoured; a building turns into rubble and ash only by being destroyed; and you "become" me only through some act of enormous psychological manipulation. But since, in the incarnation, God becomes a creature without ceasing to be God or compromising the integrity of the creature that he becomes, God must be other than a creaturely nature. This divine otherness is not simply the kind of otherness shared between two creatures, a standard over-and-againstness. Rather, God must be "otherly other," to borrow Kathryn Tanner's phrase.[6] God is not one being among many, caught in the nexus of contingent relations, but rather, as David Burrell has argued, that which is responsible for the whole of finite reality, the one who, as Herbert McCabe has said, sustains the world the way a singer sustains a song. We are skating on the edge of a paradox, for it is this very transcendence to the world that allows God to affect an incomparable closeness to worldly things. Nicholas of Cusa expressed this by saying that God, even as he remains utterly other, is the *non-aliud* (non-other), and Augustine gestured toward the same metaphysical tension when he observed that God is, simultaneously, *intimior intimo meo et superior summo meo* (more inward than my innermost and higher than my uppermost). No theologian has more beautifully evoked the noncompetitive transcendence of God than Irenaeus, who said, "*Gloria Dei homo vivens*," the glory of God is a human being fully alive, implying that God's majesty is entirely compatible with creaturely flourishing.

The closeness of God to the world is also a function of God's radical self-sufficiency. The otherly other Creator, who continually gives rise to all of finite reality, could not, even in principle, stand in a relationship of neediness with his creation. As Whitehead quite rightly saw, a process view of God is incompatible with a theology of creation. When Anselm described God as "that than which no greater can be thought," he signaled a break with the classical understanding of the divine, for the gods of ancient mythology and philosophy are superior beings to be sure, but they remain in the world alongside other things. Therefore, they could not be characterized as "that than which no greater can be thought," since they-plus-the-world would be greater than they alone. Anselm's peculiar description reflects precisely the noncontrastive and noncompetitive transcendence that we have been describing, for it implies that God-plus-the-world is not greater than God alone. The true God could not possibly need the world since nothing in creation could ever add to God's perfection.

Implications for Metaphysics

This unique understanding of God, rooted in the paradox of the incarnation, shapes the way Christians view the whole of existence. Precisely because God stands in no need of the world, all that exists apart from God is an expression and embodiment of sheerest love. Thomas Aquinas defines love as the willing of the good of the other as other. Since creatures are finite and imperfect, they remain, in regard to one another and to a certain degree, in a relationship of need, and hence their capacity to will the good of the other will always be partially mitigated or compromised. But this cannot be true of the self-sufficient Creator. Therefore the very being of the universe is testament to the purest possible act of willing the good of the other as other. The First Vatican Council, in its polemics against forms of Hegelianism that were creeping into Catholic thought in the nineteenth century, asserted that God did not make the world out of need but simply to manifest his glory.[7] Whatever has come to be, therefore, has been loved into being. Love is not an accidental relationship that a creature may or may not enter into with God; instead, love—being from and for the other—is the relationship that constitutes any and all things from the beginning.

The ontological irreducibility of relationship appears as well when we look more closely at the doctrine of *creatio ex nihilo*. As Robert Louis Wilken has indicated, one of the major points of demarcation between the metaphysical account of the earliest Christians and that of the pagan philosophers was the teaching regarding the origins of the world.[8] In most forms of classical philosophy, order comes into the universe through a divine shaping influence on some preexisting element. Thus, Aristotle's first mover draws prime matter into shape through its irresistible attractiveness, and Plato's demiurgos manipulates the primal chaos after consulting the patterns of the forms. But the Christians proposed something new—namely, a doctrine of creation from nothing, according to which God brings the whole of finitude into being, in all of its dimensions and aspects and without reference to a preexisting substrate. This implies in turn that there is nothing substantial and external with which God enters into relationship but rather that all that is not God is, essentially, a relationship to God. In his densely textured analysis of creation, Thomas Aquinas is compelled to twist and break the language of Aristotle in order to articulate this radical teaching. In response to the question of whether creation is something in the creature or perhaps between the creature and God, Thomas makes the Zen-like remark that that which receives the act of creation is itself a creature.[9] Operating beyond the categories of substance and accident, Aquinas says that creation is *quaedam relatio ad creatorem cum novitate essendi*, a kind of relation to the Creator with freshness of being.[10] The creature does not have a relationship with God; instead, it *is* a relationship with God. This novelty and distinctiveness was well expressed by Gerard Manley Hopkins when he spoke of God as "the dearest freshness deep down things."

John Milbank and his Radical Orthodoxy colleagues have helped us to see that this teaching implies, furthermore, the primordiality of nonviolence. If creation is truly *ex nihilo*, then there is nothing about it that is invasive, interruptive, or interfering, for there is no antagonistic other upon which God works. Order does not occur through any type of intrusion or conquest; instead, God brings the world to be through an entirely gratuitous and nonviolent act of love.[11] James Alison has suggested that the metaphysical doctrine of creation from nothing flows from the surprise of the paschal mystery, more precisely from the moment when the risen Jesus restores order to the frightened community of his disciples who had betrayed and abandoned him not through answering violence but through forgiveness.[12] All of this shows that the world, to the very roots of its being, exists in God, by means of a relationship, and that God can reach most intimately into things, as Aquinas puts it, "by essence, presence, and power." The intertwining, the coinherence, of God and the universe is a principal metaphysical consequence of the non-contrastive transcendence of God.

And from the coinherence of God and creation follows the coinherence of created things with one another. Because all finite reality—from archangels to quarks—comes forth here and now from the same divine generosity, the ontological ground of any one thing is identical to the ontological ground of any other. Like islands in an archipelago, we are all, despite our surface differences, connected at the depths. All creatures are ontological siblings. When he stood at the corner of Fourth and Walnut Street in downtown Louisville in 1958, Thomas Merton realized this truth and in his *Conjectures of a Guilty Bystander* gave famous expression to the realization. Seeing all the ordinary people bustling past him, it suddenly dawned on him that he loved them all not in a sentimental or emotional sense but mystically, even metaphysically. Waking from what he called "a dream of separateness," he knew that they all belonged to God and hence to one another, connected through a *point vièrge*, a virginal point where each was being created by God.[13] Understanding this coinherence for the first time, Merton exclaimed, "There is no way of telling people that they are all walking around shining like the sun."[14] It is precisely this connectedness of all creatures to one another through God that Thomas Aquinas articulates in his doctrine of analogy. Because all created beings participate in God who is *ipsum esse subsistens* (the sheer act of to-be itself), they are unavoidably related to one another by means of that shared participation. It has been central to the intellectual projects of Louis Dupré, Hans Urs von Balthasar, Alasdair MacIntyre, and many others to show how this metaphysical vision fell apart through the introduction of a univocal conception of being, which effectively placed God and creatures side by side under the general heading of existence and thereby separated them from one another. In a word, the univocal understanding of the concept of existence blinded us to the centrality and primordiality of coinherence.

Implications for Epistemology

The noncompetitive coming together of divinity and humanity in Jesus also has implications for the way we acquire knowledge. If, as the prologue to the Gospel of John insists, Jesus Christ is the visible icon of the Logos through which God has made all things, and if, as the letter to the Colossians makes clear, Jesus is the one in whom and for whom all things exist and through whom they are maintained, then Jesus is the interpretive lens through which reality is properly read. Jesus Christ is, for Christians, epistemically basic, which is to say that he functions as an epistemic trump: any account of reality that runs essentially counter to what is disclosed in the narratives about Jesus must be false. Lest this sound like sectarianism, we must bear in mind that both Augustine and Aquinas maintain that even "natural reason" is subject to Christ in the measure that the first principles and operations of the mind are nothing but a participation in the reasonability of the divine Logos, which became incarnate in Jesus. We Christians claim to know in a distinctive way, but this does not exclude us from the general human conversation—quite the contrary. It allows us to enter it more honestly, effectively, and creatively.

So what does it mean more precisely to have the mind of Christ? First, it means holding to the radical intelligibility of being. If God has made all creation through the Logos, then all existence must be stamped with form, the mark of a knower. As many have pointed out, it's no accident that the hard physical sciences emerged and came to flourish in a Christian culture, for only those who have a mystical confidence that being is intelligible will endeavor to know the world through observation, experimentation, and the forming of hypotheses. A universe without rational structure could never correlate to a scientific spirit.[15] But that upon which all scientific activity rests cannot itself be the subject of scientific investigation; it must rather be the fruit of an intuition that can be called religious only in its depth, range, and breadth. Christians name it exactly as the faithful grasp of the doctrine of creation through the Word. This is the ground for the confident humanism that has characterized Christianity at its best over the centuries. We who hold, precisely on theological grounds, to the intelligibility of being have nothing to fear from the honest and careful practice of any and all intellectual disciplines—just the contrary. When Aquinas was challenged by certain of his contemporaries who were concerned that his use of Aristotle amounted to the diluting of the wine of revelation with the water of pagan science, Thomas responded, "No, it is rather the changing of water into wine."

But Christians know, in light of Christ, how to specify more exactly the structure and content of the world's intelligibility. Because all things are made through the Logos, which is itself nothing but a subsistent relation to the Father, coinherence, and not substance or individuality, must be the basic truth of things. The wager of the Christian faith is that any philosopher, scientist, social theorist, or psychologist looking, within the confines of his own discipline, at the structure of reality will find something like being-for-and-with-the-other. Connection rather than separation, relationship rather than substance, will be disclosed as the most fundamental constitutive features of reality. In his writings on religion and science, physicist-priest John Polkinghorne has demonstrated that recent investigations by quantum physicists and chaos theorists reveal just this coinherent quality at the most elemental level of matter—a finding, he suggests, that should not surprise Christians.[16]

A further epistemological implication of the noncompetitiveness of the natures in Christ is that the act of knowing is not so much individualist but intersubjective. Over against Descartes's insistence that proper philosophy commences with the private ruminations of the isolated thinker, cut off from received tradition, sense experience, and assumption, Bernard Lonergan implied that it is not so much the *cogito* that matters as the *cogitamus*. Lonergan knew that Descartes's program of radical doubt was a fantasy, a hopelessly unrealistic and self-defeating exercise, since the act of doubt itself is made possible only through a rich complex of language, supposition, and shared conviction. Moreover, no philosopher or scientist would ever get her project off the ground had she not accepted a whole congeries of findings, data, principles, and assumptions that she herself had not verified directly.[17] In a word, every responsible intellectual project involves a community of knowers seeking the truth together: the *cogitamus* rather than the *cogito*. One of Lonergan's intellectual heroes was John Henry Newman. In his *Essay on the Development of Christian Doctrine*, Newman maintains that ideas exist not on the printed page but in the play of lively minds. The human intellect does not take in notions dumbly or passively, as though it were a *tabula rasa*; instead, it analyzes, judges, compares, assesses, and questions them. Further, by a sort of inner compulsion, it seeks to deepen and intensify this process through the establishment of a conversation with other minds.[18] In the playful, game-like exchange of insight, information, questions, and answers—beautifully exemplified in the dialogues of Plato and the treatises of Aquinas—ideas develop and human beings come to deeper understanding. This intersubjective, communitarian manner of knowing is congruent with the metaphysics of coinherence that we have been outlining. We know the complex truth of things precisely by wrapping our minds, Book of Kells–like, around one another.

A final epistemological consequence of an incarnational sensibility is a thoroughly participative view of knowing. As we have seen, the intelligibility of being is a sign that all finite reality has been thought into existence, produced through the Logos of God. But this means that at the most fundamental level there is a correspondence between knower and known, God's knowledge, as it were, informing and actualizing what it knows. Karl Rahner reiterates this idea when he says, in *Hearers of the Word*, that the meaning of existence is knowing and being known in an original unity.[19] Now this primordial coinherence of divine knower and creaturely intelligibility obtains analogically in all human acts of intellection. For Thomas Aquinas, the human subject comes to know precisely when his mind is illumined and stirred to act by an objective form, and that form is realized, illumined, and stirred to act precisely in the act of being known.[20] Knowing happens, in short, through a sort of mutual participation of knower and known, each one calling out to and perfecting the other. This mutuality is caught in the marvelous medieval dictum *intellectus in actu est intelligibile in actu*—the intellect in act *is* the actualization of the intelligible. It was this participative and mystical epistemology that was set aside in the modern period when the distantiation of subject from object, necessary for analysis, was emphasized. Descartes's concern with mastering nature through the mind is utterly alien to, say, Thomas Aquinas's desire to contemplate nature through intellectual participation. The former is made possible by a breakdown in the coinherent Christian worldview that thoroughly informed the latter.

Implications for Ethics

When the young Gregory Thaumaturgus came to Origen to seek instruction in Christian doctrine, the great teacher told him that first he must share the life of the Christians and become their friend. Only in that way would he begin to understand what Christians teach.[21] Origen shared the assumption of most sages in the ancient world that philosophy is not an academic discipline but a form of life, a *bios*. A disciple at Plato's academy was not so much a student of Platonic theory as a practitioner of a way of life centered on the pursuit of truth.[22] This tight connection between knowledge and ethical practice was maintained by Christian thinkers throughout the patristic period and into the High Middle Ages. Augustine, Bernard, Anselm, Bonaventure, and Aquinas took for granted that real advancement in knowledge of Christian mysteries is a function of an accompanying advancement in the practice of the Christian virtues. If one were to pose to any of those figures the characteristically modern question about relating theology to ethics or spirituality, I trust he would not understand the question. Nowhere is this connection between knowledge and practice clearer than in the second *Summa* of Aquinas. The great second part of the work, centered on the journey back to God, is predicated at every point upon the theological moves made in the first section, and the third part, dealing with Christ and the sacraments as the definitive way to God, is but a further specification and concretization of the second part. To speak, therefore, of Aquinas's "ethics" in abstraction from his doctrine of God or his Christology would be anomalous.[23] All of this is an elaborate way of saying that, for the classical Christian tradition, the doctrine of the incarnation and its accompanying metaphysics of coinherence have clear implications in regard to ethics, and that correct moral behavior itself conduces toward a deeper appreciation of a distinctively Christian ontology.

In order to appreciate the moral and behavioral consequences of a Christian worldview, I would like to look first at what followed ethically from a breakdown in that unified *Weltanschauung*. As I have already noted, in the late Middle Ages, figures such as Duns Scotus and William of Occam put forward a univocal conception of being, replacing the analogical understanding found in Aquinas. The most telling ontological implication of this epistemological shift was the placing of God and the world under the same metaphysical umbrella, turning God thereby into a supreme being among beings. No longer the deepest ground of whatever exists, God necessarily appeared as a rival to the world he confronted. When this supreme existent was viewed in relation to human beings, he was construed as a threat to freedom. One rubric under which modernity can be viewed is that of the struggle—sometimes explicit, more often implicit—to defend human liberty against the invasive authority of God.[24] Thus the materialist Thomas Hobbes asserted that proper political order flows not from a sense of the transcendent good but rather from individual rights grounded in desire and fear. Though he softened this view to a degree, John Locke remained in a fundamentally Hobbesian framework, arguing that legitimate government exists to defend rights, defined as those things that one cannot help but desire. A consequence of this approach, perfectly in line with the nominalist assumptions that undergird it, is that citizens are seen as individuals jealously guarding their prerogatives over against others who threaten them.

This strain of modernity came to even more radical expression in the nineteenth and twentieth centuries. For Feuerbach, Marx, and especially Nietzsche, human flourishing is made possible only through the elimination of the competitive God. Feuerbach's formula is "the no to God is the yes to man"; Marx's dictum is that religion must be sloughed off like a snake's skin before human beings can aspire to maturity and political liberation; and Nietzsche bluntly declares that God is dead because the *Übermensch*, in the sheerest exercise of his power, has killed him. Jean-Paul Sartre elegantly states this conviction in terms of a compelling syllogism: "If God exists, I cannot be free; but I am free, therefore God does not exist."[25] Lest we think that these claims remain on the level of academic abstraction, consider the decision of the United States Supreme Court in the matter of *Casey v. Planned Parenthood of Pennsylvania*. In a breathtaking defense of human freedom over against any power that might condition or direct it, the justices said, "At the heart of liberty is the right to define one's own concept of existence, of meaning, of the universe, of the mystery of human life."[26] According to this formula, the true and the good are projections of human subjectivity, constructs of an arbitrary autonomy. What we see in all of this is the playing out of the shift to a univocal conception of being and a rivalrous view of the God-world relationship. The no to God is the yes to man only in the measure that God's existence stands over against the world, impinging upon it intrusively and invasively.

However, when God is perceived not as a competitive supreme being but as the subsistent act of existence itself, then authentic human flourishing is appreciated as tantamount to a surrender to God and God's purposes. When God is correctly understood along Chalcedonian lines, then the coinherence of humanity and divinity, of subjective freedom and objective truth, becomes evident. Over against what they perceived to be the heteronomy inherent in the classical tradition, the Enlightenment philosophers advocated a bracing autonomy. Paul Tillich, reflecting the Augustinian-Christian spirit, characterized that dichotomy as simplistic and called instead for theonomy, the realization that one's deepest sense of freedom is coincident with an embrace of the God who is the ground of one's being. He knew, along with the great tradition, that the true God is not a threat to freedom but the condition for the possibility of freedom properly exercised.

In the seventh century, the monothelite controversy raged within the Christian church. This was a dispute over the nature of will in Jesus Christ. Theologians of a more monophysite bent maintained that there was but one divine will in Jesus, but others held that a key implication of the two-natures doctrine of Chalcedon is that there must be two wills, divine and human, in the Lord. After much wrangling, the fathers of the Third Council of Constantinople in 681 determined that Christ possesses two wills and two natural operations not opposed to one another but cooperating in such a way that his human freedom finds itself precisely in surrender to his divine freedom. It might seem odd to rehearse the details of this ancient theological battle, but I believe that it sheds considerable light on the problematic turn that we have been exploring. In some ways, the monothelites—those who held to the unicity of will in Jesus—anticipated the philosophers of modernity, since they seemed to hold that divine authority and real human freedom are incompatible. In resolving the dispute as they did, the fathers of Constantinople III antecedently answered Hobbes, Feuerbach, Marx, Nietzsche, and Sartre: humanity is enhanced rather than diminished when placed in tight coinherent relationship with the noncompetitive God. Divine freedom and human freedom can interlace and overlap as thoroughly as any of the designs in the Book of Kells.

Again, the proper relationship between God and human freedom is on clear display in the second part of Aquinas's *Summa theologiae*. Most of the moral philosophies and theologies of the late medieval and modern periods commence with a consideration of obligation. They are preoccupied with the limits set to freedom by the commands of God. What lies behind such a starting point is the assumption that God and human beings are alien to one another and that divine and human freedom are mutually antagonistic. But the moral section of the *Summa* does not commence with obligation, duty, or law but rather with happiness.[27] Thomas wonders what makes human beings joyful and determines that neither power, nor riches, nor reputation, nor glory, nor any finite good could ever do so. It is, he concludes, only the infinite, inexhaustible good of God that could possibly satisfy the infinite longing of the human heart. Thus, like Augustine, he shows that there is a correspondence between human desire and divine desire, between human nature and divine nature. His moral theology is predicated not on the struggle between an autonomous finite freedom and an arbitrary infinite freedom but rather on the coinherence between a human soul that finds its beatitude in God alone and the God who delights in sharing his being with creation.

We must draw one further ethical implication from the noncompetitiveness of God and the world. When asked why God creates, Thomas responds typically with the formula of the pseudo-Dionysius: *bonum diffusivum sui* (good is of itself diffusive). The good God creates because it is his nature to give. And when asked why God became incarnate in Jesus Christ, Aquinas turns to the same formula. Because it is the nature of the good to give of itself and because God is the supreme good, it is only fitting that God should give himself utterly, superabundantly, and this explains the fittingness of the incarnation. The being of God, in a word, is a being that gives. But this means that when a human being clings to God as her ultimate good, thereby finding happiness, she is conforming herself to this divine generosity. This is why, in a wide variety of his ethical writings, Karol Wojtyla, later Pope John Paul II, speaks of the centrality of the law of the gift in the Christian tradition: one's being increases and is enhanced in the measure that one gives it away. To achieve the ultimate end of the moral life is not to attain a prize that gratifies the ego; rather, it is to enter into the gracious way of being characteristic of God. One of the tragedies of our time, in my judgment, is that our presentation of the moral life remains conditioned by the assumptions and language of modernity—obligation, law, autonomy, heteronomy, divine demand—rather than by the much more traditional language of grace, coinherence, and joy.

Conclusion

In our understanding of God, the universe, the act of knowing, and human ethical behavior, we Catholics are unique. Though we can discern family resemblances in the other great religions and even in the best features of the secular culture, the Catholic vision of things is distinctive. It is born of what Chesterton called the "jest" of the incarnation, the utterly incongruous and unexpected juxtaposition of divinity and humanity. In this great coinherence of Creator and creature, we spy the pattern, the basic structure of reality; we touch and see, to borrow the language of St. John, what was from the beginning, the Word of life. Our task, as I see it, is the work taken up by every Christian generation: to narrate the story with joy and panache, to tell again and again the joke that is delightfully on us.

4

✠

The Trinity on Display in the Economy of Salvation

An Irenaean Meditation

There are many candidates for the "master idea" of the work of Irenaeus of Lyons—recapitulation, the divine economy, the unity of Scripture, God's artistry, and so on. But I would modestly propose for this title the notion of God's lack of need. Again and again, like a refrain, Irenaeus sounds this motif in his major writings. Here are a few examples chosen almost at random: "His [God's] greatness lacks nothing but contains all things";[1] "for God had no need of them [angels or other spiritual powers], in order to make what he had in advance decreed;[2] "this world is encompassed by seven heavens, in which dwell powers and angels and archangels not as though he was in need but that they may not be idle and unprofitable;"[3] "in the beginning, God formed Adam, not because he stood in need of man, but in order that he might have beings upon whom he might confer benefits."[4] In making these affirmations Irenaeus is, of course, defending the biblical conception of God over against the Gnostic claims that the high God requires various emanations and returns in order to come fully to himself. But he is doing much more. In point of fact, he is articulating the seminal idea from which his entire doctrine of God springs and from which, by extension, his entire theology comes forth. For the God who has no need is the sovereign God, the one God, the creator God, the power in whom all finite things participate. To imply even vaguely and indirectly that God has any ontological need whatsoever is to undermine all of these affirmations. The God who has no need is the only one who could be the addressee of Irenaeus's prayer in the third book of the *Adversus haereses*: "Therefore I also call upon you, Lord God of Abraham and God of Isaac and God of Jacob . . . you who are the father of our Lord Jesus Christ . . . that we should know you, who have made heaven and earth, who exercise rule over all, you are the only and true God, above whom there is no other God."[5] And this is why the biblical God of whom Irenaeus speaks is to be sharply distinguished from the Homeric mythological deities—even the highest, Zeus—for the gods are, despite their immortality and power, still subject to the constraints of fate and necessity. Whatever necessities are apparent within nature are themselves creatures of God and part of his providence.

Let us consider first the sovereignty and unity of the self-sufficient God. The God who is free of need requires no external supplementation and brooks no ontological opposition. If there were a divine or even semidivine power over against God, then God would be, logically speaking, not the fullness of perfection and would hence stand in some existential need vis-à-vis that which he is not. Borrowing the term from the Gnostics, Irenaeus says that the true God *is* the pleroma, containing all things but contained or circumscribed by nothing. And this is precisely why the oneness of God is a correlate of his self-sufficient sovereignty. The fundamental mistake of the Gnostics is to situate God within some greater totality, for even their high, unknowable God remains one reality among many within the pleroma. Irenaeus argues that the numerous aeons of which the Gnostics speak so confidently are best characterized as ideas within the mind of the one God. Several of the major Christian fathers, most notably Augustine, would follow the master of Lyons in this regard.

Further, the one God, in his ontological fullness and "opulence" (a favorite Irenaean term), is unknowable to human beings in this life. The Maker of the eye is necessarily beyond sight, and the Creator of the mind is necessarily beyond any rational measure. Though we certainly ascribe a number of names to God, these are meant in a metaphorical sense. Though we use a variety of concepts to characterize God, these are applied with extreme caution, since God can never be known "from above," that is, from the standpoint of a metaphysical framework that contains him. The ideas we use of God do not measure God; rather, they are measured by him. Some thinkers (and Irenaeus certainly has the Gnostics in mind) "stupidly" divide God into parts and present him as a composite, thereby making him easier for the analytical mind to grasp. But such a strategy is always counterindicated precisely because God is simple, fully himself at once. Though in his totality God can never be known (at least in this life), nevertheless his existence is signaled to the human mind in a number of ways. Somewhat in the manner of Anselm, Bonaventure, and Calvin, Irenaeus holds to a fundamental and universal intuition of God's existence. "For since His invisible essence is mighty, it confers on all a profound mental intuition and perception of his most powerful, omnipotent greatness. . . . All beings do know this one fact at least, because reason, implanted in their minds, moves them, and reveals to them the truth that there is one God, the Lord of all."[6] To this is added a knowledge of God that flows from the design apparent in every detail of creation, an ordering that "points to the existence and rational nature of the creator."[7] Both of these forms of knowing the divine witness to a participation metaphysic. If God is the Mind through whom the universe is created and sustained, then the logos of the human intellect must bear a trace of the primordial divine Logos, and the universe in its entirety must be stamped by intelligibility.

Now despite these mitigated modes of knowing God, authentic, saving knowledge of God comes only, Irenaeus holds, through the condescension of the divine love. "For the Lord taught us that no man is capable of knowing God unless he is taught by God."[8] In the long history of salvation, the Logos steps, as it were, into time and space and personally instructs certain chosen figures in the ways of God. This education comes to its fulfillment in the incarnation of the divine wisdom in Jesus and its perpetuation in the life of the church.

We move from this insight to the affirmation of God's immutability, since there is no further perfection to which the sovereign God could aspire, no potency in him that needs actualization. The divine unchangeability hasn't a thing to do with a supposed indifference on God's part to whatever exists apart from him. It is simply a way of stating that God cannot "improve" ontologically. One of Irenaeus's most fundamental interpretive keys to understanding the God-world relationship is that the world is made and God is unmade, which is to say the world is always growing further toward God, but God is not in any sense growing toward a reality to which he is beholden. If that were the case, the equilibrium that obtains between the luring God and the lured creation would be lost. "He who makes is always the same," and "for as God is ever the same, man, when found in God, shall ever grow towards him."[9]

Tightly linked to these notions of unity and immutability is that of perfection. Irenaeus insists that God is "equal and similar to himself, as he is all light and all mind, and all substance, and the fount of all good."[10] As the term itself suggests, the "perfect" is that which is complete and hence in need of no supplement. This is what Irenaeus means when he speaks of God as "similar to himself and equal to himself." If there were some reality that would complement God's manner of being, then God could in some way be contrasted with that reality; he would be necessarily similar to it. He would even be, in some sense, "equal" to this competitive being, since he and that being could be placed, as it were, on the same ontological background for comparison and analysis, like two human beings who, despite all their individual differences, are both instances of the genus humanity. But these terms also have a kind of internal point of reference as well. An imperfect reality, composed of parts and organic systems, is not utterly equal to itself, since the elements that make it up could be set in opposition to one another, at least conceptually. Thus the God who *is* "similar to himself" is not made up of parts, nor is he metaphysically composed in any way. To express the same idea in the language of Thomas Aquinas, this God is, in contrast to all other existing things, simple.

From Nothing into Being

On the basis of these fundamental affirmations, Irenaeus insists on the fact that the one God is the creator of the finite universe in all its modes and expressions, in both its visible and invisible dimensions. I believe it is fair to say that, given the overall narrative structures of the *Adversus haereses* and *Demonstration of the Apostolic Preaching*, this assertion of God's creation of the universe *ex nihilo* is the second master idea in the theology of Irenaeus. Though one can find some antecedents of this doctrine in Justin's pupil Tatian, Irenaeus is the first major Christian theologian to present in a developed way the idea of creation from nothing. This statement from the second book of the *Adversus haereses* is typical: "In this point, God showed his superiority to man, that while man cannot make anything out of nothing but only out of matter already existing, yet He Himself called into existence the substance of his creation, although previously it had no existence."[11] Certainly for the great Greek philosophers, "creation" is a type of making, albeit on a cosmic scale. In Plato, the demiurgos looks to the forms and finds the patterns by which he shapes inchoate matter, and in Aristotle, the prime mover draws *materia prima* to himself and thereby endows it with intelligibility. But in neither case are we dealing with the bringing of things into being from nothing. In arguing for creation from nothing, Irenaeus is giving clear metaphysical articulation to the biblical conviction, on display especially in deutero-Isaiah, that God is the creator Lord of all finite reality. But the insistence on the *ex nihilo* quality of this divine act is, as I've suggested, something of a novum. Even philosophers as biblically formed as Philo of Alexandria and Justin Martyr still held, perhaps with the Genesis account in mind, to some kind of divine shaping of preexisting matter. But Irenaeus saw to the bottom of this issue: if there were even inchoate matter coexisting eternally with God, then God would not be infinite, perfect, and simple, and his power would necessarily be limited. As the radically unoriginate, God must stand utterly over against any originate reality.

Irenaeus tells us that God in fact took from himself both the matter by which the universe is constituted as well as the patterns by which that matter is shaped. At first blush, this seems untenable: how could the utterly immaterial God take matter from himself? We must keep in mind that when we speak of spirit and matter, we are not talking about mutually exclusive types of being but rather of modes of reality at varying levels of intensity. God, who is the sheer energy of existence itself, can certainly give rise to being at a lower or less intense degree of "concentration." This might help to explain a point we shall return to later—namely, how human beings, even in their materiality, should be construed as being in the image of God. But still we are left with a puzzle. How could the utterly simple and perfect God draw being from himself in order to make the universe? Wouldn't a capacity to extract something from his own substance render God a conditioned being? Centuries after Irenaeus, Thomas Aquinas would deny that God makes the world either out of preexisting matter or from his own substance; rather, *sensu stricto*, God creates from nothing, simply by the infinity of his power and actuality. Now a problem with Thomas's view is that it seems to attenuate to the point of nothingness any real connection between the divine being and created reality. If we say that the world comes, in no sense, from God's to-be, then it seems hard to affirm that God is the creator. If we argue that it is only from God's *potentia* or power that the world comes, we're still on the horns of a dilemma, since, given the divine simplicity, any of God's attributes are identical to God's essence. I would suggest that we can retain Irenaeus's account that God draws matter and intelligibility from his own substance as long as we keep in mind the unique ontology of infinite reality. Just as, in a mathematical context, we can't speak of anything being subtracted from infinity, so in a metaphysical context, it would be nonsensical to speak of God's infinite reality being compromised or lessened by any act of "subtraction" that takes place through creation.

Thus matter comes from God, and so do the intelligible patterns that inhere in all created things. As we saw, the standard Platonist view was that the demiurgus derived the patterns of the world from his contemplation of the separately existing realm of the forms. Since Irenaeus situates the Platonic forms within the divine mind itself, he can teach that the sole Creator derives both matter and form from his own act of existing. The unicity of the Creator also precludes any and all emanationist schemas, whether of Platonic or Gnostic provenance. Irenaeus affirms that, though various degrees of ontological influence can obtain among creatures, strictly speaking, it is only God who creates. Thus all the Gnostic theorizing about the world coming through a hierarchy of aeons is, on metaphysical grounds, so much nonsense. It also runs counter—and here we come to a central Irenaean preoccupation—to the unambiguous biblical assertion that the one God made "the heavens and the earth." Over and again, throughout the *Adversus haereses*, Irenaeus shows how, for the authors of both the Old and New Testaments, there is no God beyond or higher than the God of creation. Though his usual method of demonstration is to cite texts from the Scriptures, Irenaeus does use, once again, a form of metaphysical reasoning in making this case. If, as the Gnostics argue, the fallen god of creation appealed to higher patterns in order to imbue the world with form, what would prevent us from saying that these superior aeons did not themselves appeal to higher sources of intelligibility and so on *ad infinitum*? Even within an emanationist schema, it seems, we must come finally to some divine reality that contains within itself the resources to bring about creation, and it is this Creator that the Bible simply identifies as God.

A chief implication of this view is that the universe has been made through an act of utterly generous, sheerly disinterested love. Since the world would add nothing to the perfection of a God without need, God must will the existence of the world purely for its own sake. The various dimensions of creation, both visible and spiritual, cannot be seen as the result of automatic emanations from the high God, much less as the detritus of a cosmic fall, for God would then be less than free. Irenaeus makes this point repeatedly in his refutation of both the Gnostic notion of the pleroma and the mythological conception of the gods who are desperately needy of sacrifice and praise.

The Providential Architect

From the idea of *creatio ex nihilo* flows the notion of the divine providence. If creation is the act by which God sustains the universe in its ontological foundations, providence is the somewhat less intense expression of God's presence to the universe that he has made. As Balthasar and others have pointed out, there is a very strong aesthetic sensibility in Irenaeus, and this comes through especially in his discussions of God's governance of the world. God's will, which is "the efficient and foreseeing cause of every time, place, age, and nature," invariably operates according to artistic purposes, and this is why Irenaeus typically refers to God as "architect." Whatever God orders fits into an overarching design, the contours and complexity of which we cannot readily appreciate, though hints of it appear everywhere. The following is an altogether typical Irenaean summary: "Seeing that God is vast and the Architect of the world and Almighty, he made it by a Will . . . with the novel result that the entire fullness of the things which have been produced might come into existence."[12] Though we post-Holocaust thinkers tend to feel that the classical theologians were naive in their treatment of the problem of suffering (how pat the image of the divine architect can seem in light of the sufferings that we have witnessed), I don't think that it would be right to dismiss this trope too quickly. What especially struck Irenaeus—who was, by the way, hardly unacquainted with human misery and injustice—was how a wise architect employs in his designs a balancing of the grand and the utilitarian as well as dramatic plays of dark and light. To say that all things are arranged according to an aesthetic purpose is by no means to imply that all things are neatly and predictably in place, especially when we keep in mind that the architect in question is the incomprehensible God.

From the Gnostic camp came the objection that this conception of God as monolithically one and free of any neediness implies that God is without real personality, vitality, or relationality. These same difficulties were raised, of course, in more recent times by the advocates of process theology over against what they construed as Thomas Aquinas's doctrine that God is not really related to the world. Irenaeus responds by making a move that would be repeated throughout the great orthodox tradition up to the present day—namely, to place these dynamics within God, within the interpersonal play of the Trinity and then to appreciate them as manifested iconically in creation, God as it were expressing himself in the artistry of his providence. Here the famous Irenaean metaphor of the Father and his two "hands" is appropriate: "For with him are always present the Word and Wisdom, the Son and the Spirit, by whom and in whom he freely and spontaneously made all things."[13] As John Henry Newman pointed out, Irenaeus uses the trope of "hands" to designate the consubstantiality of the Spirit and the Son with the Father, and not their mere instrumentality. It is a commonplace to observe that Irenaeus, writing in the last quarter of the second century, did not develop a fully articulated theology of the immanent Trinity along the lines of the Cappadocians, Hilary, or Augustine. To be sure, he focused much more on the economic Trinity. Nevertheless, he consistently explained God's lack of neediness vis-à-vis the world through recourse to the dynamics of the immanent Trinity.

What I would like to do next is to turn to a contemporary theologian in order to articulate more precisely the nature of these dynamics and then, in light of that clarification, to show how the Trinitarian God is, for Irenaeus, represented iconically in creation and providence.

Ratzinger's Theses on the Trinity

In his now classic *Introduction to Christianity* from 1968, Joseph Ratzinger articulates three theses that express the positive conceptual content of the Trinitarian affirmation *una essentia, tres personae*. The first thesis runs as follows: "The paradox *una essentia tres personae*—one Being in three Persons—is associated with the question of the original meaning of unity and plurality."[14] In classical philosophy, Ratzinger comments, divinity is unilaterally associated with unity, and the fallen, imperfect creation with plurality. One certainly sees this in the thought systems that Irenaeus was battling: in both Platonism and Gnosticism, emanations from the One represent disintegrations and diminutions, a falling away from primordial unity. But the Trinitarian God evades the contrast between unity and plurality, including them even as he transcends them. "God stands above the singular and the plural. He bursts both categories."[15] If God were simply one, he could be contrasted to the many and hence rendered conditioned; and if God were simply many, he could be contrasted to unity and hence be, in that measure, defined. Ratzinger draws the conclusion, "The highest unity is not the unity of inflexible monotony but rather of love, the tensive unity established by the coming together of the many."[16]

The second of Ratzinger's theses is this: "The paradox *una essentia tres personae* is a function of the concept of person and is to be understood as an intrinsic implication of the concept of person."[17] Classically, personhood is connected to mind, will, word, imagination, and love, and Ratzinger insists that all of these are grounded in intentionality: one knows something; one wills something; one imagines and loves some other. Hence, "the unrelated, unrelatable, absolutely one could not be a person." Indeed, Ratzinger finds evidence for this in the etymology of the Greek term *prosopon*, which has the sense of looking toward another. Derivatively, of course, the Latin term *persona*, with the sense of sounding through, carries the implication of directedness to another. Ratzinger draws out the implication. "If the absolute is a person, it is not an absolute singular. To this extent, the overstepping of the singular is implicit in the concept of person."[18]

The third Trinitarian thesis is the following: "The paradox *una essentia tres personae* is connected with the problem of absolute and relative and emphasizes the absoluteness of the relative, of that which is in relation."[19] Once again, in classical metaphysics, relationship was construed as accidental, a secondary qualification of substance, and hence it was rather emphatically denied of the prime substance, namely, God. One needs only to think here, Ratzinger reminds us, of Aristotle's conception of the prime mover as self-thinking thought, utterly devoid of any relationality to the world. But in the Bible, God is conceived of in a much less ontologically isolated way, even prior to creation. In the book of Genesis, God is pictured as speaking to another even in the act of creation: "Let us make man in our image, after our likeness" (Gen. 1:26). Psalm 110 begins with the mysterious phrase "The LORD says to my lord," and in the eighth chapter of the book of Proverbs we find the description of Yahweh and his Wisdom consulting together "before the beginning of the earth." There is, the great tradition concluded, a "We" in God, a play, within the very divine unity, of "dialogue, of differentiation, and of relationship through speech."[20] But if God is not only logical (characterized by Logos) but also dialogical (characterized by speech), then the category of relation must be promoted to a higher ontological plane. Ratzinger sums up, "It now becomes clear that the dialogue, the *relatio*, stands beside the substance as an equally primordial form of being."[21] Augustine acknowledged this principle when, in response to a troubling Arian objection, he clarified that there are no accidents in God and yet not all language used of God designates the divine substance. And Thomas Aquinas nodded toward the equiprimordiality of substance and relation when he argued that the simplicity of God is marked, through and through, by a play of "subsistent relations."

Irenaeus and the Iconic Manifestation of the One and the Many

With Ratzinger's pithy theses in mind, I would like to return to Irenaeus's idea that creation and the providential guidance of the world involve an iconic representation of the internal dynamics of the divine life. God does not need the world, nor is he in any kind of competition with it; rather, he loves it into being and lavishly shares his life with it. Therefore, the universe and its evolution will be marked, in every detail, by different aspects of the Trinitarian play.

If Ratzinger is right in saying that the Trinitarian God "bursts the categories" of the one and the many, then we should expect some tensive rapport between unity and plurality to be on display in the universe. And this is precisely what we find in Irenaeus's account of the *oikonomia*. The entire notion of the economy of salvation would be compromised unless there were, within creation, radical diversification, both spatial and chronological. As we saw, for the Gnostics, the very multiplicity of the created world is something of an embarrassment. The high God is supremely one, and thus the other elements within the pleroma represent a sort of falling away from that singularity. And the entire gross variety of the material order—myriad plants, animals, insects, and so on—could only be construed as the work of a lesser and morally ambiguous demiurge. But Irenaeus, committed to the biblical rule of faith, held to the unicity of the Creator of heaven and earth and therefore to the irreducible goodness of both materiality and multiplicity. He knew that they must both represent in some way God's own manner of being.

However, the plurality in God never compromises his fundamental oneness, and thus we should not be surprised to find within creation and providence a great principle of unity. Irenaeus identifies this as *anakephalaiosis*. The recapitulation is anything but an abstraction for Irenaeus, since it represents the concrete working out of a design, after the manner of an architectural or political program. Many have remarked the connection between Irenaeus's notion of the economy and central ideas in the writings of Vitruvius. Indeed, the Lyons master speaks of God "drawing up the plans for the edifice of salvation," and of God performing what is "apt," most "worthy," and most harmonious and consonant.[22] Vitruvius links the term *oikonomia* with order, disposition, shapeliness, and symmetry. For Irenaeus, God practices a kind of artistry across space and time, and nothing is finally superfluous in his work, just as the Sistine Ceiling, though overwhelming in its complexity and variety, is marked throughout by *consonantia*. There are, of course, smaller "economies" evident throughout the process, but all are governed by one overarching *oikonomia*, precisely because there is, in the end, one great *economus*. Another standard Irenaean trope is that of the musical instrument, made up of a variety of tonal colors but producing a harmony. The following is typical: "Many and various, no doubt, are the different parts of creation. These may seem, when considered separately, to be contrary and opposite to one another, but when taken in connection with the rest of creation, they form one perfect whole, just as the many discordant notes of the lyre make one unbroken melody."[23] What produces the appearance of contradiction and discord is, ultimately, our insufficient grasp of the divine musician's mind.

Most precisely, *anakephalaiosis* refers to the history of salvation, which proceeds through a number of different stages and moves to a single, definite fulfillment. Thus, to give just one example, in his education of the race,

God deigns that human beings be governed first by natural precepts, then by the law, and finally by the gospel. And this history is marked, through and through, by analogies, overtones and undertones, family resemblances, rhymes in time and space, types and antitypes, prophecies and fulfillments. The many are woven together, for those who know how to see, in a complex but unified design. As Matthew Levering has helped us to see, this unity in difference is grounded in the God who both permeates and transcends time, precisely because he is the creator of time.[24] Whereas modernity tends to construe time as a series of discrete moments, essentially unrelated to one another, the Bible reads it (and space as well) in a participatory manner, that is to say, as rooted in the creator God who effectively unifies that which he creates. Hence, on the biblical/Irenaean reading, time is not simply one thing after another but rather a web, a nexus of meaning, one moment calling out to, indicating, or echoing another; and space is not simply an empty grid occupied by a variety of objects but rather a weave of interdependence and mutual implication.

One of the designs that appears in the weave of space and time is the accustoming of man to God and God to man. For Irenaeus, the various economies of the Old Testament represent the process by which God continually lures his people into friendship with him, teaching them to think in accord with the divine mind and to move at the prompting of the divine will. But what is specially interesting is that Irenaeus appreciates the accustoming as moving in the other direction as well, God as it were learning the ways of men, condescending to the level of their minds and wills, the way a parent lowers herself in order to relate more effectively to her children. Here the metaphor of the "hands" of God is particularly apt, for Irenaeus sees the Old Testament dispensation as a gradual molding of human beings, accustoming men to the touch of God and God to the "feel" of men. This mutual touching was effortless for God and harmless for men as long as the clay was supple, but after the fall, the earth of the human heart became brittle and the molding hence became difficult for both the potter and the clay. As many have pointed out, Irenaeus is the first to read salvation history in terms of the several great covenants that Yahweh made with his people. These mutual pledges of fidelity, made between God and his servants Adam, Noah, Moses, and Christ, represent ever intensifying expressions of divine-human unity. Both the mutual accustoming and the making of covenants come to their fulfillment in the incarnation, which is the concrete embodiment of the friendship between God and the human race. Jesus is the *anakephalaiosis* (recapitulation) of salvation history, the capstone of the building, the purpose of the process, the unification of the many strands that constitute the *oikonomia*. And hence he is the *eikon* of the invisible God who is a tensive play of unity and diversity.

The Iconic Manifestation of the Personhood of God

We recall Ratzinger's second thesis, stating that Trinitarian language signals
the personhood of God, the quality of looking toward another, which obtains
within the unity of his own substance. If creation and providence manifest
the inner being of God, then we shouldn't be surprised that the *oikonomia*
would be the gradual process of making visible the invisibility of God so
that humans might become capable of looking to God. In a much-celebrated
passage, Irenaeus says that the Father is the "invisible of the Son and the Son
the visible of the Father."[25] Obviously, no creature could ever share utterly
in the mutual regard of the Father and the Son, the act by which each takes
the full measure of the other. Nevertheless, a kind of participation in it can
be enjoyed by a human being. The incarnation of the Logos makes possible
(and this is to say the same thing) the divinizing of the human being and the
seeing of God. Everyone cites the magnificent text from the fourth book of
the *Adversus haereses* to the effect that the glory of God is a human being
fully alive, but they often fail to cite what follows that quotation: "And the
life of man is the vision of God."[26] Looking at the Father through the me-
diation of the Son, we become sharers in the mutual Trinitarian regard. It is
fascinating to note how often words having to do with sight are used in the
Irenaean corpus: *manifestatio, ostentio, visio, revelatio, lux, lumen.* And it
is not merely a verbal tic or stylistic conceit that leads Irenaeus to pepper his
texts with the exhortations "see" and "you see." This is, of course, in contrast
to the stress on secrecy and privacy in the Gnostic thought world, but finally
it has to do with the dramatically public nature of the incarnation and of the
church that bears its power.

In line with his consistently evolutionary view, Irenaeus holds that this
seeing of the invisible Father through the visible icon was made possible only
through a long preparation. And it is indeed under this rubric of seeing that we
can survey the whole of the economy of salvation. Ever attentive to the details
of the biblical narratives, Irenaeus remarks that, after the fall, God admits that
he can't see Adam: "Where are you?" This signals the loss of shared intimacy
through sight. The *oikonomia* will unfold, accordingly, as God's attempt to
reconcile (eyelash to eyelash) himself with his errant human children. The
Logos, who would appear fully in Jesus, the new Adam, nevertheless made
himself visible in a variety of ways throughout Israelite history. According
to Irenaeus, it was the Logos who came to see Abraham under the terebinth
of Mamre, who visited Jacob in his dream vision, who allowed Moses to
see his back side, who operated in the dreams of Joseph, and who spoke so
eloquently out of the burning bush. Relatedly, it was the Logos who appeared

in the visions (the typical Irenaean word) given to the prophets. Both Justin and Irenaeus relate these manifestations in the minds of the prophets to the manifestations of the forms that occur in the minds of the philosophers. The signal difference is that the prophets actually crossed the bridge into the realm of the forms, whereas the philosophers saw that land only from a distance. This is why the prophets never appeal to argument or other indirect forms of manifestation. For the Lyons master, they were "witnesses to the truth, above demonstration and worthy of belief." What the prophets saw, to state it precisely, were the forms of the divine *oikonomia* stretching across space and time, all the rhymes and rhythms of God's providential artistry. In these various ways, the Logos was gradually, and with infinite patience, revealing his light to the fallen and compromised eyes of the human race. Irenaeus knew that a direct showing of the Logos to sin-sick eyes would be like the introduction of a spelunker, lost for days in the darkness of a cave, to the direct illumination of the sun.

And therefore, Israelite eyes, accustomed over many centuries to look upon the Logos, were finally, in the fullness of time, able to see him when he appeared: "The Word became flesh and dwelt among us, full of grace and truth; we have beheld his glory, glory as of the only Son from the Father" (John 1:14). For Irenaeus, it is crucially important that the Son of God appeared visibly and publicly and that his revelation took place according to a series of events open for investigation. His miracles, his table fellowship, his interaction with sinners, his confrontation with his enemies, his trial and execution, and the gestures of his resurrected body were all luminously available to those who had eyes to see. Each of these constituted an aspect or profile of the super-saturated phenomenon (if I can borrow Jean-Luc Marion's phrase) of the incarnate Word. Looking upon the Word, the first visionaries were able to "see" the invisibility of the Father ("he who has seen me has seen the Father") and hence were able to participate in the Son's looking toward the Father within the inner life of the Trinity. As a kind of afterglow of the full manifestation of the Logos, we have, argues Irenaeus, the sacramental and liturgical life of the church, which is, like the incarnation itself, colorful, visible, and public. Through these visible means, believers continue to gaze upon the Logos and hence upon the Father.

The Iconic Manifestation of the Absoluteness of Relativity

Ratzinger's third Trinitarian thesis holds that the play between the one divine essence and the three divine persons signals the absoluteness of relativity, the co-primordiality of substance and relation. If God *is* a set of relationships, then we shouldn't be surprised that, in accord with the Irenaean principle, the *oikonomia* involves the iconic manifestation of relationality. The first place to look is Irenaeus's treatment of creation, the inaugural act in the drama of God's self-presentation. As we saw, Irenaeus is the first major Christian theologian to defend a doctrine of *creatio ex nihilo*, setting him rather dramatically apart from the metaphysical tradition that surrounded and preceded him. But Irenaeus saw clearly that *creatio ex nihilo* is a corollary of God's lack of need and of God's omnipotence. No matter how highly they construe the power and majesty of God, Plato, Aristotle, Philo, and Justin still have to maintain that God does not have supreme power precisely in the measure that he requires something that is ontologically co-basic with him in order to create. Thus Irenaeus concludes that the properly omnipotent God could not possibly make the universe in the manner of an artist shaping some already existing substrate but rather must give rise to the very matter that he in turn molds.

Now what follows from this is God's immediacy to the world. If God truly creates from nothing, then there is no aspect of creation that is not, from moment to moment, coming forth from God and, quite literally, nothing standing between creatures and their Creator. Though Irenaeus does not put it quite this way, it seems impossible to avoid the conclusion that the creature who is being created *ex nihilo* must be construed not so much as a thing that has a relationship to God but *as a relationship*. Many centuries after Irenaeus, Thomas Aquinas would state this idea explicitly. In the disputed question *De potentia Dei*, Thomas specifies that creation is "*quaedam relatio ad creatorem cum novitate essendi*." Another key implication of the doctrine of creation from nothing is the connection of all created things to one another by the deepest bonds. All finite realities are ontological siblings precisely in the measure that they are all simultaneously coming forth from the same divine ground. In light of this principle, Irenaeus celebrates not only the diversity of things (as we saw) but also the fundamentally unbreakable connection that obtains among them. In a word, the entirety of the finite realm *is* a manifestation of the sheer relationality that constitutes the divine being.

To transpose this to a moral and spiritual register, there is no place that one can run from the presence of God, no ontological ground on which one can finally stand in resistance to God's creativity. "Where shall I go from your Spirit? . . . If I ascend to the heaven, you are there!" Irenaeus expresses this through the trope of the right hand of God, which holds up the sinner even when that creature, in rebellion, "takes the wings of the morning and dwells in the uttermost parts of the sea." And this analysis provides the best angle of vision into Irenaeus's understanding of sin. One of the principles of the master, stated over and over again in the *Adversus haereses*, is that God makes and man is made. The human being *is* a relationship to the God who is continually making and shaping him; essential to the good life is an acceptance of this state of affairs. At the heart of original sin, therefore, is the tendency toward self-creation and self-deification and the concomitant refusal to be shaped. Thus, the moral twisting is grounded in a more fundamental metaphysical violation, a refusal of the relationship to God that one is. Now we see still another way to interpret the *oikonomia*—namely, as God's steady attempt to draw his human creatures back into an acknowledgment of their inescapably relational nature. The covenants, the law, the temple, the teachings of the prophets, and the adventures of the patriarchs are all trainings in this salutary relationality with the God whose substance is relationship. The heroes of Israel are those who embody this truth. Thus Enoch and Elijah rather naturally make a heavenly journey under the aegis of God, and the three young men thrown into the furnace place themselves confidently in the divine hands.

All of this is recapitulated in the new Adam. Whereas the first Adam disobeyed and hence withdrew into a kind of metaphysical shadowland, the second Adam obeyed the Father and lived out of the deepest truth of things. And this did not merely indicate the way things are; it effected a change in a world marked by division. Irenaeus uses the following words to indicate what the union between divinity and humanity in Christ produced in the wider creation: "unite," "join together," "fuse," "make one." The obedient relationality on display in Jesus knits a broken creation back together precisely in the measure that it incarnates the relationality that God is.

PART 2

THEOLOGY AND PHILOSOPHY

5

---✠---

To See according to the Icon of Jesus Christ

Reflections on the Catholic Intellectual Tradition

The influential twentieth-century theologian Hans Urs von Balthasar commented that the greatest tragedy in the history of the church was neither the rupture between the Eastern and Western branches of Christianity in the eleventh century nor the Protestant Reformation of the sixteenth century but rather the split between theology and spirituality that occurred at the end of the thirteenth century. Up to the year 1300, roughly speaking, the most important spiritual writers were precisely the theologians: Paul, Origen, Chrysostom, Gregory of Nyssa, Irenaeus, Augustine, Anselm, Thomas Aquinas. If you had asked Aquinas, for example, to name the difference between his systematic theology and his spirituality, he wouldn't have understood the question. But after 1300, theology evolved into a more strictly academic university discipline, and what we have come to call *spirituality* branched off into a distinctive form of thought. It is extremely instructive that, after this watershed year, the people we consider the most important "spiritual" writers—Meister Eckhart, Johannes Tauler, Jan Ruysbroek, Teresa of Avila, John of the Cross, Blaise Pascal, Thérèse of Lisieux, Thomas Merton—were not academic theologians. The sad consequence of this division is that we do not tend to appreciate the transformative, salvific dimension of our theology. We tend not to see that the dogmas of the faith are a primary means by which we become grafted onto Christ and through which we properly see the world. I would share with Balthasar and Henri de Lubac the conviction that the re-pairing of the division between theology and spirituality is a pressing concern of our moment in church history. It is this healing, especially in regard to the Catholic intellectual life, that I would like to explore.

Jesus as Logos Made Flesh

I love the clever cartoons in the *New Yorker* magazine. But there are some times when, though I have seen all the characters and understood fully the caption, I don't understand why a given cartoon is funny—I don't "get" it. Then, although I have seen no new feature of the design nor grasped a new word of the caption, I see the pattern that obtains, the light goes on, and I smile. The philosopher Ludwig Wittgenstein said that the most puzzling prob-lem in all of philosophy is how we manage to see something *as* something, precisely what is at stake in "getting" a joke. He illustrated the issue with his famous example of the "duck-rabbit" design, a simple drawing that, squinted at from one perspective and the right suggestion in mind, looks like a duck and, perceived from another angle and with a different suggestion, becomes a rabbit. Such perception involves the transcendence of the merely empirical or measurable—this feature or that—and rises to the far more elusive grasp-ing of a formal structure.

The prologue to St. John's Gospel includes the assertion that Jesus Christ is the incarnation of the Word of God (*ho Logos tou Theou*). This means that Jesus is the iconic representation of the very mind of God, the enfleshment of the pattern according to which God fashioned the universe. In the first chapter of Paul's letter to the Colossians we find a similarly bold claim in regard to Jesus. We are told that he is the "image (*eikon*) of the invisible God," the one in whom "all things were created, in heaven and on earth . . . [and] all things hold together" (Col. 1:15–17). Infinitely more than one prophet among many or one spiritual teacher alongside others, Jesus is the lens through which the whole of reality is properly read, the means by which we correctly see the universe *as* something. Balthasar said that Christ "is the unchangeably valid blueprint in every situation in the world and in history."[1] These maximalist metaphysical claims carry the implication that the narratives and doctrines concerning Jesus are epistemically basic. To state this negatively, the Jesus presented in the New Testament must function as an epistemic trump, that is to say, the truthful pattern that cannot be finally gainsaid by any rival system, philosophy, or overarching perspective. This claim by no means disallows insights from other points of view and intellectual disciplines, but it does rule out the possibility that those views or disciplines could, at the end of the day, fundamentally contradict what is presented in and through Jesus Christ. This is why the Catholic tradition, at its best, has exhibited a generosity in regard to mythic, philosophical, and scientific claims to truth, seeing them as *logoi* coherent with the *Logos*. But Jesus is the final and definitive pattern by which reality is interpreted—the manner in which we "get" God and the world, and the dynamics of our own spiritual transformation. That claim stands at the heart of the Catholic intellectual tradition. I would like to expand upon this assertion by examining four specific doctrines that flow from the Catholic belief in Jesus as the Logos of God: first, God's nature as noncompetitively transcendent to the world; second, radical humanism; third, creation from nothing; and fourth, the paschal mystery.

The Noncompetitive Transcendence of God

The most elemental insight to which we come on the basis of the incarnation is what I term the "noncompetitive transcendence" of God. The claim made throughout the New Testament and confirmed by the early tradition is that this man Jesus, the prophet from Nazareth, is also God. In him, God became human, without ceasing to be God and without compromising the integrity of the creature he became. The Council of Chalcedon, in 451, gave classic expression to this paradox when it taught that in Jesus two natures—divine and human—come together in the unity of the divine person, "without mixing, mingling, or confusion." In saying this, it was holding off forms of monophysitism (according to which Jesus's divinity overwhelms his humanity), forms of Nestorianism (according to which Jesus is a human person with a rich relationship to a divine person), and forms of Arianism (according to which Jesus is an amalgam of divinity and humanity, along the lines of mythological figures such as Achilles and Hercules). The upshot of this very distinctive teaching is that God cannot be thought of along the lines of a worldly nature, an ordinary thing in the world, for such a reality would be competitive with others of the same type; they would be mutually exclusive on the ontological level. An antelope, for example, can become a lion, but only by being devoured, or a podium can become a pile of ashes, but only by being destroyed through flames. But in Jesus, God *became* a creature in a completely unthreatening, noninvasive, nonviolent way; proving that the true God is not so much somewhere else as somehow else. He is not simply other but, to borrow Kathryn Tanner's phrase, "otherly other," transcendent according to a mode of transcendence that goes beyond spatial, modal, quantitative, or any other type of creaturely differentiation.

This is precisely why the great theologians of the Christian tradition do not typically refer to God as the highest being, which is to say, one being among others, or in David Burrell's phrase, "the biggest thing around." Rather, they tend to use the mysterious and evocative language of "being itself." Thus Thomas Aquinas calls God not the *ens summum* (highest entity) but *ipsum esse subsistens* (the sheer act of to-be itself). And St. Anselm spoke of God as "that than which nothing greater can be thought." Though this designation seems to indicate the highest being, upon closer examination it amounts to a deconstruction of the doctrine of the *ens summum*, for the supreme being plus anything else in the world would be greater than the supreme being alone. If Anselm's definition holds, then God plus the world is not greater than God alone, which could not possibly be the case were God one being among many. *Ipsum esse* is, in Augustine's magnificent phrase, *intimior intimo meo et superior summo meo*, that is to say, simultaneously closer to me than I am to myself and higher than anything I can possibly imagine. Being itself is utterly unlike any of the beings in the world, and it is the most intimate ground of all that exists in the world. The prophet Isaiah catches this tension when he speaks forth these words of Yahweh: "For as the heavens are higher than the earth, / so are my ways higher than your ways, / my thoughts higher than your thoughts" (Isa. 55:9 NABRE), and "Can a mother forget her infant. . . ? / Even should she forget, / I will never forget you. / See, upon the palms of my hands I have engraved you" (Isa. 49:15–16 NABRE). This entire tradition of theological speech finds its ground in the self-designation of God in Exodus 3:14. When Moses asks his mysterious interlocutor for his name, he is wondering which god he is dealing with, which of the many local deities has addressed him. But the true God disallows just this sort of question as he speaks his famous non-answer: "I AM WHO I AM." The implication seems to be that this God is not one deity among many, one existent alongside others, but rather the one whose nature is to-be.

The spiritual concomitant of this theological description is that the divine transcendence is not competitive to the world and to the human endeavor. On the contrary, the distinctive otherness of God is what makes creaturely flourishing possible. The prophet Isaiah, once again, catches this paradox when he says, in regard to human action, "LORD . . . / you have accomplished all we have done" (Isa. 26:12 NABRE). We notice in this formula that there is absolutely no tension between our very real accomplishments and God's active providence in and through them. This fundamental noncompetitiveness between infinite and finite freedom was too often lost sight of in the famous debates between Jesuits and Dominicans in the sixteenth century in regard to divine foreknowledge and human freedom. Christians can and should say that our freedom is utterly compatible with God's serene direction of the universe according to his eternal plan. In the stories and dramas of the ancient Greeks, this tension between divine and human achievement is taken for granted and provides the theological matrix for the narratives. The God disclosed in the biblical tradition, however, is the condition for the possibility of the richest humanism.

Radical Humanism

There is, in fact, no philosophy, religion, or social theory in history that is more radically humanistic than classical Christianity. An adage that can be found in a variety of the fathers of the church is this: *Deus fit homo ut homo fieret Deus* (God became human so that humans might become God). None of the humanisms of antiquity, the Renaissance, or modernity ever held out to human beings the prospect of a comparable flourishing. I would like to make this clear by narrowing my focus a bit and concentrating on the issue of finite freedom in relation to God.

A few centuries after the Council of Chalcedon, a controversy arose in the church over the arcane question of the number of wills in Christ. Some, in the interest of defending the Lord's divinity, held that there was but one divine will in Jesus, which had effectively replaced his human freedom. These advocates of the one will were called monothelites. But the orthodox church condemned monothelitism as heretical and taught, in line with Chalcedonian instincts, that there were, in Christ, two wills, a fully constituted human freedom and a fully integral divine freedom. The opponents of monothelitism intuited that a key implication of the incarnation is that human liberty is not suppressed by the proximity of divine liberty but rather enabled by it. We are, in fact, freer the more fully we surrender to the divine will.

A major preoccupation of the early modern philosophers was a defense of human freedom over against what was taken to be an oppressive and arbitrary divine freedom. This concern was given classical expression in Kant's celebration of our autonomy over against all forms of heteronomy, including and especially that of the church. Obedience to the categorical imperative involved, for Kant, not a submission to divine authority but an acquiescence to the deepest moral instincts of one's own will. Hence, it was the highest form of autonomy. The theological concomitant of this valorization of autonomous freedom was the Deism that beguiled the best minds of the period. God exists, the Deists said, not as a power brooding over the cosmos, the political society, and the self-expressive human will, but rather as a distant clockmaker isolated in an indifferent transcendence. In time, even this marginalized divinity came to be seen as a threat to human liberty, and the peculiarly modern form of atheism emerged as a result. Ludwig Feuerbach, the inaugurator of this trajectory of thought, opined that God was nothing but the neurotic projection of an idealized self-understanding, the perfect human writ large and imagined as an independently existing being. The no to God, therefore, was the yes to man, in his famous formula. The young Karl Marx was such an ardent disciple of Feuerbach that he punningly urged his contemporaries to be "baptized in the fiery brook," the *Feuer-bach*. As he developed his own philosophical perspective, Marx took for granted Feuerbach's assessment of religion as fundamentally dehumanizing. The "opium of the people," religious faith was tantamount, he thought, to a fantasy from which the human race would have to awaken in order to commence the hard work of economic and political liberation. Sigmund Freud was another who enthusiastically raced down the Feuerbach autobahn. In his *Future of an Illusion* (whose title pretty much gives away the game), Freud taught that religion is a waking dream, a wish-fulfilling fantasy that would have to be dissolved were the human race to make any realistic progress. This school of thought is given perhaps pithiest expression in the syllogism constructed by the most famous existentialist of the twentieth century. In his *Existentialism Is a Humanism*, Jean-Paul Sartre reasoned as follows: if God exists, I cannot be free; but I am free, therefore God does not exist. Sartre makes explicit what had been implicit from the beginning of the modern period, namely, that the no to divine freedom is the yes to human freedom. What I hope to have made clear is how thoroughly this entire trajectory of thought represents the repudiation of the noncompetitive interpretation of divine and human freedom implied by the tradition of Christian orthodoxy.

I'll specify the tension between these two construals of finite freedom in relation to God by glancing at the work of the contemporary Dominican moral theologian Servais Pinckaers. Pinckaers argues that the distinctively modern understanding of liberty, which we have sketched, has its roots in the late medieval speculation of William of Occam. Occam held that freedom is best understood as a kind of indifference of the subject in the presence of competing values. Someone is free in the measure that she hovers above the yes and the no and makes a choice on the basis of no compulsion either interior or exterior. This interpretation of freedom as choice and self-expression Pinckaers calls "the freedom of indifference." This Occamist theory represented, however, a major departure from a classical and biblical understanding of liberty. On this earlier reading, liberty is not so much self-expressive choice as the disciplining of desire so as to make the achievement of the good first possible and finally effortless. In this sense, I am a free speaker of English, for I can say, in that language, whatever I want to say; and Michael Jordan was a free basketball player, for he could do whatever he wanted in response to the shifting demands of the game. This more classical interpretation Pinckaers calls "freedom for excellence." In light of this clarification, we see immediately that the two types of freedom are oriented in entirely different ways toward the law and the objectively good. For the freedom of indifference, law and the good will be seen as threats, for they necessarily represent a limit to the range of self-determining choice. But the freedom for excellence is not threatened by the objectively good but rather finds itself precisely in relation to it. Michael Jordan became freer in the measure that he internalized the objective structure of the game that he played.

Pinckaers's distinction allows us to see more clearly why modernity became increasingly hostile to God. The liberty advocated by modern thinkers was, practically without exception, the autonomous self-legislating and self-expressive freedom of indifference. Such liberty could not, in the long run, tolerate the interference of the supreme objective good, namely, God. The resolution of the monothelite controversy makes sense only against the background of a "freedom for excellence" construal of human liberty. The supreme objective good is not a limitation for authentic liberty but precisely the condition for its possibility. In light of these clarifications, we can make sense of Paul's paradoxical claims that he is the "slave of Christ Jesus" (Rom. 1:1 NABRE) and that "For freedom Christ has set us free" (Gal. 5:1) And we can understand St. Irenaeus's ecstatic summary of Christian faith: "The glory of God is a human being fully alive."

Creation from Nothing

Another elemental Catholic notion, deeply rooted in the doctrine of God's noncompetitive transcendence and hence in the fact of the incarnation, is that of creation from nothing. If we look in the mythological, philosophical, scientific, and theological accounts available throughout the ages, we find a wide variety of theories in regard to the origin of things. The biblical and Christian account is distinctive: God makes the whole of the finite order *ex nihilo* (from nothing), that is to say, not from any preexisting substrate. Since God is *ipsum esse subsistens*, then everything that exists besides God is derived in the entirety of its being from God.

Now several conclusions can be drawn on the basis of this assertion. First, all things in the universe are marked by a fundamental intelligibility or know-ability. Since all finite existence has come into being through God, and since God is a person endowed with intellect and will, the created universe is not dumbly there; rather, it is marked with formal structure, since it has been thought into being. The medievals expressed this idea with customary laconi-cism: *omne ens est scibile* (all being is knowable). Christians know that all acts of knowledge here below are acts of re-cognition, thinking again what has already been thought by a more primordial knower. As John Polkinghorne, Peter Hodgson, Stanley Jaki, Albert Einstein, and Joseph Ratzinger have all acknowledged, it is absolutely no accident that the modern physical sciences emerged precisely in the universities of the Christian West, that is to say, out of a thought-world in which the doctrine of creation is a structuring element. No scientist could commence her work unless she had the confidence, born of a theological intuition, that the world she is going out to meet is endowed with intelligibility. Mind you, this insistence on the presence of form in all finite things has nothing to do with claims that the cosmos is "orderly," even less with theories of "intelligent design." It is getting at something much more fundamental, namely, that all things have been made through the power of the Word. In light of this, we can see why the conflicts that break out from time to time between religion and science are so tragic and nonsensical. Understood properly, the sciences rest upon inescapably religious intuitions, and religion, consequently, can only benefit from the perceptions of scientists.

A second conclusion that one can draw from the doctrine of *creatio ex nihilo* is that nonviolence is metaphysically basic. In all the ancient mythic and philosophical accounts of the beginning, we find something like a pri-mordial warfare as the matrix out of which order emerges. God or the gods wrestle some opposing force into submission, and from that struggle comes the world we know. Often enough, the universe is made from the remains of the conquered powers. Even in the more austere philosophical accounts, traces of the mythological story remain. Thus, in Plato the demiurgos shapes mat-ter in accord with the heavenly forms that he contemplates, and in Aristotle the prime mover draws recalcitrant prime matter into shape. Overtones of these old narratives and theories can be heard in popular stories from the *Epic of Gilgamesh* to *Rambo* and *Dirty Harry*, in which chaos is wrestled into order through an invasive act of violence. But there is none of this in the Christian account of *creatio ex nihilo*. Rather, God makes the whole of the created universe in a sheerly generous act, by the power of his Word, and in opposition to nothing at all. The ground of order, therefore, is not violence but love. A derivative point is that relationship is more ontologically basic than substance. Aristotle articulated the commonsensical position that substances—individually existing things—are primordial, and that relationship—what obtains between or among substances—is secondary. But the doctrine of *creatio ex nihilo* turns this around, since creatures *are*, to the depths of their being, relationships to God, the source from which they continually flow. Thomas Aquinas defined creation as *quaedam relatio ad creatorem cum novitate essendi* (a kind of relationship to the Creator with freshness of being), and this has to imply that relationality, or what Charles Williams called "coinherence," is the basic ontological form.

A third implication of the doctrine of creation from nothing is the interconnectedness of all created things to one another through their common center in God. As I have been arguing, God is not a supreme being alongside other beings but rather *ipsum esse*, the sheer act of to-be itself, in which and through which all finite things are constituted. This means that as I find my center in God, I simultaneously find your center, the center of everyone else, and indeed the center of brother sun and sister moon. When St. Francis used that evocative phrase, he was not indulging in sentimental poetry but rather articulating an exact metaphysical position: because of the creator God, all things in the cosmos are ontological siblings to one another, connected by a bond deeper and more abiding than anything that divides them. We can find this metaphysical view vividly depicted in the rose windows of the gothic cathedrals. At the center of the rose, invariably, is an image of Christ, and then wheeling around that center in ordered harmonies are the various pictures and designs of the window, all of which are connected to one another and to the center through spokes or some other feature of the design. The rose is meant to be a portrait of the properly ordered cosmos: all things linked to the center and, through that center, to one another. Williams's coinherence obtains not only in regard to God's relation to each creature but to the rapport among creatures. Catholic social teaching, articulated with special clarity by the modern popes from Leo XIII through John Paul II, flows from this metaphysical perception. Each individual is worthy of respect and is the subject of inalienable rights precisely in the measure that he is created by God. Moreover, the essential bond among creatures grounds the moral obligation to care for the common good. As Ambrose of Milan put it, "If you have two shirts in your closet, one belongs to you; the other belongs to the man who has no shirt." To live in accord with this teaching is not simply to be ethically upright; it is to live in accord with the grain of the universe.

The Paschal Mystery

A final feature that I would like to consider is what the liturgical scholars of the twentieth century called "the paschal mystery," the passage of Jesus from death to resurrection. In a certain sense, this phrase is a shorthand for the heart of Jesus's existence and mission. If we Catholics squint at the world through the lens of Jesus Christ, and if the paschal mystery speaks the deepest truth about Jesus, then this dynamic of cross and new life is of central importance for our understanding of the way things most fundamentally are.

If we are to plumb the depths of this mystery, we must attend to both dimensions of it. The Son of God appeared on the earth—God's own self in human form—and we killed him. A basic motif of the Gospels is that Jesus was, from the beginning of his life to the end, massively opposed. Any illusion that all is fundamentally well with us, that we are perfectible through our own efforts, is shattered by this truth. In a very vivid sense, our sin becomes apparent to us by way of contrast with the light and truth of Christ. The Gospels display this dynamic with ruthless insistence. At the news of the Messiah's birth, Herod and all Jerusalem tremble, and that wicked king tries to stamp the child out. In Luke's account of the nativity, Jesus's lordship is implicitly placed in tension with the lordship of Caesar Augustus, and the battle between these two kings is a leitmotif of that entire Gospel. From the moment that Jesus appears on the public scene, forces rise up to oppose him: the scribes, the Pharisees, Jewish collaborators, Roman officialdom, often his own disciples. And these powers are interpreted by the Gospel writers as but diplomats and agents of a more primal power, the spiritual person whom Jesus confronted in the desert just after his baptism. The devil has two great names in the New Testament, and both are telling. He is referred to as *ho diabolos* (the scatterer) and *ho Satanas* (the accuser). As we have seen, the primordial form of reality, on the Catholic reading, is coinherence, the coming together of the many in love. The power that is opposed to this is therefore a dividing, scattering force.

When Jesus emerged publicly and began preaching the kingdom of God, he was taken to mean something very specific, namely, that the tribes of Israel, scattered by sin, were being gathered. In the second chapter of the prophet Isaiah, we find the prediction, "the mountain of the house of the LORD / shall be established as the highest of the mountains . . . / and all the nations shall flow to it" (v. 2). The Israelite hope was that, in the Messianic era, Israel would become a godly nation gathered around the common worship of the true God at the temple on Mount Zion, and that this united Israel would become, in turn, a beacon to the other nations of the world. Jesus's entire preaching and ministry should be read under this rubric of the great gathering. He went out consistently to the margins of society in order to lure the lost sheep of the house of Israel, and he hosted festive suppers to which were invited both the rich and the poor, both male and female, both saints and sinners, both the righteous and the unrighteous. This open table fellowship was the concrete acting out of the kingdom prophecy of Isaiah and an implicit critique of a religious society predicated upon exclusion, domination, and stratification. Again and again, the parables of Jesus give narrative expression to this new kingdom way of being. In the story of the prodigal son, for example, we hear how a gracious father, through patient love, attempts to draw back into the embrace of his compassion two sons who, in different ways, had wandered far from it. And in the teaching of Jesus, the gathering motif is central. The rhetorical high point of the Sermon on the Mount is Jesus's insistence that the love of his followers must be like that of God himself, extending to both friends and foes, shining on the good and the bad alike. The commandment to love one's enemies takes on a special urgency when we conceive of it against the background of the creation metaphysics that we outlined above, for even the direst of opponents are, in the deepest ground of their being, ontological siblings. Therefore, the injunction to love one's enemy is much more than an ethical demand; it is an encouragement to live according to the coinherence that constitutes the grain of the universe. Once again, the opposition that Jesus faced brings into sharp relief a basic form of human dysfunction: our preference for the patterns of exclusion, domination, division, and violence. As St. John put it, "The light has come into the world, and men loved darkness rather than light" (see John 3:19).

The second great title for the devil, as we saw, is *ho Satanas* (the accuser), a name that Jesus explicitly uses in the Matthean account of the temptation. As René Girard has pointed out, all sinful human societies are predicated, to varying degrees, on the scapegoating mechanism. We tend to find a sense of community precisely through a common blaming of someone or some group that we perceive, because of their "otherness," to be a threat. This scapegoating dynamic is evident everywhere from small conversation circles to the nation state. We notice how consistently in the Gospels, Jesus undermines and interrupts just this sort of phony society. The story of the woman caught in adultery is especially instructive (see John 8:1–11). The scribes and Pharisees, who had seen the woman in the very act of adultery, stand for the scapegoating mechanism, and the angry crowd that gathered around them, eager to throw the stones, represent the ersatz unstable and violent sort of community that is formed by that mechanism. How deftly and thoroughly Jesus interrupts the process with his words and gestures of forgiveness. When Jesus says that he has come to divide, setting mother against daughter and father against son, that he has come not for peace but for the sword, he should be taken to mean that his purpose is to break up false, dysfunctional communities so that the true community, based upon forgiveness and love, can emerge. In a word, Jesus draws the scattering and accusing powers of the sinful world out into the open where he can do battle with them, and he makes vividly present, by his own actions and words, another way of being in the world, the way of the kingdom, God's order.

The struggle against Jesus, which commenced at his birth and continued through his public ministry, reached a climax when the prophet from Nazareth made a triumphal entry into Jerusalem. The scattering and accusing powers came out in full force to oppose this pretender to the title of Messiah. A conspiracy of Judean and Roman authorities, abetted by the betrayal of his closest followers, brought Jesus to the cross. On that instrument of torture, Jesus fought the final battle, but not with the weapons of the world. Rather, he willingly took upon himself all the darkness of sin, the violence of the world, the scattering and accusing energy, and he swallowed it up in the divine mercy: "Father, forgive them; for they know not what they do." In this, he manifested himself as the true king of the world, a truth that Pontius Pilate, in a supreme irony, announced to all the nations in Hebrew, Greek, and Latin. Now, what prevents the cross of Jesus from being just one more example of failed idealism, another instance of a good man "ground under by the wheel of history"? How do we know that Jesus's kingdom has triumphed over the powers of domination, exclusion, scapegoating, and fear? We know because Jesus rose from the dead through the power of the Holy Spirit. N. T. Wright has commented that, within the context of first-century Judaism, there would be no clearer proof that a person was not the Messiah than that person's death at the hands of Israel's enemies. Therefore, that Christianity survived precisely as a Messianic movement implies that something absolutely extraordinary happened after the death of Jesus. The only finally satisfying explanation, Wright concludes, for the perdurance of the belief that the crucified Jesus is the Messiah is the bodily resurrection of Jesus from the dead. Without this fact, Christianity, as a historical phenomenon, remains inexplicable.

What is theologically important about the resurrection—and this comes through in all the Gospels—is that God's power is greater than the sinful powers of the fallen world. When the risen Jesus presents himself to his disciples, he always shows his wounds, so as to demonstrate human resistance to grace, but then he says, "Shalom," peace. In the *shalom* of the risen Jesus, we know that nonviolence, coinherence, compassion, and love are more powerful than hatred, division, scapegoating, and the ways of violence. We know that God's order is restored not through answering violence but through forgiving love. And that is why Paul can say in his letter to the Romans, "I am sure that neither death, nor life, nor angels, nor principalities, nor things present, nor things to come, nor powers, nor height, nor depth, nor anything else in creation will be able to separate us from the love of God" (Rom. 8:38–39). And this is why the first Christians can refer to Jesus, not Caesar, as the *Kyrios*, the Lord. And this is why Paul can hold up the terrible Roman cross, a symbol of the violence and heartlessness of a fallen world, and say, "For I decided to know nothing among you except Jesus Christ and him crucified." The cross now becomes a kind of taunt: "You think that frightens us? God's power is greater than any power you can throw at us!" Thus, the resurrection of Jesus from the dead is the ratification of the vision of reality that we have been presenting.

Conclusion

Contemporary theologian Stanley Hauerwas has said that the task of the Christian church is to tell the world what its story is. Its story is that of creation, fall, and redemption, and the interpretive key to that narrative is Jesus of Nazareth, the crucified and risen Lord. Without knowledge of Jesus, people are like actors who don't know what play they're in. Therefore, Christianity is not a set of private convictions that we cultivate inwardly or whisper among ourselves. It is the message that the whole world needs to hear. We who have heard it must become agents of subversion and transformation. "Go therefore and make disciples of all nations, baptizing them in the name of the Father and of the Son and of the Holy Spirit, teaching them to observe all that I have commanded you; and lo, I am with you always, to the close of the age" (Matt. 28:19–20).

But the moment this call for a public declaration of Christian faith is heard, many in our culture—especially within the academy—draw back. Isn't religion best construed as a private matter, a subjective conviction? And isn't it, at the very least, bad form to announce it in the public forum? Doesn't talk of Jesus's metaphysical and epistemic primacy smack of intolerance, intellectual obscurantism, and bigotry? Wouldn't this sort of rhetoric awaken the terrifying ghost of religious violence, a specter that the intellectual founders of modernity were passionate to exorcise? With these questions in mind, I

would like by way of conclusion to draw some implications from my forego-
ing observations.

I argued that God stands in a noncompetitive relationship with the universe that he has made. This means that *ipsum esse*, while wholly determining the to-be of the finite world, lets that world be in its own integrity and
independence. In an analogous manner, theology stands in a grounding but
noncompetitive relationship with the other sciences, determining them even
as it lets them be. In his *Idea of a University*, John Henry Newman claimed
that theology, precisely in the measure that it speaks of the creator God who
impinges on the whole of finite reality, has to do with the entire circle of university disciplines. This does not mean, of course, that theology determines
the method and analytical procedure of the particular sciences, but it does
indeed mean that theology provides an ultimate matrix of meaning for those
disciplines and sets an essential limit to their pretension to be the interpretive
lens for the whole. Newman warned that theology, once displaced from the
center of the university disciplines, would in very short order be replaced
by a science unworthy of that position and that this transition would have
disastrous effects for the entire life of the university. Though there isn't a
distinctively Catholic way of doing biology or calculus or law in the technical sense, there is indeed a Catholic manner of understanding the epistemic
framework for those sciences. In saying this, Newman echoes St. Bonaventure,
who held that Christ the Logos stands at the center of physical, mathematical,
and metaphysical endeavors. For both Bonaventure and Newman, theology
stands in relation to the other academic disciplines as *ipsum esse* does to
created reality: simultaneously grounding and liberating.

As I argued above, religion was seen by many of the founders of modernity as a limitation on academic freedom. One has only to remember Kant's
clarion call to his contemporaries to quit their intellectual kindergarten and
sapere aude (dare to know) free from the constraints of received traditions,
especially of the religious variety. But this entire style of argumentation, practically taken for granted in the contemporary academy, is predicated upon
a construal of freedom as indifferent choice. To follow a line of argument
wherever it leads, to think outside of any determining framework and free
of any prejudice, is the epistemic practice congruent with a moral practice
of radical self-determination. It is also, as Hans-Georg Gadamer showed so
convincingly, a fantasy. The Catholic intellectual tradition, which assumes the
epistemic primacy of Jesus Christ, cannot accept the principle of academic
freedom in this modern sense, but it most emphatically embraces it in the
classical and biblical sense that Pinckaers characterized as the freedom for
excellence. To accept Jesus Christ as epistemically basic is to orient all modes

of knowing toward their proper good and hence to make them free. Newman's reflections on how mathematics becomes fussy and self-preoccupied when dissociated from sacred geometry and how the arts become perverted once divorced from sacred beauty are particularly apposite here.

As hinted above, one of the most significant motivations for the modern privatization of religion was the conviction that religion, due to its fundamental irrationality, is inevitably violent. In the wake of the events of September 11, this Enlightenment characterization has come once more to the fore in both the popular and the high culture. From this conviction flowed the etiquette of inclusion and tolerance in regard to faith that holds sway, especially in the contemporary academy. What happens, then, when Catholics declare the epistemic primacy of Jesus Christ? Would this not lead in short order to divisiveness and even violence? By way of response, I would first observe that modern toleration is a far cry from the biblical virtue of love, which is, as Thomas Aquinas specified, the willing of the good of the other as other. Love includes, therefore, the desire to share the good of truth with others and positively excludes a bland indifference—a "live and let live" attitude—in regard to what Paul Tillich called "ultimate concern." To declare the epistemic primacy of Jesus Christ is to evangelize the minds of others, willing for them what is intellectually the greatest good. This, it seems to me, is the indispensable task of Catholics everywhere, but especially in academic institutions.

Now we must be careful to attend to the second part of Aquinas's definition: love wills the good of the other *as other*. This means that love always respects the integrity, individuality, and dignity of the one it addresses. To evangelize, therefore, through aggression and intimidation or by means of institutional coercion is directly repugnant to the way of love. Moreover, the Logos that the authentic Catholic intellectual seeks to declare is none other than the divine reasonability made most fully manifest in the forgiveness offered by the crucified Jesus and the *shalom* spoken by the risen Christ. To resort to violence in order to spread the Logos is to fall into self-contradiction.

What is the task of the Catholic intellectual? It is to evangelize the mind, to speak of God's noncompetitive transcendence, of the nonviolence of creation, of the God-given intelligibility of the real, of sin, death, and the resurrection of Jesus from the dead. It is, in a word, to declare the truth in love.

6

✠

A Tale of Two Cardinals

Avery Dulles's Creative Engagement with the
Thought of John Henry Newman

Even the most cursory glance at the work of Avery Cardinal Dulles reveals the influence of John Henry Newman. So many of Newman's major themes—faith and reason, theological method, religious epistemology, apologetics, ecumenism—are Dulles's principal preoccupations. Newman is one of the most-cited authorities in the writings of Dulles, but what is perhaps most remarkable is how Newman's thought, even when not explicitly referred to, functions so consistently as a structuring element in Dulles's speculations. As many have pointed out, there is a fascinating analogy between the lives and careers of these two princes of the church. Both were converts from Protestantism—Newman from High Anglicanism and Dulles from Presbyterianism—both pursued careers as distinguished university scholars, both were public intellectuals and controversialists, both curiously transcended the customary categories of left and right, and both became cardinals in their later years. What I would like to do in the course of this chapter is to explore just two major areas where Avery Dulles incorporated and developed the thought of John Henry Newman: the nature of religious epistemology and the tensive play

between theology and ecclesiastical authority. My hope is that this proves to
be more than simply an academic exercise, for I am convinced that the way
that Cardinal Dulles used Cardinal Newman is especially clarifying in regard
to some of the ecclesial and intellectual problems that bedevil us today.

Religious Epistemology

From the beginning to the end of his career, John Henry Newman opposed
the frontal assaults of the representatives of Enlightenment reason against the
bulwark of classical Christianity. But it is fascinating to observe that he did not
do so through an intellectual retrenchment, a retreat into premodern styles of
argument. Rather, in a manner remarkably anticipatory of the postmoderns
of the twentieth century, he demonstrated the limitations, blind spots, and
aporias of Enlightenment reason itself. This same Newman-style engagement
of the modern critics of Christianity is on full display in Cardinal Dulles's
meditations on postcritical theology, his 1992 text *The Craft of Theology*.

On Dulles's reading, the properly critical period commenced with the
overthrow of the authority of Aristotle in the realm of science, effected by
Bacon, Galileo, and others. It was then given philosophical form and specificity through the work of Descartes and Spinoza.[1] Descartes's strategy in
the *Discourse on Method*—the bracketing of all received moral and intellectual traditions in the interest of finding an indubitable foundation for
knowledge—became paradigmatic for practically all modern philosophy.
If Descartes's and Spinoza's form of epistemological foundationalism was
intuitional and rational, that of John Locke and David Hume could be characterized as empirical. Those influential British philosophers engaged in a
similar skeptical bracketing of traditional claims to certitude but averred that
all legitimate knowledge was based not so much in Cartesian intuitions but
in direct perception or the memory of direct perception. Philosophers from
both camps articulated a form of rational religion justifiable precisely on these
foundationalist grounds. (The explicit atheism of Feuerbach, Nietzsche, Marx,
and Freud would develop later.) Malebranche, Spinoza, Kant, and Descartes
himself all presented versions of religion rooted in self-evident first principles;
Locke offered an empirically verifiable religion in his *Reasonableness of Christianity*, and many Deists followed his lead. Many intelligent Christians of
the eighteenth and nineteenth centuries perceived, of course, that these new
rationalist construals of biblical religion undermined the dogmatic structure
of a properly revealed faith, and they reacted accordingly. One has only to
consult the condemnations of rationalism in both the Syllabus of Errors and

the official documents of Vatican I to see a Catholic version of this resistance. However, Cardinal Dulles points out that the scholasticism of this period, though used ostensibly to counteract the foundationalist rationalism of the Enlightenment, actually mimicked and mirrored that very form of thought. In a manner quite alien to Aquinas himself, the scholastics of the time searched for indubitable rational grounds for belief, clinching arguments upon which the claims of faith could be based: "The neo-scholastic theology of the nineteenth and early twentieth centuries . . . was heavily infected by Cartesian rationalism and mathematicism."[2]

Of course, a second path lay open to thoughtful Christians as they contemplated the critiques of the moderns, and this was to adopt the modern method explicitly and to ground the claims of Christianity in something like self-evident intuitions. The most influential and important practitioner of this approach was Friedrich Schleiermacher, who met the cultured despisers of religion with the mollifying observation that the dogmas and doctrines of classical Christianity were but symbolic manifestations of the underlying and universally held feeling of absolute dependency. In this, he proposed a religious version of the Cartesian *cogito*. The Schleiermacherian style proved very popular among academic theologians in the nineteenth and early twentieth centuries, inspiring the projects of, among many others, Ritschl, Otto, Tillich, and Rahner. Critics over the past two hundred years have consistently argued that very few of the cultured despisers of Christianity have in fact been persuaded by Schleiermacher and his disciples and, more important, that his subjectivist epistemology has resulted in a fatal positioning of revelation by neutral psychological experience. The theological projects of Karl Barth and Hans Urs von Balthasar, for instance, center on a critique of Schleiermacher's method. It appeared, therefore, that the engagement with modernity on the part of Christians—either to blame it or to praise it—resulted in a problematic compromise with it.

But Avery Dulles points out that in the middle of the twentieth century a new approach began to emerge, one that might be characterized as postmodern or postcritical. In a philosophical context, Wittgenstein, Foucault, Hans-Georg Gadamer, and Michael Polanyi were the key players, and among the theologians, Balthasar and George Lindbeck led the way.[3] Over against the rationalism and subjectivism of the Cartesian school, these thinkers emphasized the importance of the nonrational and the prerational in every concrete act of knowing. For example, Gadamer argued that prejudice necessarily played a constructive role in the commencement of any conversation or the interpretation of any text. What the Cartesians tried desperately to eliminate—unexamined tradition, prerational conviction, preconception—Gadamer blithely reinstated.[4] In point of fact, he argued that the *cogito* itself would be impossible without a whole set of assumptions and linguistic conventions accepted, perforce, without definitive proof. For his part, Foucault delighted in demonstrating the often brutal and irrational motivations that animated the purportedly enlightened social practices of early and late modernity. And Lindbeck, following Wittgenstein here, insisted that certain communal practices and a definite form of life inevitably shaped the consciousness of even the most isolated and skeptical Cartesian knower.[5] In all these ways, the postmoderns questioned the pretensions of modern reason to be critical, neutral, and untainted by ungrounded convictions.

Cardinal Dulles associates himself with this postcritical style and urges that it be used in the formulation of a proper theological method. In a sense, the adoption of this new approach would allow the Christian theologian to cut the Gordian knot of the modern problem and to articulate the faith without being positioned by liberal assumptions. With the help of Polanyi, Dulles lays out several basic aspects of this approach.

First, whereas the critical or modern method was "animated by a bias toward doubt . . . with the implied assumption that the royal road to truth consists in uprooting all voluntary commitments," the postcritical program commences with a kind of prejudice in favor of faith and the adoption of a hermeneutic of trust rather than suspicion. If the Cartesian attitude was understandable in the period following the wars of religion, it is, Dulles argues, a distinct liability now "when moral and religious convictions have been thoroughly eroded by skepticism."[6]

Second, Dulles comments, in a Gadamerian vein, that the critical program, formed by modern skepticism, itself rested on a fiduciary basis, that is to say, a whole network of assumptions and convictions such as "the postulates of Euclidean geometry and the testimony of the senses."[7] Here one thinks of the standard postmodern observation that every act of sensible perception is theory-laden rather than neutral.

Third, Dulles holds that "it is impossible to apply the critical program consistently," precisely because systematic doubt is "repugnant to human nature."[8] Since we don't have anything approaching apodictic proof for even the most ordinary facts of experience—the existence of an external world, the "reliability of physical and behavioral laws," the forward progress of time—we can't possibly endure over the long haul the epistemic asceticism that Descartes requires. One thinks here of Jacques Maritain's famous critique of the implicit "angelism" in much of modern epistemology and anthropology.

Fourth, Cardinal Dulles observes that the strict critical program overlooks the necessarily social dimension of even the simplest act of knowing.[9] Upon reading Descartes, Spinoza, or Kant, one has the impression that authentic knowledge can be achieved by the individual in isolation from his community and from his tradition. But those paradigmatically modern thinkers themselves were, in point of fact, massively shaped by the conversations they had with both the living and the dead, the *cogito* necessarily giving way to the *cogitamus*.

Fifth and most fundamental, Dulles maintains that "the critical program overlooked the tacit dimension of knowledge," giving no "cognitive value to what Pascal meant by 'the reasons of the heart.'" Does one know best in a detached, objective, basically disinterested manner; or does one know most effectively through a subtly interlocked weave of analysis, instinct, feel, and passion? To opt for the latter position is to be postcritical. In her *Upheavals of Thought*, Martha Nussbaum convincingly shows how her fiercely emotional reaction to the news of her mother's death carried an epistemic valence, telling her truths about her mother and their relationship that objectively analytical reason never could.[10] To construe emotion as merely expressive or to consign it to the level of the irrational is, for the postcritical Nussbaum, fatally to overlook the role that it plays in coming to know the truth of things.

In making these claims, Dulles shows himself a disciple not only of Michael Polanyi but very much of John Henry Newman. As I suggested above, Newman was, if I can put it this way, proto-postmodern or proto-postcritical in his approach, and in regard to the program just outlined he was a significant forerunner. In his late-career masterpiece *A Grammar of Assent*, Newman explicitly took on the empirical foundationalism of John Locke. In his epistemological writings, Locke had argued that, were philosophy and science to remain responsible and not bogged down by obscurantism and superstition, assent and inference ought to be tightly correlated. This means that the act of accepting a proposition as true ought to have a valence coordinated with the quality of argument used to justify it, so that if the evidence for a given proposition is clinching, the assent to it ought to be absolute, and if the evidence is less persuasive, the assent should be mitigated, and so on. To do otherwise, Locke insisted, was to be not only intellectually suspect but morally blameworthy as well.[11] Newman, who deeply admired Locke, admitted that syllogistic or strictly demonstrative ratiocination plays an essential role in bringing the mind to assent, but he insisted, over against Locke, that the act of assenting ought never to be coordinated reductively to the quality of inferential support. Though syllogisms often point correctly in the direction of truth, they are in themselves typically inconclusive, since they commence with generalizations that cannot reach to particular cases. "All men have a price; Fabricius is a man; therefore Fabricius has a price" is a valid bit of reasoning precisely in the measure that the peculiarities of Fabricius are subsumed under the umbrella term *man*, but Fabricius just might be that one peculiar man who does not have a price. The upshot of this is that assent is often, even typically, given independently of strict inference. Sometimes, Newman said, "men are loud in their admiration of truths which they never profess"; or to turn it around, some people will assent enthusiastically to propositions for which there are, at best, very bad arguments.[12] In regard to the way that human beings actually come to assent, formal inference—what Locke insisted upon—is supplemented by what Newman called informal inference, that is to say, the whole range of hunches, intuitions, experiences, and suppositions "too fine to avail separately, too subtle and circuitous to be convertible into syllogisms."[13] In Newman's famous example, one comes to assent unhesitatingly to the proposition that Great Britain is an island through certain kinds of formal inference complemented by a number of prerational or nonrational hints: every map of Europe represents Great Britain as an island; the entire written history of the country assumes this insularity; every reasonable person that one converses with takes it for granted; one's own explorations confirm it, and so on. For the instinct of the mind that governs the process of informal inference Newman coined the term "illative sense," from the Latin *ferre*, *latus*, "to carry." The illative sense is the epistemic counterpart to phronesis in the moral life, for both constitute a feel for the particular, for this pointed judgment of truth in the one case, for moral rectitude in the other. It is an intuition for the trajectory of converging probable arguments.

In light of these insights from the *Grammar of Assent*, I would like now to return to the five qualities of a postcritical method and note their resonance with Newman's theory. Dulles's postcritical approach, as we saw, favors faith and rests upon a hermeneutic of trust rather than one of suspicion. Newman takes for granted that, due to the illative sense, the vast majority of people are untroubled in the assents they make to myriad propositions for which there is no clinching inferential support, and he assumes that few of them could even begin to articulate with rational clarity precisely why it is they make such confident intellectual moves. He cites with approval the adage that a good judge should hand down his decisions firmly and confidently but that he should resist the temptation to give the reasons for those decisions, for his judgments are undoubtedly correct, though the justifications are largely unknown, even to him. What does this represent but a hermeneutic of trust in regard to ordinary (and not so ordinary) moves of the mind?

Next, Dulles's postcritical epistemology assumes that a "fiduciary" basis remains in place even for the most disinterested, neutral, and "objective" intellectual projects. Newman argues in the *Grammar of Assent* that we regularly assent to the "furniture of the mind," that whole range of basic assumptions concerning experience, the laws of nature, the syntax of language, and so on, though, once again, we can summon nothing like apodictic arguments on their behalf. When Descartes, in that heated room in Ulm, formulated and executed his program of systematic doubt, he couldn't, even in principle, seriously doubt the furniture of his mind, especially language itself, which made the doubting possible.[14] In his study of Newman, Dulles reminds us that "in his own day, Newman felt called upon to combat the myth of an autonomous realm in which reason, operating without presumptions, would deliver incontestable conclusions. He showed that in concrete matters reason always depends upon presumptions, and that these presumptions are by no means self-evident."[15]

We saw, third, that Dulles's postcritical method resists the angelism that suggests that radical doubt can be seriously sustained. In the *Grammar of Assent*, Newman explicitly scores Locke for just this sort of angelism, when he argues that perhaps in a higher world inference and assent are as tightly correlated as Locke says they should be, but that here below real human beings do not countenance so rigorous a correspondence. Indeed, one could argue easily enough that were the Lockean recommendation followed faithfully, we would give confident assent to practically nothing at all. Newman counters Locke not deductively and abstractly, or even on moral grounds, but pragmatically, insisting that real, embodied people just don't think this way.

We'll return to the fourth principle in a moment, but we recall that the fifth and final feature of Dulles's postcritical method was an insistence on the tacit dimension of knowing, all the ways that the reasons of the heart involve themselves in the process of coming to assent. The illative sense is nothing but the faculty for sorting through and assessing precisely these nonrational intuitions and perceptions. In this regard, Pascal's *raisons du coeur* (reasons of the heart) meet Newman's *cor ad cor loquitur* (heart speaks unto heart), and both clearly inform Avery Dulles's postcritical epistemology.[16]

In order to explore Newman's influence on the fourth of Dulles's principles, we have to leave the confines of the *Grammar of Assent* and consult Newman's mid-career masterpiece, *An Essay on the Development of Christian Doctrine*. It is in the context of this treatment of the living quality of ideas that the *cogitamus* dimension of knowing comes most clearly to the fore. In line with the *Lebensphilosophie* of the period, Newman insisted that a real idea is never a static given, a fixed Platonic form. Rather, he argued, ideas exist neither in a transcendent realm nor on the printed page but in "the play of lively minds."[17] Whereas Hume held that the mind is a kind of empty theater in which impressions and sense data appear for neutral viewing, Newman opined that human intelligence is a lively, active, inquisitive power, constantly sifting and weighing evidence, making judgments, asking and answering questions. It should come as no surprise that Lonergan's analysis of the highly energized agent intellect in *Insight* should have come after multiple readings of Newman's epistemology. Now this restive intellectual process obtains not simply within the individual mind but also intersubjectively in the play of conversation and debate. One thinker tosses an idea, already refined and analyzed, to an interlocutor who turns it, wonders at it, further refines it, and then passes it to another thinker who does the same. Newman compares this conversational development of the idea to the unfolding and deepening of a river over time.[18] Remarkably anticipating Husserlian phenomenology, Newman comments that a real idea is equivalent to the sum total of its possible aspects.[19] Just as an adequate representation of a physical object, say the Sears Tower, would have to include a range of profiles, perspectives, and aspects, so an even relatively adequate understanding of an idea would have to include a startling number of that notion's dimensions. And therefore real understanding takes place rarely in a flash of intuition but rather gradually, in the play of analysis and conversation, stretching across both space and time. But this means that the individual thinker, isolated in the confines of his subjectivity—in a word, the ideal Cartesian philosopher—is by no means the optimal knower. Rather, it is the one who situates himself within the context of a lively conversational community who will know best. As I've been suggesting, Newman is implicitly critical here of Descartes and his disciples, but he is critical as well of Luther and his followers, those who would maintain that the individual, in isolation from the believing community across the ages, can come to a sure grasp of the complex ideas that make up the Christian creed. In a word, Protestant "private judgment" strikes Newman as epistemologically counterindicated. We recall that the fourth of Dulles's postcritical principles was precisely a prejudice in favor of the social dimension of every act of knowing. I hope to have shown that this prejudice could not be more Newmanesque.

The Play between Magisterium and Theology

A theme that both John Henry Newman and Avery Dulles touched upon frequently in their writings was that of the tensive play between ecclesial authority and theological freedom. Both wrote during roiled times, when authority, both secular and sacred, was being questioned vigorously and when the claims of intellectual freedom were being pressed with particular vehemence. Avery Dulles did some of his most seminal and influential work during the sixties and seventies of the last century, precisely at the moment when the tension between ecclesiastical authority and academic liberty came to a head over issues of sexual morality. One has only to think of the two waves of the Charles Curran dispute, the first of which took place just after the publication of *Humanae vitae*, and the second of which unfolded during Cardinal Dulles's years as Curran's professorial colleague at Catholic University. Dulles's analysis of this thorny problem bears everywhere the mark of John Henry Newman's influence, especially in its balance and its keen sense of history.

Newman argued throughout his career that it is precisely because Christian ideas exist in the intersubjective play of lively minds that doctrine naturally develops, implicit dimensions of key notions becoming explicit only gradually. Cardinal Dulles shares this same perspective: "The message of Christ has to be proclaimed in new situations and interpreted for new audiences who have their own perspectives and their own questions."[20] Just as the oak tree is implicit in, but by no means reducible to, the acorn, so, for example, the fully unfolded idea of the incarnation is grounded in but not simply identical to the biblical stories and reflections concerning Jesus's identity. This is why the Protestant principle of *sola scriptura* struck Newman as deeply inadequate. Though the notion of doctrinal development strikes the contemporary reader as relatively liberal, for Newman it was in service of a defense of Catholic doctrines and practices that seemed, to many of his contemporaries, aberrational. Thus Newman managed successfully to hold off both a doctrinaire conservatism that would imagine Christian ideas as simply a deposit handed on unchanged from generation to generation and an undisciplined liberalism that would construe doctrine in a purely relativistic manner.

But Newman perceived something else in this context, and it constitutes one of the greatest strokes of genius in his work. He noticed that ecclesiastical authority is a concomitant and not an opponent of doctrinal development, that the two ideas, so often seen as mutually exclusive, are in fact mutually implicative. As in nature so in the intellectual order, development can be either positive or negative. A body can unfold in such a way that its essential integrity and orderly functioning are compromised, and an idea can develop in a manner incongruent with its proper nature. In the first case, a physician capable of diagnosing the problem and dealing with it effectively is required for the health of the body, and in the second case, an authority capable of discerning ideational corruption and of dealing decisively with it is requisite for the healthy development of a doctrine. From his youth, Newman knew that the Bible itself, open to such a wide variety of interpretations, could not be this authority. Dulles emphatically agrees with this: "Scripture alone, however, was never intended to be, and has not proved to be, a self-sufficient rule of faith."[21] When he was an Anglican, Newman held that antiquity (roughly the consensus of the greatest fathers) could serve this evaluating function, but as he was making the turn to Catholicism, he realized that the words of the fathers, however moving and truthful they were, could never function as a living voice and hence could not definitively adjudicate disputes regarding development and corruption. At the close of the *Apologia pro vita sua*, in his general answer to Mr. Kingsley, Newman maintains that the presence of an infallible ecclesiastical authority follows logically from the very idea of revelation.[22] If God revealed certain truths necessary for salvation, and if doctrine unfolds somewhat unpredictably and precariously over time, then it follows that God must provide for an authority sufficiently strong and clear to guarantee the integrity of those truths. Further, this authority must be active, infallible, and personal if it is to have the required effect. If I may shift the metaphor from the organic to the sociological, doctrinal development is something like a game, and ecclesial authority something like a referee. No basketball team has ever brought the ball up the court in precisely the same way, and each individual game unfolds in a distinctive manner, but integral play is presided over by a judge, whose purpose is the enforcement of the rules and the maintenance of the game's essential form. Precisely because the play flows, the authority of the referee is required, and precisely because the game is current and lively, the referee must have a voice and it must be definitive in its pronouncements. In *The Craft of Theology*, Dulles articulates the role of the magisterium in a distinctly Newmanesque way: "The Church, as the bearer and interpreter of revelation, has the capacity to approve what is consonant with, or reject what is dissonant with, the word entrusted to it. The organ that authoritatively expresses the mind of the Church is known as the ecclesiastical magisterium."[23] Again, this role is required not to keep doctrine from developing but to monitor and encourage healthy development.

Now Newman was obliged to engage the objections of his skeptical contemporaries who worried that the acceptance of an infallible ecclesiastical authority would imply the intellectual subservience of the human race, a retreat into premodern obscurantism. He responded, in the *Apologia*, with this remarkable statement: "The energy of the human intellect does from opposition grow; it thrives and is joyous with a tough elastic strength under the terrible blows of the divinely-fashioned weapon and is never so much itself as when it has lately been overthrown."[24] Just as the energy and verve of a river come from its firm banks, and just as the excitement of an athletic competition is made possible by the unbending quality of the game's rules and obstacles, so the effervescence and creativity of the intellect are grounded in the very limits set to it. Without defined banks, the swift-flowing river would devolve into a lazy lake; without borders infallibly defined, the theological mind, Newman holds, would devolve into idle speculation and relativism. David Tracy has argued that the theological community can, through critique, peer review, book reviews, and so on, effectively police itself, free from the interference of ecclesial authority, which is seen today, at least in the West, as arbitrary and invasive. Newman, it seems to me, would have little patience with that position. Asking theologians to monitor their own discussions would be akin to asking baseball players to umpire their own game. Paul commented that his apostolic authority was given to him "to edification and not to destruction," and in this Newman finds the perfect characterization of ecclesial authority's role vis-à-vis theological investigation: "Its object is not to enfeeble freedom or vigor of human thought in religious speculation, but to resist and control its extravagance."[25] Once again, Cardinal Dulles concurs with this basic line of thought. Commenting on the regnant perception of the rapport between magisterium and theology, Dulles says, "Tensions can arise between the hierarchical authorities and theologians. From some literature one gets the impression that the two groups are engaged in a perpetual contest, and that every advance of one group is achieved at the expense of the other. The magisterium, according to this scenario, would be asking theologians to 'knuckle under,' to abandon their own judgment and sacrifice the integrity of their own discipline. . . . This journalistic portrayal of the relationship is a caricature."[26] For both Dulles and Newman, the play of magisterium and theology is not a zero-sum game but rather a tensively harmonic relationship.

What, for Newman, are the limits to ecclesiastical authority? What prevents it from morphing into authoritarianism? A first restriction is that the church's infallibility ought not to extend beyond the definite circle formed by the moral law, the principles of natural religion, and the apostolic faith.[27] If it tries to assert itself outside this relatively narrow range, or if it seeks too precisely to determine the concrete implications of these foundations, it oversteps. Further, the official teaching authority of the church—the pope in union with an ecumenical council—has existed only a relatively few times in the long history of the church. And the extraordinary magisterium involving a papal statement *ex cathedra* had, in Newman's time, been invoked precisely once, in the declaration of Mary's immaculate conception. The point is this: the awful power of infallible definition is employed only carefully and rarely, lest it interrupt unnecessarily the healthy flow of the theological conversation. Just as a bad referee can intervene too frequently in the game and hence compromise its natural rhythm, so the ecclesial authority can hover too fussily over the give-and-take, the experimentation and speculation, involved in doctrinal development. In the *Apologia*, Newman avers that a theologian or apologist, wishing to forward a new idea that he considers helpful for his day, welcomes the opportunity to write, to think, to debate, and to launch his views into the public forum. He would be cowed into inaction were he to feel that "an authority, which was supreme and final, was watching every word he said and making signs of assent or dissent to each sentence as he uttered it."[28]

In his meditations on the prudential norms that ought to govern the utterances of the magisterium, Avery Dulles observes that "until the twentieth century, ecumenical councils and dogmatic decrees were rare. Popes issued relatively few doctrinal decisions and then only at the end of a long process of theological discussion."[29] And then he continues, very much in the spirit of John Henry Newman: "Unless the authorities exercise great restraint, Catholics can easily feel overwhelmed by the multitude of views they are expected to profess. . . . Wherever diversity seems to be tolerable, theologians and others should be given freedom to use their own good judgment."[30] Finally, he invokes Newman directly: "Newman and, later, Pope John XXIII were fond of the ancient dictum: *In necessariis unitas, in dubiis libertas, in omnibus caritas.*"[31] In his stress on the importance of a lengthy process of intellectual sifting, largely uninterrupted by interventions of ecclesial authority, Dulles shows himself, again, a disciple of Newman. In the *Apologia*, the nineteenth-century cardinal gives a rich description of the gradual steps by which a controverted theological question comes, at long last, to be adjudicated by the highest ecclesiastical court. He observes that a controversial position might be defended by a local preacher or professor and the question allowed to smolder and burn while Rome takes no action. Eventually, the issue might be taken up by a professor at another seat of learning, where it is mulled over while Rome takes no action. Next, it may be formally condemned by a theological faculty of a major university and still Rome remains silent. If the question continues to be divisive, the local ordinary might attempt to resolve it, while Rome does nothing. Finally, only if he is unsuccessful, might the bishop present the matter to the Roman doctrinal authorities for their judgment.[32] The very salutary thing that has happened in this long and slow process is that the issue has been so weighed, considered, turned over, seen from multiple perspectives that, when Rome makes its decision, it is usually but a ratification of the truth that has already emerged. Dulles's conclusion is very close in spirit to Newman: "The magisterium can avoid issuing too many statements, especially statements that appear to carry with them an obligation to assent."[33]

Newman articulates a final restriction on the potentially tyrannical exercise of ecclesiastical authority, namely, the inescapable dependence of that authority on the work and expertise of the theological community. He makes the keen historical observation that the great formulators of doctrine have not, for the most part, been popes, bishops, and magisterial officials. "Authority in its most imposing exhibition, grave bishops laden with the traditions and rivalries of particular nations or places, have been guided in their decisions by the commanding genius of individuals, sometimes young and of inferior rank."[34] Thus Origen, Irenaeus, Tertullian, and Augustine formed the mind of the ancient church more than any pope, and their teachings grounded the decisions of the great early councils. Thomas Aquinas, a humble Dominican friar, had the profoundest impact on the shaping of the medieval church, and his formulations significantly shaped the statements of the Council of Trent on original sin, justification, and the sacraments. One of Newman's heroes, the young deacon Athanasius, gave form to the church's eventual magisterial determinations against Arianism. Newman's overall point is that the infallible teaching office of the church, far from putting theological creativity to bed, positively calls it forth and relies upon it.

Once more, Dulles couldn't be in more enthusiastic agreement with his predecessor. In *The Craft of Theology*, he shows this dependence of authority upon theology in even greater historical detail than Newman. "What would the documents of Trent look like had it not been for the work of papal theologians such as Lainez and Salmeron? What would Vatican I have been able to say without the preparatory texts supplied by Franzelin, Kleutgen, and others? How would Vatican II have been able to accomplish its task in the absence of Congar, Phillips, Rahner, Murray, and their colleagues?"[35] He goes on to comment that nearly every papal encyclical was made possible through the efforts of theologians who prepared drafts and responded to questions and that no Roman congregation or episcopal doctrinal commission could do its work without the contribution of numerous theological researchers. More to it, Dulles insists that theologians are indispensable to the proper interpretation and reception of dogmatic statements uttered by the magisterium. Dulles thereby makes his own Rahner's observation that every doctrinal statement of the church is in one sense an end to discussion but in another sense very much a beginning of further conversation, clarification, and interpretation.

Conclusion

In his intellectual autobiography, *A Testimonial to Grace*, Cardinal Dulles gives us a gripping account of his journey from a somewhat world-weary materialism to a vibrantly imagined Catholic faith. To be sure, there was a powerfully academic dimension to this itinerary. To give just one example, Dulles's reading of Plato and Aristotle when he was still a student played a decisive role in moving him to accept the ideas of order in nature, final causality, and objective morality, all of which would prove key in his eventual conversion to the faith. However, in one of the most lyrical passages in the book, Cardinal Dulles describes the manner in which he first came to give what Newman would have called "real assent" to the idea of God, and this involved much more than mere reason. He speaks of a walk that he took one gray February afternoon when he was an undergraduate at Harvard.

> As I wandered aimlessly, something impelled me to look contemplatively at a young tree. On its frail, supple branches were young buds attending eagerly the spring which was at hand. While my eye rested upon them the thought came to me suddenly . . . that these little buds in their innocence and meekness followed a rule, a law of which I as yet knew nothing. How could it be, I asked, that this delicate tree sprang up and developed and that all the enormous complexity of its cellular operations combined to make it grow erectly and bring forth leaves and blossoms? The answer was new to me: that its actions were ordered to an end by the only power capable of adapting means to ends . . . a Person of whom I had no previous intuition.[36]

I quote this passage at some length because it discloses so beautifully a Newmanesque account of assent. There was undoubtedly an intellectual aspect to this coming to see—inferential reason was clearly operative—but there was something else as well. There was beauty, the quality of the day and time, the pensive mood in which the young searcher found himself, that particular tree with its early spring buds—and all of these elements and many others came together along with formal ratiocination to produce the moment of breakthrough and vision that Cardinal Dulles describes. What guided this rational and other-than-rational process was none other than Newman's illative sense. It is my conviction that an apologetics for a postcritical age will involve just this sort of confident use of both the rational and the affective, both the discursive and the intuitive, both the theological and the artistic in the process of bringing people to faith. Both John Henry Newman and Avery Dulles witness to this truth.

In the expanded 1996 edition of *A Testimonial to Grace*, Cardinal Dulles adds a chapter on the contemporary situation in the church. He acknowledges that the intellectual acumen of the theological community in seminaries, universities, and other institutions of higher learning has perhaps never been greater. Theology in one sense is vital and creative. However, he observes as well that the relationship between theology and the magisterium has become strained and tendentious. He says that central teachings of Vatican II on the role of the pope and bishops, the divine constitution of the church, the necessity of the sacraments, and so on are "widely contested or ignored" in the theological community.[37] Furthermore, many in the West consider the church a purely human society capable of changing its structure and teaching at the whim of the faithful, much as a modern political state can change its leaders and constitution through majority vote. This falling apart of creative theology and authoritative magisterium has led to a polarization and politicization of the life of the church, giving rise to the battles between liberal and conservative Catholics. Cardinal Dulles sees this split as one of the bitterest fruits of the postconciliar period, and he insists that only when it is healed will the church regain the confidence and balance necessary for effective evangelization. No theologian would be more helpful in this regard than John Henry Newman.

The new evangelization will depend greatly upon the right understanding of both religious epistemology and the rapport between theology and authority. I hope that this tale of two cardinals has contributed, however modestly, to that understanding.

7

✠

John Henry Newman
among the Postmoderns

In my study of certain contemporary thinkers who would qualify themselves as postmodern or postliberal, I have frequently encountered points of contact with the thought of John Henry Newman. This should not strike us as too surprising, for both Newman and the postmoderns share a distrust of modernity, that is to say, of the Cartesian-Kantian intellectual project. At the same time, I have found that elements in the thought of Newman serve to correct excesses, both rhetorical and substantive, in the writings of the postmoderns. In a word, Newman moves among these contemporary thinkers in a most provocative and illuminating manner. It is the stimulating "conversation" among them that I would like to explore in this chapter. I will focus on three topics dear to postmoderns: the question of epistemological foundationalism, the problem of the centrality and "positioning" quality of theology, and the issue of a conversational model of truth. I will set these themes in dialogue with key texts of John Henry Newman, the first with *An Essay in Aid of a Grammar of Assent*, the second with *The Idea of a University*, and the third with *An Essay on the Development of Christian Doctrine*. My hope is to show, in at least a preliminary way, the extraordinary relevance of Newman for the contemporary theological and philosophical dialectic.

Foundationalism and Anti-Foundationalism

In his *Biglietto* speech of 1879, Newman famously commented that his entire
intellectual life could be characterized as a battle against liberalism in matters
of religion. And he helpfully specified precisely what he meant by that slippery word *liberalism*.[1] He took it to mean the view that no real knowledge is
possible in the area of theology, that the assertions of religious people are, at
best, expressions of feeling and subjective conviction or, at worst, the distillate
of irresponsible thinking. What Newman sensed at the heart of the liberal
attitude was an unwarranted restriction of the range and scope of reason
so that the distinctively religious way of grasping truth would not count as
rational. We can find something very similar in the work of postliberal theologians today, often expressed as a dissatisfaction with the foundationalism
of modern epistemology.

William Placher, one of the most articulate of contemporary postliberals, comments that foundationalism has two basic forms, theoretical and
empirical, the latter associated with Locke and Hume and the former with
Descartes.[2] Cartesian foundationalism is the claim that all legitimate knowledge is finally reducible to intuitions known with immediate certitude. Thus,
on the basis of the indubitable and subjectively grasped *cogito*, one can
move, by careful logical steps, to further insight. Any claim made outside
the discipline of this method should not qualify as reasonable. Lockean or
Humean foundationalism, on the other hand, is the contention that valid
knowledge is grounded not in rational intuition but in the immediacy of
sense experience. Once again, the purpose of this epistemological restriction is carefully to censor claims to authentic knowledge, allowing only
those assertions that are either self-evident or logically connected to what
is self-evident. Despite their differences, foundationalists of both stripes
come together in holding that only through this strict, rational *askesis* can
the Western mind be cleared of humbug and obfuscation. It would be fair
to say that the principal, but by no means exclusive, target of both forms of
foundationalism would be the superstitious and uncritical claims of religion.
Now some responded to the challenge of modernity by trying to articulate
Christian theology within narrow foundationalist strictures. Locke's own
The Reasonableness of Christianity, which had a decisive influence on the
development of eighteenth- and nineteenth-century Deism, Kant's *Religion
within the Limits of Reason Alone*, which strongly marked much of liberal
Protestantism in the nineteenth and twentieth centuries, and Schleiermacher's
Glaubenslehre, which set the tone for the work of both Paul Tillich and Karl
Rahner, are obvious cases in point.

Finding inspiration in both Karl Barth and Hans Urs von Balthasar, many postliberals, on both sides of the Catholic-Protestant divide, are deeply impatient with these accommodationist theologies, precisely in the measure that they remain suspicious of the foundationalist assumptions that undergird them. When Christianity is accepted as reasonable only on these narrow terms, it quickly turns into a shadow of itself, an ideology vaguely reflective of modern convictions. The strategy employed by many postliberals is to question the supposed irreducibility of Cartesian and empiricist foundations. Thus they argue that the *cogito*, which Descartes took to be epistemically basic, is in fact a function of a whole set of psychological conditions and cultural presuppositions, including and especially language itself. Would, for example, the *cogito ergo sum* of Descartes have been possible without the *si fallor sum* of Augustine, and would the experience of doubt have been possible without the multivalence of the Latin word *dubium*? Similarly, they claim that even ordinary sense experience—what Locke and Hume took to be epistemically basic—is in fact "theory laden," that is to say, shaped by expectation, determined by an individual's power of perception, necessarily taken in perspective. It too is in a complex interdependent relationship with an array of presuppositions and conditions. Many postliberals enjoy Wittgenstein's taunt to his modern colleagues that "when you discover the foundations, you find that they are being held up by the rest of the house."[3]

In fact, Wittgenstein is the principal philosophical influence on postliberalism, particularly in his stress, in his later work, on discrete games of language. In his puzzling but strangely compelling texts from the 1930s and 1940s, Wittgenstein argues that there is no absolute, rational substructure for all language (as he had maintained in the earlier *Tractatus Logico-philosophicus*) but rather that each language is like a game with a unique set of rules, disciplines, and characteristic moves. If this is true, then whatever Descartes meant by the *cogito*, whatever Hume meant by immediate sense experience, and whatever Schleiermacher meant by the feeling of absolute dependency were not absolute foundations but rather functions of a game of language and form of life in which each of those thinkers was already implicated. This Wittgensteinean reconfiguration is meant not to conduce toward relativism (as many critics of postliberalism fear) but rather to break the shackles that had been placed on reason by a finally unreasonable concern for certainty and universality. Placher comments that a postliberal would clearly hold that the range of truth is universal but that the access to truth can be, in fact usually is, particular. So slavery is wrong, always and everywhere, though it was the specificity of the biblical narratives and the witness of particular Christian people that permitted us gradually to see that universal truth.[4]

We see here, in this postliberal preoccupation with overcoming unnecessary intellectual restrictions, a clear link to John Henry Newman, who similarly resisted the imperialistic tendencies of the regnant liberalism of his time. Newman's chief interlocutor in *A Grammar of Assent* was one of the founders of empirical foundationalism, namely, John Locke. As we saw, for Locke, all legitimate knowledge is either direct sense experience or what can be shown through strict inference on the basis of sense experience. The upshot of this epistemology is that the intensity of one's assent to a given proposition should be directly proportionate to the quality of the empirical/inferential support that one can muster for it. Thus, if one has a clinching argument, one should fully and enthusiastically assent; if one can muster only a somewhat persuasive demonstration, one should be restrained in assent; and if one can find no inferential support, one should simply and honestly refuse to assent. Locke famously concluded that it would be not only irrational but immoral to allow one's assent to move outside of a strict correspondence to its inferential ground. It is, of course, with this Lockean position that Newman strenuously disagrees.[5] In a journal entry for October 30, 1870, Newman tells us that he made nineteen separate beginnings to this text before finding the right path. The breakthrough occurred while he was vacationing on the shores of Lake Geneva, when he resolved to commence the project not with the problem of certitude (as did modern philosophers from Descartes to Kant) but with the act of assent.[6] This shift freed him, for he saw that in actual practice assent, *pace* Locke, is often given utterly, even when untethered to unambiguous inferential justification.

Newman specified this insight by exploring the relationship between what he called formal and informal inference. The former corresponds, to some degree, to Locke's sense-based demonstrations, but more precisely to the Aristotelian syllogism, that rational mechanism by which we can draw conclusions, in a fairly rigorous way, from properly juxtaposed universal and particular premises. Newman has great respect for the power of the syllogism, commenting that it quite reliably shows the mind the direction in which the truth lies.[7] But he is quick to observe that, except in the case of the most banal sort of mathematical demonstration, this type of formal reasoning is rarely conclusive or definitive. The problem is that syllogisms invariably commence with a generality or an abstraction—for instance, all men have their price—which serves to describe with reasonable accuracy the vast majority of individuals within that class. But it will, almost necessarily, fail to catch each and every one. In *A Man for All Seasons*, Cromwell confronts the Duke of Norfolk with trumped up evidence against Thomas More: "We have reason to believe that when he was a judge, Sir Thomas took bribes." The Duke, reflecting a rather Newmanesque suspicion of generalities, responds, "Damn it man, he's the only judge since Cato who didn't take bribes."[8] Newman states the problem this way: "Thus it is that the logician, for his own purposes . . . turns rivers, full, winding, and beautiful, into navigable canals. To him dog or horse is not a thing which he sees, but a mere name suggesting ideas."[9] Accordingly, the syllogism, because its major premise is not oriented to the individual, cannot with full adequacy reach to the individual in its conclusion. It lies, in Newman's words, "open at both ends."[10] What the psychologically astute Newman notices—and this in many ways is the hinge on which the entire text turns—is that despite the less than perfectly satisfying quality of any and all inferential demonstrations, full assent is frequently given. So what bridges the great divide between imperfect formal inference and confident assent? Newman's answer: informal inference guided by the illative sense. By "informal inference" he means that largely intuitive process by which the mind gathers and assesses a wide variety of nonrational and quasi-rational elements—gut feelings, hunches, instincts, experiences, testimony of reliable witnesses, venerable traditions, the example of beloved people—as part of its search for truth. These are consulted along with the findings of more strictly disciplined ratiocination, and it is the combination of informal and formal inference that produces assent. What Newman termed the "illative sense" is none other than that "feel" or instinct of the mind—comparable to phronesis in the moral life—according to which one pushes toward the truth.[11]

In making these observations, Newman has effectively turned Locke on his head. Whereas the empiricist had implied that standard religious claims could not be counted as rational since they were not justified through strict, sense-based inference, Newman has shown that all manner of knowing, from the most ordinary to the most sophisticated, would be similarly discounted were Locke's principle obediently followed. Not unlike Jacques Maritain in his critique of Descartes, Newman holds that Locke's evidentialism (what postliberals would call foundationalism) is a type of angelism, a denial of the embodied/spiritual, rational/arational way that human beings actually think. Through this neat little *tu quoque*, he has cleared the ground for religious assertions and the legitimacy of assent to religious propositions. Just as Placher and his colleagues hold off liberalism through the questioning of foundationalism, Newman does so through the dismantling of evidentialism.

Theology as a "Positioning" Form of Discourse

One of the most remarkable books of theology to appear in the last thirty years is John Milbank's *Theology and Social Theory*. It has spawned the so-called

Radical Orthodoxy movement, involving figures such as Catherine Pickstock and Graham Ward, and it has inspired already a mountain of literature, both pro and con. In the preface to this *magnum opus*, Milbank thanks a number of people, including Rowan Williams, now former Archbishop of Canterbury, who, he said, taught him theology. He also tells us that he stands in the great tradition of Anglo-Catholicism and explicitly mentions the influence of one J. H. Newman.[12] A particular mark and virtue of Milbank's approach is the setting into conversation of the classical Catholic metaphysics of participation and a number of themes in continental postmodernism. There is a motif developed throughout *Theology and Social Theory* that reminds one rather vividly of Newman—namely, the "positioning" relationship that theology ought to have with the other intellectual disciplines.

In the introduction to his text, Milbank comments that "the pathos of modern theology is its false humility," by which he means its tendency to surrender its claim to be a metadiscourse, or what the medievals would have characterized as its "queenly" role.[13] At least from the time of Schleiermacher, liberal or modern theology has tried to justify itself in terms of some antecedent philosophical system, but this has resulted in a compromising of theology's properly dominant position. To claim such dominance is not intellectual bravado but simply logical consistency. Precisely because theology speaks of the creator God who is responsible in a sustaining way for the whole of finite reality, it must be a metadiscourse and must impinge in a controlling way on every other form of human inquiry.[14] Once, in the thrall of its falsely modest modern assumptions, theology abandons that positioning responsibility, it necessarily finds itself positioned by some other discipline. But this is essentially incoherent and destabilizing, since it is tantamount to a controlling of the Creator by a creature. In the modern form, theology devolves into "the oracular voice of some finite idol, such as historical scholarship, humanist psychology, or transcendental philosophy," becoming the limit case or furthest expression of those studies.[15]

Milbank explores this theme most thoroughly in terms of theology's relation to the social sciences, but in a very illuminating chapter, "Founding the Supernatural," he examines the rapport between theology and transcendental anthropology as it was analyzed by Catholic thinkers in the twentieth century. In the 1940s and 1950s both Henri de Lubac and Karl Rahner tried to push beyond the two-story account of nature and grace that had been bequeathed to Catholic theology by nineteenth-century neo-scholasticism. Both accordingly defended a more integrated view of the nature-grace relationship. Milbank feels, however, that de Lubac was far more successful in this enterprise, since his program involved a "supernaturalizing of the natural," while Rahner's turned into a "naturalizing of the supernatural."[16] In his groundbreaking work *Le surnaturel*, de Lubac showed that, for both Augustine and Thomas, human nature can be properly understood only in a highly paradoxical way as that which finds its fulfillment in something that utterly exceeds its natural capacities: *ultimus finis creaturae rationalis facultatem natura ipsius excedit*.[17] To put it more exactly, the desire for the beatific vision is "natural" to us, but the satisfaction of that desire depends not on the exercise of our virtues but upon an utterly supernatural gift. Where this paradoxical anthropology is most fully on display, for de Lubac, is in the dynamics of Christ's own being, in the play between his divine and human natures, and it is therefore only through participation in him in his historical concreteness that we can hope to realize our deepest desires. The natural longing of the soul is supernaturalized by being drawn into the specificity of what Balthasar called the *concretissimus*, the irreducibly unique Jesus of Nazareth.

Milbank contrasts this to the Rahnerian approach. In book after book, article after article, Rahner focuses on the *Vorgriff* of being as the transcendental horizon for every particular act of knowing. Then he relates the specifics of Christian revelation to this intellectual dynamic, generally appreciating the former as explications of what is implicitly given in the latter. The result, according to Milbank, is that the Christian theologian is not compelled to look with attention at the real, concrete Christ, since he is but the richest expression of something that is already known independently of him. Transcendental anthropology positions and judges the contents of revelation.[18] This effective drawing of the supernatural into the confines of the natural is what bothers Milbank about Rahner—and, it should be noted, what bothered Balthasar about his former Jesuit colleague. And this Rahnerian method—hugely influential in the years just after the Council—opened the door, according to Milbank, to a whole series of compromises of the primacy of biblical revelation, most notably the use in liberation theology of Marxist social theory to understand the meaning of "kingdom of God" in Jesus's preaching. The connecting point between Rahner and liberation thought is, of course, the work of German political theologians, especially Johann Baptist Metz, one of Rahner's closest disciples.

Though Newman is mentioned nowhere beyond the preface to *Theology and Social Theory*, it is not difficult to see his influence on this aspect of Milbank's work. If Milbank's concern is the drawing of theology under the influence of a secular discipline, Newman's was, if anything, more basic and dramatic, namely, the exclusion of theology from the circle of university disciplines altogether. In the lectures given at Dublin on the occasion of the inauguration of the Catholic University of Ireland, later collected as *The Idea of a University*, Newman combats the then prevalent view that theology is not a form of knowledge and should not, accordingly, be a subject of study at the university level. Critics had maintained that it would be as absurd to have a chair of religion as it would to have a chair of "fine feeling, sense of honour, patriotism, maternal affection, or good companionship."[19] Newman argues vigorously for the properly intellectual pedigree of theology. He does so first through a clever twist of the *tu quoque*: "For instance, are we to limit our idea of University Knowledge by the evidence of our senses? Then we exclude ethics; by intuition? We exclude history; by testimony? We exclude metaphysics; by abstract reasoning? We exclude physics."[20]

But then he turns the argument around. Does not theology in fact rely, in part, on empirical data, on the testimony of historical witnesses, on the ratiocinations of metaphysicians, on the intuition of conscience? On what grounds, therefore, should one feel obliged to exclude religious knowledge from the university conversation?

Then Newman turns up the heat. Not only does theology belong in the circle; it belongs in the center, precisely because it articulates the truth about a creator God, who is not one being among many but that primordial reality responsible for the to-be of whatever else exists and that, therefore, impinges upon all finite things. To say that God is creator is to imply that he is the one

> who is sovereign over, operative amidst, independent of, the appointments which he has made; One in whose hands are all things, who has a purpose in every event, and a standard for every deed, and thus has relations of his own towards the subject matter of each particular science which the book of knowledge unfolds; who has with an adorable, never-ceasing energy implicated Himself in all the history of creation, the constitution of nature, the course of the world . . . and who thereby necessarily becomes the subject-matter of a science, far wider and more noble than any of those which are included in the circle of secular education.[21]

Anticipating Milbank by a century and a half, Newman is implying that theology must be a metanarrative or it loses its soul. In this regard, both Newman and Milbank carry forward the teaching of St. Bonaventure who, in the thirteenth century, argued that Christ is the center and organizing principle of the many sciences studied at the medieval university. As incarnate Logos, Bonaventure urged, Jesus is the archetype around which the physical, mathematical, and metaphysical sciences revolve. Thus, without reference to Christ, the physical scientist, for example, could say many true things and accumulate much accurate data, but his mind would be in error in the measure that he fails to relate his findings to the deepest truth of the physical universe.

The final move that Newman makes is to show how theology, once extricated from its proper position at the center, is necessarily supplanted by one of the particular disciplines, resulting, as Milbank clearly saw, in a destabilizing of the system. A sign of this destabilization is the corruption of the arts and the sciences. Thus painting and architecture become extravagant, undisciplined, and self-absorbed when they are freed from their relationship with religion, and economics and politics become coarsened and self-indulgent when untethered to their ultimate moral ends. Furthermore, these compromised disciplines will inevitably begin to dictate terms to theology. "Any secular science, cultivated exclusively, may become dangerous to Religion; and I account for it on this broad principle that no science whatever, however comprehensive it may be, but will fall largely into error if it be constituted the sole exponent of things in heaven and earth."[22] Newman and Milbank agree that there seems to be no alternative: theology is either positioning or positioned; it is either queen or the "oracular voice of some finite idol."

A Conversational Model of Truth

One of the characteristic marks of modernity is a sort of introspective individualism. In his *Discourse on Method*, Descartes tells us that the *cogito* came to him after he had retreated alone into a heated room in the German town of Ulm and explored his inmost consciousness.[23] Having bracketed history, tradition, received ideas, and even that most elemental conversation with the outside world that is sense experience, Descartes discovered, in his solitude, the foundation stone of true philosophy. This archetypally modern move is repeated in Kant's uncovering of the categorical imperative in the very structure of his will and apart from any indications from nature, action, inclination, or the moral tradition. In his *Three Reformers*, Jacques Maritain expressed the view that this Cartesian starting point is but the secular version of Luther's justification by grace through faith. Like the French philosopher, the German reformer discovered the surest ground of his life and thought in his deepest interiority and apart from tradition and community.

Most late moderns and postmoderns are distinctly uneasy with this epistemological individualism. In *Method in Theology*, Bernard Lonergan, an ardent disciple of Newman, commented that in the actual unfolding of a scientific project, it is not so much the *cogito* that matters as the *cogitamus*. Real intellectual achievement is rarely if ever individualist but rather the result of complex conversations with a community of both the living and the dead. No physicist, for instance, would ever get his research off the ground unless he assumed the truth of myriad propositions, equations, and empirical observations that he had never personally verified.[24] A late modern such as Jürgen Habermas proposes a theory of communicative action, according to which authentic knowledge emerges in the conversational play of a properly constituted intellectual community. Relying on the work of Paul Ricoeur and especially Hans-Georg Gadamer, David Tracy holds that theological truth is the result of the self-regulating discussion of qualified conversation partners gathered around the classic texts, persons, and events of the Christian tradition.[25] And for those formed in the phenomenological tradition—Heidegger, Gadamer, Levinas, Derrida, and their disciples—conversation is necessarily ingredient in the process of coming to truth, precisely because we know only by intuiting the essence of a thing through the successive viewing of a manifold of appearances. It is only in the intersubjective sharing of perspectives that the fullness of truth comes gradually, if asymptotically, into view.

Much of this, it seems to me, is anticipated in the writings of John Henry Newman. Congruent with the *Lebensphilosophie* that was regnant in Europe by the middle of the nineteenth century, Newman placed great stress on the lively, evolutionary, and intersubjective quality of human thinking. Though these themes are present in writings from practically every segment of Newman's career, they are especially evident in the Oxford University Sermons and in the magnificent *Essay on the Development of Christian Doctrine*. In the opening sections of the *Essay on Development*, before he turns to properly theological matters, Newman analyzes the development of ideas in general. Unlike Platonic forms or Kantian *a priori* notions, real ideas grow and unfold like living organisms. This is because they exist neither in a self-contained metaphysical realm, nor in the structures of consciousness, nor dumbly on the printed page, but rather in the play of a lively, inquisitive mind: "It is the characteristic of our minds to be ever engaged in passing judgment on the things which come before us. No sooner do we apprehend than we judge: we allow nothing to stand by itself: we compare, contrast, abstract, generalize, connect, adjust, classify: and we view all our knowledge in the associations with which these processes have invested it."[26] Lonergan commented that there are two kinds of emptiness, that of the box and that of the stomach. The former is dumb, uninterested, entirely passive, while the latter is full of energy, purpose, and concentrated interest. The classical epistemological tradition might be right in saying that the mind, prior to sense experience, is empty, but it is—Lonergan and Newman would insist—empty like a stomach, not a box, since it actively seeks out what it wants and knows what to do with it once it gets it.

Moreover, a particular mind, having taken in an idea through active assessment, enters subsequently into a game with other minds, tossing the
idea back and forth, engaging in a rambunctious intersubjective process of
questioning, wondering, answering, critiquing, and arguing. In this way, the
innumerable facets of a complex idea are brought to light. Anticipating Husserl by fifty years, Newman says, "The idea which represents an object or
supposed object is commensurate with the sum total of its possible aspects,
however they may vary in the separate consciousness of individuals," and he
clarifies that "ordinarily an idea is not brought home to the intellect as objective except through this variety."[27] In a word, the sort of lively conversation
that we have been describing is the condition for the possibility of conceptual
clarification: ideas become purer, weightier, more luminous as they unfold.
This is why Newman consistently rejected the Protestant suggestion that one
should return to the origins of the church in order to discover an authentic
Christianity: "It is indeed sometimes said that the stream is clearest near the
spring. Whatever use may fairly be made of this image, it does not apply to
the history of a philosophy or belief, which on the contrary is more equable,
and purer, and stronger, when its bed has become deep, and broad, and full."[28]
It is in this context, of course, that Newman makes what is perhaps his best-
known remark: "In a higher world it is otherwise, but here below to live is to
change, and to be perfect, is to have changed often."[29] The living thing under
consideration is an idea, and its perfection is a function of its development
in the course of a lively conversation across both space and time. We can see
that, just as surely as he quarreled with Luther's antiquarianism, Newman
would contest Descartes's anti-traditionalism. Whatever ideational value the
cogito has would be a function of the long conversation that produced it and
the equally long conversation required to understand it. Now if all of this is
true of ideas in general, it is *a fortiori* the case in regard to the theological
ideas at the heart of Christianity, intricate and densely textured notions such
as incarnation, redemption, Trinity, grace, and the mystical body. These concepts will require the whole of the history of the church and the exertions
of the subtlest theological minds in order to be expressed with even relative
adequacy. In making these claims, Newman clearly anticipates the postmodern
advocates of a dialogic model of truth.

However, he also corrects them in his insistence that this playful and ef-
fervescent discussion must be limited and directed by an authoritative voice
lest it devolve into idle, and finally unproductive, academic chatter. We saw
that Tracy holds to the self-regulating capacity of the responsible theological
conversation. I believe that this confidence would have struck Newman as
unwarranted. It is precisely because doctrine unfolds that it is also subject

to the danger of corruption, false development. As a careful historian of the church, Newman was acutely aware of these errant branches that occasionally grow from the living tree of the Christian tradition and of the need to cut them lest they compromise the integrity of the organism. The pruner of the tree is the authoritative church, the *ecclesia docens*. Protestants held that the Bible is a sufficient rule for the life of the church; when he was an Anglican, Newman felt that Christian antiquity could be the criterion for distinguishing true from false belief. What became clear to him as he was making his transition into Roman Catholicism was that only a living, personal authority could adequately function as the determiner of ecclesial belief, and this is what he found in the infallible authority of bishops and the pope. I cannot help but see a connection between this authoritative referee and the living voice of the conscience required for the guidance of the moral life and the active, phronesis-like "voice" of the illative sense necessary for the proper functioning of the knowing process. In all three cases, a restless energy becomes focused—and hence more powerful—through the disciplining influence of a judge. Freed from authority, the moral, intellectual, and ecclesial projects would lose purpose and verve, much as a raging river, having overflowed its banks, rather quickly spreads out into a lazy lake.

Newman's liveliest presentation of the mutually enhancing play between the theological conversation and ecclesial authority can be found in the final chapter of the *Apologia pro vita sua*, entitled "A General Answer to Mr. Kingsley." Having established that the infallibility of the church is a divine gift designed to preserve the deposit of revelation, Newman considers the objection that submission to such authority would imply "the intellectual subservience of the human race." He responds with one of the most remarkable statements in his *oeuvre*: "The energy of the human intellect does from opposition grow; it thrives and is joyous with a tough elastic strength under the terrible blows of the divinely-fashioned weapon and is never so much itself as when it has lately been overthrown."[30] Muscles develop as they press against a resisting force; a tennis player improves when he faces someone who can skillfully return his shots; a debater progresses only when he confronts an opponent who can confound him. So the lively play of the theological conversation is not enervated by authority but is instead most itself precisely in the measure that authority blocks it and sets limits to it. More to the point, infallibility is "brought out into act" only through the lively exercise of theological reason. A sluggish, jejune, and dull-minded conversation would not even draw the attention of the infallible authority. Thus, Newman concludes, "[Infallibility's] object is not to enfeeble the freedom or vigour of human thought in religious speculation, but to resist and control its extravagance."[31]

There is a strain of postmodernity—represented most thoroughly by Jacques Derrida and his disciples—that rules out, as a matter of principle, any limitation that authority would impose on the infinitely open-ended play of interpretation. This is the conversational model of truth run amok, for it has allowed truth to evanesce into a phantom. John Caputo, one of America's most perceptive commentators on Derrida, has remarked that deconstruction is essentially a messianism without a Messiah, that is to say, an openness to what is *l'avenir* (to come), coupled with an absolute conviction that it can never finally appear.[32] Newman's balanced epistemology, including the indispensability of both intersubjective conversation *and* infallible authority, confirms what is constructive in the postmodern critique of modernity, even as it holds off a weirdly self-destructive element within it.

Conclusion

I hope to have shown that John Henry Newman, in his implicit anti-foundationalism, insistence that theology has a positioning relationship vis-à-vis other academic disciplines, and understanding of the dynamic rapport between infallible authority and the conversation of theologians, anticipates key features of the postmodern dialectic. My further hope is that the demonstration of these correspondences inspires a more careful reading of this great nineteenth-century teacher, so that those who are presently engaged in the rough and tumble of theological debate can draw from him not only intellectual inspiration but also strength and a sense of *joie de combat.*

8

✠

Biblical Interpretation and Theology

A Meditation on Irenaeus, Modernity, and Vatican II

One can witness in recent years a growing consensus that a one-sided, historical-critical approach to the sacred Scriptures is inadequate. Figures as diverse as Brevard Childs, Walter Brueggemann, Jon Levenson, Gary Anderson, Francis Martin, Robert Louis Wilken, and Joseph Ratzinger have indicated how, in various ways, the dominance of historical criticism in the postconciliar period has led to a diminishment of the Bible in the life of the church. Common among many of these critics is the conviction that too much recent biblical scholarship involves a severing of the ties between exegesis and dogmatic theology. For many historical critics, exegesis is typically construed as the concern of technically trained experts in ancient language, philology, and culture, while theology is characterized as, at best, a spiritual reflection only vaguely related to the intentions of the Bible's authors or, at worst, a later overlay that effectively obscures those intentions. Many of these contemporary critics—Wilken, Martin, and Ratzinger spring most readily to mind—complain that the richly typological and theologically integrated understanding of the Bible that held sway among the fathers of the church and the medieval doctors has been almost completely eclipsed by modern biblical criticism. What I would like to do in this brief chapter is to argue for the reintegration of exegesis and theology in the spirit of the fathers and the medieval masters of the *sacra pagina*, fully acknowledging as I do so the legitimate gains of the modern historical-critical approach. In his paper from a conference on biblical interpretation in 1988, then cardinal Joseph Ratzinger held that this sort of work would be the task of an entire generation of theological scholarship.

I will proceed in three steps. First, I will explore the groundbreaking and massively influential work of St. Irenaeus of Lyons, the second-century genius who set the tone for the distinctively patristic style of biblical exegesis that remained more or less in place until the beginning of the modern era. Second, I will analyze the metaphysical and epistemological shifts that occurred in the early modern period and opened the door to a mode of biblical interpretation rather strikingly at odds with the classical method. Third, against this backdrop, I will look at the Vatican II document *Dei verbum* in hopes of finding a path forward, a means of incorporating the historical-critical method into the context of a patristic-ecclesial method of interpretation. My hope is that a careful reading of *Dei verbum* discloses not simply a blandly both/and approach nor a facile "beyondism" but rather a creatively integrated reading of the ancient and the modern.

The Biblical Theology of Irenaeus of Lyons

It is entirely appropriate to refer to the theological project of St. Irenaeus as biblical. Unlike Origen, who wrote a generation later, or even Augustine, Irenaeus was not endeavoring to fit Christian revelation into a preexisting philosophical framework or even to establish a correlation with one. Rather, his theology is nothing but a sustained and reasoned reflection on the ideas, assumptions, images, history, and metaphor that constitute the biblical world. The typically modern dilemma of relating theology or doctrine to biblical exegesis would have struck Irenaeus as anomalous, for Irenaeus's theology is not an alien system of thought imposed on the Bible but rather the making plain of the inner logic of the Bible itself. For him, the Bible is indeed the "soul" of theology (to use the Vatican II expression), and theology is the proper interpretive lens of the Bible, the two existing in a kind of circumincession. Irenaeus pithily expresses this relationship with the phrase—found frequently throughout his writings—*regula fidei* (rule of faith). The *regula*, a primitive

form of the creeds that would emerge out of the later councils, is a set of
convictions, assumptions, and narrative content that grows organically out of
the biblical witness itself. A kind of canon within the canon, the *regula fidei*
allows the prospective interpreter to find his way through the often confusing
thicket of the scriptural world. It has, accordingly, a sort of mystagogic function, indicating the structuring architecture of divine revelation.

For the sake of simplicity and clarity, I shall examine one form of the *regula
fidei* found in the first book of the *Adversus haereses*. It begins as follows:
"The Church, though dispersed throughout the whole world, even to the ends
of the earth, has received from the apostles and their disciples this faith in
one God, the Father Almighty, Maker of heaven, and earth, and the sea, and
all things that are in them."[1] The affirmation of God as creator of the entire
universe—the totality of all that is not God—is, of course, the ground for
Irenaeus's fierce opposition to the Gnostics, who held the existence of a high
God, beyond speech and knowledge, from whom had come forth, through a
long series of emanations, a fallen and compromised divinity who was responsible for the material realm. This lesser god they identified with Yahweh of the
Old Testament. It was the signal merit of Irenaeus to have perceived that the
Gnostic notion of God remains fundamentally irreconcilable with the narrative logic of the Bible. Two important consequences follow from this assertion
of God's creativity. First, since God is creator and unique (the one God), it
follows that all of finite reality must come from him. In a word, he creates *ex
nihilo* and not in the manner of the Platonic demiurgos or the Aristotelian
prime mover, both of whom effect some preexisting matter or energy that is
ontologically co-basic with them. In making this claim, Irenaeus departed
from practically the whole of the philosophical and religious tradition that
preceded and surrounded him. Even the Jewish philosopher Philo, who was
deeply grounded in the biblical revelation, held back from speaking of *creatio
ex nihilo*, insisting that Yahweh fashioned the world out of some sort of prime
matter. Now if God is, in the proper and radical sense, creator, then God is
simultaneously and completely other than the world *and* present to the world
in the most intimate way possible. The one who made the universe *ex nihilo*
could never be identified as a reality within the universe. He is neither one
being among many nor the totality of existing things; by the same token, the
Creator *ex nihilo* must stand in the most ontologically intimate relationship
with anything that exists outside himself, since quite literally nothing stands
between him and that which he makes. Augustine would express this paradox
as follows: God is both *intimior intimo meo et superior summo meo*. One
could sum up the situation by speaking, with Robert Sokolowski, of God's
noncompetitive transcendence or, with Kathryn Tanner, of God's "otherly"

otherness, an echo of Nicholas of Cusa's claim that God, the *totaliter aliter* (completely other), remains the *non-aliud* (non-other).

The second great implication of the doctrine of creation is that all of finite reality—spiritual as well as physical—is good and marked by a participation in the reasonability of the Logos. This too tells against the Gnostics, who held that matter is ontologically compromised, but it also expresses the biblical conviction that all created reality is, in some sense, a bearer of God's presence and implicated in the story that God wants to tell. If all finite being comes forth here and now from the creative ground of God, then all things are necessarily connected to one another through God and are woven together according to God's intelligent purpose. The book of Wisdom states this truth as follows: "God's wisdom stretches from end to end mightily and orders all things sweetly" (AP, see Wis. 8:1). On the modern telling, space is simply the empty arena in which extended things situate themselves haphazardly, and time is simply the linear unfolding of event after event. But on this Irenaean/biblical reading, space and time participate in the eternal reasonability of God and hence take on a narrative density and luminosity.

After affirming the unity and creativity of God, the *regula fidei* goes on to assert the truth of the incarnation, the enfleshment of the Son of God. "And in one Christ Jesus the Son of God, Who became incarnate for our salvation."[2] It is most important to note that there is a tight logical connection between the doctrines of creation and incarnation, for it is only the creator God who can possibly enter into a personal union with a finite nature in such a way that the finite nature is not compromised or overwhelmed. The incarnation becomes thereby the fullest manifestation of Sokolowski's noncompetitive divine transcendence. For Irenaeus's purposes, the incarnation displays the fundamental logic of God's relationship to his creation: nonviolent, alluring rather than imposing, enhancing rather than domineering. It is this dynamic that most basically distinguishes the biblical story from the Greek and Roman narratives of divine-human relationships, a point emphatically made by Augustine in *The City of God*. The doctrine of the incarnation also implies that the true God does not despise matter but rather desires to transfigure it under the influence of spirit. The *regula* states the purpose of the incarnation explicitly: "To gather up all things in Himself and to raise the flesh of all mankind to life."[3] It will belong to the structuring logic of the biblical story that matter is not to be escaped from but rather transformed and raised to a higher ontological pitch through more intense participation in the divine manner of being.

Next, the *regula* affirms the existence of the Holy Spirit and specifies that God the Father, through the Son and the Spirit—that is to say, needing no help from creatures—"makes, disposes, governs, and gives being to all things."[4] The principal actor in the biblical narrative is this tri-personal God who shapes the whole of his creation purposefully and lovingly, according to the manner of an artist or storyteller. Since he is noncompetitive, his action is utterly compatible with the free and purposeful action of his rational creatures. Again, the Irenaean God accomplishes his end sweetly, through allurement.

Now this *regula*, Irenaeus insists, was not so much his work but that of the apostle John, the mentor to Polycarp, who in turn taught Irenaeus himself. "The disciple of the Lord [John]therefore desiring to put an end to all such doctrines [Gnosticism], and to establish the rule of truth in the Church" handed on this formula.[5] Time and again, Irenaeus characterizes his work as the handing on of the apostolic teaching; in fact, his short summary of the *Adversus haereses* bears the straightforward title *Demonstration of the Apostolic Preaching*. In a word, the *regula* does not represent a philosophical consensus or an externally imposed matrix of interpretation but rather the apostolically ratified distillation of the essential biblical worldview, the fundamental metaphysics that St. John and his companions insisted must undergird the biblical story. This is why, for Irenaeus, these "doctrinal" claims are not the least bit distorting but clarifying. Indeed, apart from them, the biblical witness would remain opaque and the essential story murky and open to misinterpretation. To suggest that the *regula fidei* should be set aside in order to allow the authentic intention of the biblical authors to emerge would have struck Irenaeus as so much nonsense.

We might sum up the sense of the *regula* with the word *participation*. The universe in its entirety—both its spiritual and material elements—participates in the to-be of God, and through this common participation all created things are related to one another. Moreover, God's providence and governance conduce toward an even richer creaturely share in the divine life. In an oft-repeated formula, Irenaeus says that God is unmade but the creature made, that is to say, continually molded and shaped so as to participate ever more fully in God's life. And since the Bible is the story of God's dealings with creation, the Scriptures themselves participate in the divine Logos, and particular parts of Scripture participate in one another, contributing to the whole of divine revelation. The Bible, consequently, ought never to be read simply as a congeries of unrelated tales, prophecies, histories, and words of wisdom, drawn from a variety of sources and in response to differing historical situations. Though it might seem that way "from the ground," it takes on coherence and consistency when read from the standpoint of the divine author. Thus, the Bible is a *symphonos*, a sounding together of tones and melodies, under the direction of the supreme artist. Also, since we the readers of the Bible participate in the divine being and are subject to the divine governance, we should expect the scriptural narrative to be illuminating for us. Finally, given that God is the author of both the Bible and history itself, we shouldn't be surprised to find a whole set of figural or typological correspondences throughout the scriptural witness. We should expect that God will speak in a distinctive accent and according to certain characteristic patterns and rhythms. These hermeneutical assumptions bring Irenaeus quite close to the rabbis of the intertestamental period who, as James Kugel argues, operated out of four fundamental convictions—namely, that God in a very real sense is the author of the whole Scripture, that the Bible is consistent with itself, that its meaning is often cryptic, and that it has relevance for us today.[6]

With this entire interpretive apparatus in place, Irenaeus reads the Scripture. He interprets Adam and Eve as children or, perhaps better, teenagers—good but inexperienced and hence easily deceived. God allowed them to fall so that through the pain of their sin they might come to deeper life. This approach, so different from the mainstream of the tradition, which followed Augustine, was picked up by Hegel, Kierkegaard, Tillich, and Teilhard de Chardin in the modern period. But it was perfectly in accord with Irenaeus's own instincts concerning the goodness and all-powerfulness of God who makes and the malleability and educability of the creature who is made. The rest of the biblical story is the account of the process by which the Father, using his two hands, the Son and the Spirit, shaped the descendants of Adam and Eve back into friendship with God. This shaping is delineated by Irenaeus according to a number of covenants and elections throughout salvation history. God made a covenant with the whole world at the time of the flood, and then with Abraham as he formed a people after his own heart, and then with Moses as he drew Israel from slavery to freedom, and finally with David as he established a kingdom that would last for all ages. These various figures, on Irenaeus's reading, were approached by the Word who was, as it were, gradually accustoming the human race to the divine presence. And hence the various covenants with the Old Testament figures were anticipations of the incarnation, the full accommodation of divinity to humanity and humanity to divinity.

As the divine Logos incarnate, as the culmination of the process of the shaping of Israel to God's friendship, Jesus is, in person, the recapitulation of time and history. The notion of *anakephalaiosis*, rendered in Latin as *recapitulatio*, is one of the master ideas of Irenaeus's biblical theology. Jesus draws all the strands of history and revelation together in himself, preserving and repeating them even as he brings them to fulfillment. Thus, he is the new Adam, the one who participates fully in the reality of Adam, including physicality and alienation from God, even as he draws all that was implicit and potential in Adam to completion. And Mary the mother of Jesus is the new Eve, sharing in the reality of the first Eve even as she redirects the momentum of her forebear's sin. Jesus, too, is the recapitulation of creation. In his resurrection from the dead, he heals, renews, and elevates the fallen world. The recapitulating Christ is himself the interpretive key of the whole Scripture, since he is the Logos made flesh, the very embodiment of the *regula fidei* in all its dimensions. When this key is lost, the various pieces of the biblical revelation remain disconnected, or as was the case with the Gnostics, they are assembled erroneously. According to Irenaeus's famous trope, the Gnostics, lacking the proper pattern, turned what should have been the beautiful picture of a king into a depiction of a fox.

Irenaeus bequeathed this extraordinarily integrated manner of biblical interpretation to the great tradition. It was repeated and enhanced by Origen and Chrysostom in the east and Jerome and Augustine in the west, to name just the most prominent figures. And it continued its vigorous development through the high Middle Ages to the work of Thomas Aquinas. I would like to say just a word about Thomas, arguably the most important of the medieval *magistri sacrae paginae*. Within the context of the very first question of the *Summa theologiae*, Thomas wonders whether it is appropriate that the Scriptures have a variety of senses. In his response, he clarifies, in line with Irenaeus's approach, that the author of the Bible is God and that God can use words to designate things (as any human author could do) but that he can also use things to designate things. When this latter correspondence takes place, we speak of the Bible's spiritual sense, which is subdivided into the moral, the allegorical, and the anagogical. For our purposes, what is interesting here is the implicit affirmation of a participation metaphysic undergirding the biblical hermeneutics. One "thing," which is to say a person, place, or event, can speak allegorically, morally, or anagogically of another thing precisely because all created reality is interdependent and coinherent, drawn together by the common implication in divine causality and governance. Were God not, in this strong sense, creator and governor of the cosmos, the integrity and coherence of the biblical witness would collapse. Also, Thomas's concentration on the intentionality of the divine author shows him to be a disciple of Irenaeus. Like his patristic forebear, Thomas doesn't deny for a moment that fully engaged human authors have written the various texts of the Bible, but he sees their efforts as a participation in the noncompetitive and intelligent direction of the divine mind.

The Shift to a Modern Mode of Interpretation

Many have told the story of the emergence of a new, typically modern, approach to biblical interpretation in the seventeenth and eighteenth centuries, but insufficient attention has been paid to the shifts in the metaphysical base that made this transition possible. In recent years, many etiologists of modernity have indicated the figure of Duns Scotus as decisive. Writing just a generation after Thomas Aquinas, Scotus consciously departed from Thomas and opted for a univocal rather than an analogical conception of being. On this reading, God was construed as one being among many, the supreme instance of the genus "existence." In accord with his analogical conception, Thomas had denied that God could be situated in any genus, including that of being, since God is not *a* being but rather that in whom essence and existence coincide, *ipsum esse* rather than *ens summum*. But in the context of Scotus's conception, God is indeed *ens summum*—the highest being among beings—and hence the essential ontological link between God and creatures was compromised. Scotus's successor William of Occam would present his fundamental ontology as follows: *praeter illas partes absolutas nulla res* (except for absolute parts, there is no real thing). In other words, the connection that obtained, on Thomas's interpretation, between God and those finite things that participate in him had been eliminated, and only absolute things—both divine and nondivine—remained. This univocal conception of being had massive implications for the way that one viewed not only individual existing things but also time itself. History, which had been seen as participating in the intelligent providence of God, came to be seen as purely linear, a series of isolated and essentially disconnected events. If God were to involve himself in history, it would be in an interruptive and occasional manner.

The metaphysical view that we've been sketching was inherited by the Protestant reformers, who were largely formed in schools dominated by some version of Occam's nominalism. It is on clear display in Luther's and Calvin's one-sided emphasis on the divine transcendence, in their suspicion of mysticism, and in their stress on the isolated individual, in his interiority, confronting the grace and freedom of God.

But it is in the philosophers of the modern period that the breakdown of a participation view is most obvious. When they speak of God—and they do it often—modern thinkers tend to construe God as a supreme being only distantly related to the concerns of the world. Think of the cosmic designer proposed by the Deists or of Descartes's perfect being or Kant's metaphysically inaccessible moral postulate. The dissolution of the participation metaphysics can break in the opposite direction as well, God becoming not so much a distant supreme being but nature or finite reality considered as a totality. We see this kind of pantheist mysticism clearly in Baruch Spinoza, who said, "*Deus sive natura*" (God or nature), as though the terms were simply interchangeable. On this Spinozan reading, there is no longer a tensive participatory relationship between the God who is *ipsum esse* and the world that he continually makes. Rather, "God" is simply another way of talking about the world. And there is accordingly no dramatic play of infinite and finite freedoms, but rather all is determined as the outflowing of God: *natura naturans*.

I believe that it is not accidental that the founder of modern biblical criticism was this same Spinoza. I don't think for a moment that all historical criticism is reducible to the Spinozan system, but I do indeed think that insufficient attention has been paid to the Spinozan assumptions that often inform, consciously or not, the work of historical biblical critics across the centuries and up to the present day. What precisely is that system? In his hugely influential *Tractatus Theologico-Politicus* of 1670, Spinoza laid out a series of hermeneutical principles that, as James Kugel comments, "became the marching orders of biblical scholars for the next three centuries."[7] First, Spinoza determined that "all knowledge of Scripture must be sought from Scripture alone."[8] In making this recommendation, he was trying to get rid of Jewish midrash and Christian allegory and typology, all of which led to "absurdities." The Bible ought to be read straightforwardly and literally on its own terms. Second, he advised that the biblical interpreter should attend carefully to the language and conceptual world of the biblical authors themselves, careful not to project his own thinking and presumptions onto the text. Third, Spinoza counseled that the biblical hermeneut must seek to understand the mind and historical context of authors of the Scriptures and of the communities that they were addressing. Finally, he urged that the sane interpreter of the Bible must rid himself of the assumption that the Scriptures are consistent with themselves and admit that they are, in fact, filled with anomalies, inconsistencies, and inaccuracies. As Kugel remarks, "It is not difficult to see that the program outlined by Spinoza calls for the systematic dismantling of the Four Assumptions mentioned earlier," assumptions basic to Irenaeus's manner of exegesis.[9] Is the Scripture cryptic and allusive? Not at all: Scripture should be taken to mean what it says without complication. Is Scripture applicable to us today? Not at all: the Bible can be understood properly only in the context of its own time. Is Scripture unified and harmonious? By no means: one should assume that the Bible is a collection of disparate texts, written by a wide variety of authors to a wide variety of audiences for a wide variety of purposes. Is Scripture authored by God? One would never guess it from Spinoza's exclusive stress on the human authorship of the biblical books.

Those on the other side of the postparticipation divide—namely, the Deists—ran rather gleefully with Spinoza's recommendations. Thomas Jefferson, David Hume, Voltaire, and many other Deists took apart the classical sense of the Bible with a certain relish. Hume's meditations on the Pentateuch are typical: "A book presented to us by a barbarous and ignorant people written in an age when they were still more barbarous, and in all probability long after the facts which it relates . . . resembling those fabulous accounts which every nation gives of its origin."[10] From Hume, it is a very short step to Reimarus and Strauss and their unambiguously debunking program. Perhaps no modern more pithily summarized the Spinozan revolution than Benjamin Jowett, who in 1860 opined, "Scripture has one meaning—the meaning which it had in the mind of the Prophet or Evangelist who first uttered or wrote, to the hearers or readers who first received it."[11] As Jon Levenson has pointed out, this hyperconcentration on the intention of the historical author within his historical period, and in abstraction from the wider literary, theological, and metaphysical context, has led effectively to the relegation of the Bible *to* the past. And this was, in the minds of many, precisely Spinoza's purpose.

What I would like to stress is how the Spinozan program for biblical interpretation is grounded in the postparticipation metaphysical program embraced by Spinoza and most of his modern philosophical colleagues. If God is no longer a person (or at least not a person with much of an interest in the world), and if he is no longer the Lord of history, exercising a providential governance over things that are distinct from him even as they participate in him, then the Spinozan assumptions are valid. And since there is no ongoing work of the Holy Spirit, doctrinal or dogmatic rules such as Irenaeus's *regula* are distorting.

I would like to draw attention to another strain of modern biblical interpretation which has had a rather massive impact on much theologizing—both Catholic and Protestant—over the past two centuries. It runs from Friedrich Schleiermacher, the founder of liberal Protestantism, through Adolf Harnack and Rudolf Bultmann, and its chief characteristic is neo-Marcionism, or a radical de-Judaizing of the Scripture. It is by no means accidental that the principal philosophical influence on Schleiermacher was none other than Spinoza, who had, to say the least, an ambiguous relationship with his own native Jewish religion. Even the most casual survey of Schleiermacher's major works shows that he was surprisingly neglectful of the Old Testament. What he wanted to establish, of course, was a ground for religion outside of what he took to be the ambiguous historical claims of positive revelation. Certainly Lessing and Kant influenced him in this regard, but he was shaped above all by the devastation caused by the wars of religion that ravaged Europe in the wake of the Reformation. It appeared as though neither Protestants nor Catholics were able to adjudicate their disputes through reasonable appeal to their Sacred Scriptures, and therefore in the interest of peace, Schleiermacher wanted to find a new interpretive context for the claims of religion. He discovered it in the universally shared feeling of absolute dependency, an intuition described in the Bible but by no means essentially tied to it. This allowed him to declare independence from what his contemporaries held to be increasingly incredible and suspect Scriptures. Here is Schleiermacher's own assessment of the believability of classical biblical hermeneutics: "Do you hope that the traditional views of the messianic prophecies and indeed of types will be found credible by those who have come to a sound and lively view of historical matters? I cannot believe it."[12] But finally this is of no matter because, "of all that I praise and feel at its [religion's] work, hardly anything can be found in the Holy Books."[13] Furthermore, Schleiermacher dismisses the patristic/medieval method of interpretation with a wave of his hand: "To those who would seek to restore the fallen walls of their Jewish Zion and its Gothic pillars, I say that we must discover the essence of religion in personal experience."[14] Indeed, so dispensable is the Old Testament that Schleiermacher can say, "Christianity does indeed stand in a special historical connection with Judaism; but as far as concerns its historical existence and aim, its relations to Judaism and heathenism are the same."[15]

It would be hard to imagine any of the first Christians finding that last statement anything but breathtakingly wrongheaded. What this signals is the keynote for most of the theological liberalism of the past two centuries, namely, the disassociation of Christianity from its Old Testament roots. N. T. Wright has commented that most of the Christology of the modern period has been essentially Marcionite in form, and we can see the truth of this assertion borne out in the remarkably unbiblical Christologies of Paul Tillich, Karl Rahner, and David Tracy, to name just a few representative cases.

A century after Schleiermacher, Adolf von Harnack made explicit the implicit Marcionism of his predecessor. Harnack said that Marcion was his "first love," and he gleefully embraced the heresiarch's program of de-Judaizing, commenting that Marcion saw "the religion of Jesus Christ corrupted by the addition of the Old Testament . . . resulting in a syncretistic catholicism that differed sharply from its founder's view that all traditions, doctrines, and forms were essentially indifferent." Thus, for Harnack, Marcion was "the first Protestant," who rightly perceived that "the Pauline antithesis of righteousness by faith and not by works leads logically to the rejection of the Old Testament."[16] Like his master, Harnack proposed that the god of the Old Testament was uncouth, angry, and lacking in refinement.

Something very similar is on display in the exegetical and theological work of Rudolf Bultmann. Like most moderns, Bultmann rejected the classical apologetic argument that miracles and prophecies grounded Christian truth claims. These have been eliminated by serious historical criticism, but their disappearance poses no problem to authentic Christianity, which is based, on Bultmann's reading, upon God's eschatological act of salvation proposed in Christ. In point of fact, the vitiating of the Old Testament is something of a liberation for Christianity, for it allows us to appreciate the soteriologically significant Jesus. "As the eschatological deed of God, Jesus makes an end of all ethnic history as the sphere of God's dealing with man." This reading compels Bultmann to deny explicitly Paul's contention that the church is grafted onto the tree of Israel: "For the history of Israel is a closed chapter; it is not our history and the events which meant something for Israel mean nothing more to us." And this line of reasoning brings him quite close to the most radical teaching of Schleiermacher: "It is true that, in a certain sense, the history of Israel has become part of our western heritage, but the same is also true of Greek history, so that it might be said that the Spartans fell at Thermopylae for us and that Socrates drank the hemlock for us. Jerusalem is not a holier city for us than Athens or Rome." Because the Jewish background is dispensable to the presentation of Christianity, it can be replaced "by other illustrative material, drawn perhaps from Greek tragedy or modern philosophy."[17] And this, of course, is just what Bultmann did, substituting Heideggerian anthropology for the Bible. One would be hard pressed to find a more thoroughgoing embrace of Marcionism—or a more complete rejection of the patristic/medieval manner of biblical interpretation.

Having surveyed the development of some strains of modern biblical interpretation, I would like to consider the work of the man generally regarded as the dean of contemporary Catholic biblical exegesis, Raymond E. Brown. I would like to be eminently clear from the outset of this analysis that I don't think Brown is Schleiermacher, Harnack, or Bultmann. He had benefited from the numerous and vociferous critiques of those players and had been formed in the broad Catholic tradition of biblical reading. Nevertheless, I'm convinced that Brown shares certain assumptions and basic moves with his modern forebears and that these have rendered his approach problematic. In his programmatic essay on hermeneutics in the *Jerome Biblical Commentary*, and in any number of books and articles from the sixties, seventies, and eighties, Brown laid out and defended his vision of modern historical criticism. He construed it as, basically, the attempt to discover, through the use of philology, literary analysis, historical investigation, redaction criticism, and so on, what precisely was the communicative intention of the author or redactor of a biblical text as he addressed his particular audience. This intention Brown identified with the literal sense of the scriptural text. He spoke readily enough of the *sensus plenior*, the fuller sense, corresponding to what God intended to communicate through a text, even beyond the explicit intention of the author, but he never developed this in his own exegetical writings, leaving its explication to theologians and spiritual writers. Proper biblical scholarship, he felt, is limited to the determination of "what a given text meant," while theology or spirituality can sort out what a text might mean in the present situation: "The meaning of the Bible . . . goes beyond what the authors *meant* in a particular book. Not only scholarship but also church teaching and tradition enters into the complex issue of what the Bible *means* to Christians."[18]

What concerns us in this program is, first, the exaggerated bifurcation between biblical exegesis and theology, as though the latter is in, at best, a tenuous relationship to the former. If one had asked Thomas Aquinas to distinguish between his systematic theology and his biblical analysis, I'm quite sure he would have been puzzled. As we've seen, he was known precisely as a *magister sacrae paginae*, and his theology is best characterized as an elaborate and sustained study of the Bible. Moreover, his more formal biblical commentaries are shot through on every page with theology. Though Brown phrases his position here carefully, one can't help but sense in his sharp division of exegesis and theology the Spinozan desire to interpret the Bible purely on its own terms and from within the context of its own history. And this gets to a second and deeper objection. When Thomas and the fathers before him were endeavoring to exegete the Scripture, they were not going after, primarily, what the historical authors intended but rather what the divine author intended. They realized, of course, that God worked through the secondary causality of intelligently engaged human beings, but their real focus was on the God in whom both history as such and the biblical authors participated. In light of their creation metaphysics, they realized that history cannot be construed simply in a flat, linear manner but rather as an iconic manifestation of the eternal purposes of God. And this is precisely why they chose not to focus exclusively or even primarily on the intention of historical authors but rather on the divine author working trans-historically through them. Here is Matthew Levering's formulation of this position: "The problem with this view [Brown's account of historical critical exegesis] is that 'what it meant' is inscribed with the triune God's creative and redemptive presence so profoundly as to defeat any strict version of the past tense: the past, as history . . . is participatory."[19] Nicholas Lash commented on contemporary Catholic biblical scholarship in a very similar vein: "There is . . . a sense in which the articulation of what the text might 'mean' today is a necessary condition of hearing what the text 'originally meant.'"[20] This is true because, in a participation framework of understanding, the Holy Spirit, who stands outside time, is the author, simultaneously, of history, text, and interpretation.

In light of these clarifications, it is instructive to consult the section of Brown's article on hermeneutics where he discusses the characteristically patristic mode of biblical interpretation. In regard to Origen and the Alexandrian school in general, Brown says, "A good part of his allegorical exegesis was based on the theory that the Old Testament was christological in many passages. . . . This writer does not share the view that Origen's exegesis can really be revived for our time."[21] There is, of course, something breathtaking, and typically modern, about this blithe dismissal of fifteen hundred years of biblical interpretation. For Irenaeus, his patristic colleagues, and the doctors of the Middle Ages, such a denial of christological density to the Old Testament would be tantamount to Marcionism and would result in a seriously skewed reading of the Bible as a whole. From the standpoint of a participatory exegesis, which places a stress on the divine authorship of both the Bible and the history of salvation itself, the christological character of the Old Testament is taken for granted as the indispensable propaedeutic to the appearance of the Word made flesh.

Dei Verbum

Having analyzed, however briefly and inadequately, the classical patristic mode of biblical hermeneutics and the modern approach that in so many fundamental ways departed from it, I would like to turn now to a consideration of the Vatican II document on divine revelation, *Dei verbum*. When scholars survey the recent history of official ecclesial statements on biblical hermeneutics, they customarily cite *Dei verbum* and Pius XII's *Divino afflante spiritu* as relatively "liberal" documents in the measure that they allow for an openness to the historical-critical method. They often cite, by way of contrast, *Dei filius* of Vatican I and *Providentissimus Deus* of Leo XIII as relatively "conservative" statements. Without denying for a moment *Dei verbum*'s embrace of certain aspects of the modern approach, I would like to suggest that the document's overall thrust is much more in the direction of a patristic, participation mode of interpretation. It is precisely the bringing together of the two styles in a noncompetitive but still asymmetrical manner that constitutes the chief virtue of *Dei verbum*.

The first chapter of *Dei verbum*, which deals directly with the question of revelation, brings us promptly into an Irenaean perspective, for it speaks of God's gradual self-manifestation through his Word, culminating in the enfleshment of that Word in Jesus Christ. The document specifies that the purpose of this manifestation is none other than the drawing of human beings into friendship with God and participation in the divine life. Then comes that distinctively Irenaean word *oeconomia*, which is repeated like a refrain throughout *Dei verbum*: "*Haec revelationis oeconomia fit . . .*" One could not speak coherently of an economy unless there were an *economus*, some great mind and personality responsible for the rational arrangement of nature and history. The very term therefore sums up a participative view of time and space. Next, *Dei verbum* specifies that this pattern or economy of salvation unfolds *gestis verbisque*, by both gestures (acts) and words. It thereby implies that revelation is never simply a verbal or intellectual matter but an affair of factual history. In Thomas Aquinas's language, God has authority over both words and "things" and can use both for his communicative purposes. Now this means, *pace* the moderns, that history cannot be construed in a purely linear way but must be interpreted as a coherent and artistically driven narrative, filled with allusions, anticipations, rhymes, echoes, meanings that double back upon themselves, typologies, and prophecies.

On *Dei verbum*'s reading, this participatory view of history and nature is rooted in the creative power of the Word. God witnesses to himself through the orderliness and beauty of the created world and, in a more pointed way, through salvation history. *Dei verbum* mimics Irenaeus in laying out the contours of sacred history, commencing with the call of Abraham and the other patriarchs, the giving of the law through Moses, the summoning of the prophets, and finally the arrival of the Messiah. And like the second century master, the Vatican II document characterizes this *oeconomia* as a succession of covenants made between God and his people. This summation is *Dei verbum*'s version of Irenaeus's *regula fidei*. The participatory metaphysics is further emphasized in the second chapter's discussion of the relationship between Scripture and tradition. In one of the most celebrated of its passages, *Dei verbum* affirms that Bible and tradition form together one great source of revelation, since both flow from the Holy Spirit, which is to say, from a power who properly transcends time and hence can effectively unite them. The pivotal third chapter, which treats explicitly of biblical inspiration and interpretation, situates itself thoroughly within a patristic framework. We hear that the sacred books were written under the influence of the Holy Spirit and hence *Deum habent auctorem* (have God as their author). That this does not amount to a naive literalism is made clear in the immediately subsequent observation that "God employed human agents, using their own powers and faculties in such a way that they wrote as authors in the true sense, and yet God acted in and through them." The ground for this paradoxical assertion is in the consistently biblical teaching that God relates to his creation noncompetitively, allowing it to flourish on its own even as he works through it. Perhaps the clearest Old Testament statement of this principle is in the twenty-sixth chapter of Isaiah when the prophet states, "You [LORD] have accomplished all we have done" (see Isa. 26:12 NABRE) But, as we've seen, the idea comes to richest and most dramatic expression in the New Testament claim that God became human, without ceasing to be God and without compromising the integrity of the creature he became. The Council of Chalcedon honored this biblical logic when it spoke of the two natures in Jesus coming together without mixing, mingling, or confusion. It thereby held off the triple threat of monophysitism (a one-sided stress on divinity), Nestorianism (a one-sided stress on humanity), and Arianism (a compromise of the two). The negation of all three positions was made possible by the distinctively biblical belief in God as creator. Extrapolating from this discussion, we can say with *Dei verbum* that the true God is capable of working decisively through intelligent, created causes but in such a way that the full integrity and purposefulness of those causes is not compromised. On a more Nestorian reading of inspiration—prominent in much of modernity—one might speak of an independent human author speculating according to his lights, with perhaps a vague relationship to a distant God. On a monophysite reading, one might speak—as fundamentalists and literalists do—of a God who uses human agents in a domineering manner, essentially eliminating their own intelligence. Both fall short of the participative view on display in *Dei verbum*.

We must be exceptionally careful here, since Chalcedon, even as it insisted on the separation of the natures, did not simply lay them out side by side. Rather, it affirmed a certain asymmetricality in their rapport, since both natures are actualized precisely by the divine personhood of Jesus. In Christ, God uses a human nature in an instrumental way, but it would never be appropriate to reverse the logic and speak of a human Christ using his divine nature instrumentally. The divinity of Jesus does not suppress his humanity, but it does control and transcend it. And this relationship most fully expresses the biblical logic of divine-human relationality, including that which obtains between divine inspiration and human authorship. All of this is meant to call into question Raymond Brown's insistence that one can and should do biblical exegesis with an exclusive focus on the intentionality of the human authors. The one-sidedness of this approach amounts to a violation of both the noncompetitiveness and the asymmetricality of the Chalcedonian theo-logic. In light of this clarification, it is interesting to note the ideological bias in Norman Tanner's translation of a line from paragraph 12 of *Dei verbum*. He renders *quid hagiographi reapse significare intenderint et eorum verbis manifestare Deo placuerit* as "what meaning the biblical writers actually had in mind; that will also be what God chose to manifest through their words."[22] In point of fact, the *et* by no means entails an equivalency between divine and human intention. A much fairer rendering would be "what the sacred authors really intended to signify and what it pleased God to manifest through their words." In authentic scriptural exegesis, the primary focus is on the manner in which God has used a human instrument to communicate *his* meaning.

Nodding vigorously in the direction of modern criticism, *Dei verbum* emphasizes the crucial importance of attending to authorial intention and literary genre in biblical interpretation. One should never approach a more straightforwardly historical text such as First Samuel with the same hermeneutical assumptions that one might employ to survey a text such as the book of the prophet Jonah. But then it immediately affirms what would come to be called "canonical criticism," insisting that the Bible as a whole must be used as the interpretive matrix for any part of Scripture. Over against Spinoza (and Brown), *Dei verbum* maintains that "Holy Scripture requires to be read and interpreted in the light of the same Spirit through whom it was written." This principle is clearly violated in the measure that the recovery of the mind of the historical authors is the exclusive preoccupation of biblical hermeneutics.

Chapter four of *Dei verbum*, which treats of the Old Testament, is deeply Irenaean in spirit. It speaks of God's intention to save the world through the preparation of a "plan or *dispensatio*," and then specifies, once more, that the plan unfolds according to a series of covenants and elections. Furthermore, it employs the explicitly Irenaean notion of God's "accommodation" to man in order to explicate the different modalities of Old Testament revelation. In paragraph 15 of chapter 4, *Dei verbum* uses the Irenaean term *oeconomia* to describe the structuring logic of both salvation history and the Bible itself, and it states clearly, again in a distinctly Irenaean manner, that this *oeconomia* is directed to Christ. To be sure, the Old Testament texts have their own spiritual integrity, but they are particularly reverenced by Christians in the measure that "in them our salvation in Christ is hinted at under signs and symbols." Echoing Augustine's famous formula, *Dei verbum* says that because God is the *inspirator et auctor* of both Testaments, he brings it about that "the new Testament should be hidden in the old and the old Testament should be made manifest in the new."

In the sixth and final chapter of *Dei verbum* we find a discussion of the role of Scripture in the life of the church today. The council fathers call for helpful translations of the Bible so that all believers can have easy access to the Word of God, and then they explicitly recommend the study of the church fathers, both east and west, as a privileged way of coming to know the meaning of Scripture. How at odds this is with Raymond Brown's blithe dismissal of patristic analysis. And they call for a sort of *circumincessio* of biblical exegesis and theology, each one conditioning and informing the other. When they speak of the Bible as the "soul of theology," they imply that Scripture animates theology and that theology instantiates and gives concrete expression to the meaning of Scripture. The Spinozan/modern separation of exegesis and dogmatics is thereby implicitly called into question.

Conclusion

Like so many of the other texts of Vatican II, *Dei verbum* is best read under the rubric of *ressourcement*, the recovery of the biblical and patristic roots of the Christian faith. The great *ressourcement* theologians of the twentieth century, many of whom were *periti* at the council, tended to engage modernity in an oblique manner. Unlike their liberal colleagues, who endeavored to present Christian theology in a straighforwardly modern form, the *ressourcement* masters—de Lubac, Balthasar, Ratzinger, Daniélou—attempted to assimilate the best of modernity to the patristic form of the faith. They took modernity in, but they adapted and corralled it, making it ancillary to classical Christianity. This is just the method followed by the authors of *Dei verbum* in regard to characteristically modern modes of biblical analysis.

And it is precisely this vibrant, patristically flavored participatory exegesis that is meant to bear great fruit in the liturgy. In *Sacrasanctum concilium* 24, we find the frank assertion that "the importance of Scripture in the celebration of the liturgy is paramount." The conciliar fathers remind us that the readings at Mass are derived from Scripture, as are the psalms and, more indirectly, the prayers that are recited and the hymns that are sung. The Bible is the soul of the Mass as it is of theology. When in paragraph 35 the fathers call for a "fuller, more varied, and more appropriate approach to the reading of the Scripture," they are not asking simply for more of the Bible but for the integral, organic, richly typological reading that we saw advocated in *Dei verbum*. The proof of this is in the practical norms that followed the council, according to which a patristically flavored typological relationship is meant typically to obtain between the Old Testament reading and the Gospel at Mass.

The liturgy is, in a very real sense, the proper home of the Bible, the place where the Scriptures are most effectively presented and understood. This is in no sense to gainsay the importance of more technical exegesis, even of a modern sort, but to insist, in the spirit of Irenaeus and the other fathers, that the Bible is above all God's word, God's story told according to his intention and for his purpose.

PART 3

LITURGY AND EUCHARIST

9

✠

The Eucharist as the *Telos* of the Law in the Writings of Thomas Aquinas

No careful student of the life of Thomas Aquinas can doubt that the Eucharist played a central role in the saint's spirituality. Thomas would begin his day by celebrating the Mass and then would typically assist immediately afterward at a second Mass offered by his socius, Reginald of Piperno. It is said that he could rarely get through the liturgy without shedding tears, so intense was his participation in the reality of Christ's sacrifice. At the prompting of Pope Urban IV, he wrote—at least according to the scholarly consensus—a remarkably beautiful and theologically precise office for the newly instituted feast of Corpus Christi, the language and cadences of which are present in the liturgical life of the church to the present day. During the investigations prior to Aquinas's canonization, Reginald of Piperno said that though Thomas was the most brilliant man he had ever known, he was convinced that the saint's wisdom came much more from the intensity of his prayer than the diligence of his study. He added that he would frequently see Aquinas resting his head against the tabernacle, lost in contemplation, especially when he was wrestling with a particularly thorny theological problem. One of the most enduring and poignant legends concerning Aquinas has to do, at least indirectly, with the Eucharist. After he had finished the questions from the third part of the *Summa* dealing with the Blessed Sacrament, he placed the text at the foot of the cross in the Dominican chapel at Naples, as if to ask for judgment. According to the story, a voice spoke from the crucifix saying, "You have written well of me, Thomas, what would you have as a reward?" Aquinas responded, with admirable and typical laconicism, "*Nil nisi te*"—"nothing but you."

The treatise on the Eucharist—questions 73–83 of the *tertia pars* of the *Summa theologiae*—is one of Thomas's most insightful and adventurous theological undertakings, and it is one of the last pieces he wrote. He completed it probably in the summer of 1273, just months before the experience of December 6 of that year, which brought his writing career to an end. Thomas is, of course, one of the most cohesive and systematic thinkers in the tradition, and thus it is usually quite possible to show the variety of ways that any one section of the *Summa* relates to any other. What I would like to do here is to explore a perhaps surprising connection, namely, the link between Thomas's densely textured doctrine of the Eucharist and his teaching on law. Aquinas consistently refers to the Eucharist as the prime sacrament of the New Law. As such, he insists, it stands in relation not only to the other sacraments of the New Law but also to those antecedents of the New Law that can be found in the moral, judicial, and ceremonial precepts of the Old Law. And both the Old and New Laws are grounded in that eternal law that is identical to the divine mind itself and in turn is reflected in both the natural law and the human positive law. Through the exploration of these connections, I hope to make plain the way in which the Eucharist functions for Aquinas as the ultimate *regula* of the spiritual life for those of us on the pilgrim journey toward God.

The Nature of the Law

In accord with the familiar characterization, the *prima pars* of the *Summa theologiae* has to do with the great *exitus* of all things from the divine principle, and the *secunda pars* and *tertia pars* have to do with the ordered *reditus* of creation back to the source from which it came. This return—which has both a natural and a supernatural dimension—takes place in accord with law, or a reasoned *ordo* grounded finally in the dynamics of God's own self-understanding. Thus one could argue that the bulk of Thomas's masterpiece—whether it is treating of freedom, virtue, vice, the commandments of the Old Testament, or the sacraments of the New Testament—is finally about law.

The formal treatise on law commences with question 90 of the *prima secundae* and runs through question 114 of that same section. In the *respondeo* to question 90, we find a tightly formulated definition: "Law is a kind of rule and measure of acts, according to which one is drawn toward acting or restrained from acting."[1] But, Thomas continues, since the primary rule of free acts is the intellect, it follows that law, in all its expressions, pertains to reason. Moreover, since all action is directed ultimately to the end of happiness and since the happiness of any one agent is linked to that of every other, it follows that the *regula* of action—the law—has to do with the common or universal good. From these considerations, Thomas derives a somewhat more expansive definition: "Law is an ordinance of reason, for the common good, made by him who has care of the community, and promulgated."[2] As I have already intimated, the ground of all law is the eternal law, that reasonable *ordo* by which God governs the whole of the cosmos in his providence, drawing all things to their ends individually and with an eye toward the common good. The natural law, in turn, is that participation of the eternal law discoverable within the structures of the human moral consciousness, an ethical intuition by which we properly seek certain fundamental goods and avoid their opposites. And the human law is the positive specification of the natural law, formulated and promulgated for the realization of the common good in specific political and cultural circumstances. The manner in which positive human law nests in the natural law and thus finally in the eternal law shows how even the simplest traffic ordinance, rightly instituted, is an ingredient in the *reditus* of all things to God. Most treatments of Thomas's doctrine of law stop at this point, but this is unfortunate, for it overlooks the influence of the properly supernatural law, which supposes and perfects the natural law of which we have been speaking.

Besides the more familiar forms of law, there is what Aquinas calls "the divine law," that peculiar form of rational *ordo* revealed in the pages of the Scriptures, both Old Testament and New. In the fourth article of question 91, he lists a variety of reasons why this modality of law was necessary. I will examine the first and most important. Since we are directed by law toward our final end, and since that end is properly supernatural, we require a law whose specifications go beyond what reason can attain or perceive. We need, in other words, an *ordo* that is proportionate to the ultimate happiness that God desires for us. One can remark an analogy between this argument and the one found in the very first question of the *Summa*, dealing with the necessity of a properly *Sacra doctrina* beyond the philosophical disciplines. Though much truth concerning God can be discovered through metaphysical speculation, no saving or supernatural truth can be found in that manner. Thus, paradoxically, both the mind and the will need to be drawn beyond their own powers in order to realize their proper ends, the former through theology and the latter through the divine law. Though a kind of relationship with God can be established on the basis of the natural perceptions of the intellect and will, authentic friendship with God can come only through a divine gift, what Thomas typically calls *gratia*. The divine law is this properly gracious direction of the will by God's reason.

The Nature and Purpose of the Old Law

Thomas's fundamental approach to the issue of the Old Law is Pauline, which is to say that he sees the Old Law in all its modalities as preparatory for and prefigurative of the New Law that would appear in Jesus Christ. In question 99 of the *prima secundae*, Thomas delineates the three basic forms of the law revealed to the patriarchs and prophets of the Old Testament: the moral precepts, the judicial precepts, and the ceremonial precepts. First, one has only to glance at the Decalogue to realize that God's revealed law contained ethical directives: "You shall not kill; you shall not steal; you shall not commit adultery." The primary purpose of human law is to foster some sort of friendship among human beings, expressed as basic justice; and the purpose of the divine law is to cultivate friendship between human beings and God. But friendship, Aquinas maintains, is possible only between those who bear some similitude to one another, since likeness is the reason of love. It follows therefore that "there cannot be any friendship of man to God, who is supremely good, unless man become good; wherefore it is written 'You shall be holy, for I am holy.'"[3] Thus, it is reasonable that the Old Law should foster the cultivation of moral virtue. It is worth noting that, for Thomas, the precepts of the Decalogue correspond, more or less, with basic intuitions of the natural moral law. This overlap between revealed and naturally discoverable ethical truth is analogous to the overlap between revealed and naturally discoverable speculative truth that Aquinas calls, in the *prima pars*, the *preambula fidei*. In both cases, God deigns to reveal truths that can, in principle, be plumbed through reason, precisely because most people, due to the limitations of their intellectual capacities, require a divine supplement and inspiration.

Now the judicial precepts of the Old Law are specifications of the second table of the Decalogue, since they govern, through precise legislation, the complex arena of human interaction. They derive their binding power not through reason alone (since their exact requirements can seem rather arbitrary) but primarily "in virtue of their institution," that is, through the authority of the one who promulgates them, namely, God himself. Like all the commands of the Old Law, these judicial precepts are intended to foster friendship with God, but they achieve this end distinctively, by rightly ordering human relations in light of the divine sovereignty over all things. However, Aquinas is clear that these judicial requirements were not intended to be perpetual—as were, for instance, the moral precepts of the Old Law—but were rather designed to prepare a particular people for the coming of Christ. Once Christ had come, this legislation lost its binding force, as can be seen in the letters of the apostle Paul.

The ceremonial precepts constitute the third major subdivision of the Old Law, and I will spend more time examining these, since the Eucharist is best seen in relation to them. If the judicial precepts specify the second table of the Decalogue, the ceremonial laws specify the first, since they have to do with the right worship of God. How precisely should one honor God above all things, keep his name holy, and remember the Sabbath day? The answers to these questions are found in the ceremonial precepts, which are "determinations of the moral precepts whereby man is directed to God."[4] In the second article of question 101, which deals with the figurative quality of the ceremonial precepts, Thomas exposes the essential features of this aspect of the Old Law. The ceremonial requirements have to do with the correct worship of God, and worship is twofold, both interior and exterior. Interior worship is a matter of joining our intellects and affections to the truth of God; whereas exterior worship is a kind of ordering of the body so as to awaken and confirm the interior attitude of praise. Precisely because we are composites of body and soul, both modes of worship are necessary, and each implies the other. In this life, Thomas clarifies, we cannot look directly at the divine reality and so we stand in need of illumination through "sensible figures." In the old dispensation, ceremonial gestures and signs accomplished this external office, but they were also figurative in a double sense. First, they foreshadowed the sensible form of Christ who was to come, and more distantly, they evoked that perfect praise that would take place in the heavenly realm where all figures are overcome and the divine truth appears as such. "For in the state of future bliss, the human intellect will gaze on the Divine Truth in itself. Thus the external worship will not consist in anything figurative but solely in the praise of God, proceeding from the inward knowledge and affection."[5] This double figuration is a theme to which we shall return, for it shows that even those sacraments of the New Law, deriving their power from the incarnation, are themselves but anticipatory of something more perfect, namely, the bliss of the heavenly worship. Thus, the ceremonial precepts had a literal sense for the Jewish people of the Old Covenant and a symbolic sense for Christian believers and for the saints in heaven.

Now the ceremonial laws have to do with three dimensions: the worship of God in itself (sacrifices), those instruments pertaining to worship (sacred things), and the sanctification of those who offer the worship (sacraments and observances). I will focus on the first of these. The basic spiritual purpose of a sacrifice was to direct the mind of the worshiper to the God from whom all things come as a gift. By offering the first fruits of the harvest or herd, the sacrificer was acknowledging his radical dependence upon the divine Creator for all good things. A second and derivative purpose of sacrifice was the turning away from idolatry. By sending a burnt offering to the true God, the sacrificer was signaling his refusal to honor any rival gods: "Hence it is that the precepts about the sacrifices were not given to the Jewish people until after they had fallen into idolatry, by worshipping the molten calf."[6] Both of these rationales have to do with the literal sense of the sacrifice, that is to say, with the actual shaping of the Israelite people. But there was, as we have seen, a more symbolic and anticipatory meaning. All sacrifice is an acknowledgment of God's gifts through a return of some portion of those benefits. But God's greatest gift is that of his only begotten Son, and thus the most perfect sacrifice is the return of that gift to the one who gave it; and this is precisely what takes place through the sacrifice of the cross. Therefore, in the deepest symbolic sense, the various sacrifices of the old dispensation were prefigurements of the radical self-offering of Christ the Son: "And thus all the other sacrifices of the Old Law were offered up in order to foreshadow this one individual and paramount sacrifice—the imperfect forecasting the perfect."[7]

I would like to pause for comment at only two other places within the remarkably dense question 102. The first objector in article three maintains that there can be no suitable cause assigned for the sacrifices of the old order, since God stands in need of nothing outside of himself. To this claim, Thomas responds emphatically that God did not desire these things for himself, as though he required them in any sense, but rather that through them his people might be rightly ordered. This clarification is most important precisely in the measure that the sacrifices of the Old Law anticipate the sacrifice of the cross and the representation of that sacrifice in the Eucharist. Anselm's many detractors notwithstanding, God the Father accepted the sacrifice of his Son not in order to effect some change in himself or to satisfy some deficit (all of that would run contrary to God's immutability) but rather to draw the fallen world into justice or right order. The sacrifices of the Old Law were for the Jewish people; the cross was for the world; and the Eucharistic sacrifice is *propter homines*. All sacrifices break, as it were, against the rock of the divine self-sufficiency and redound to our benefit.

The second theme upon which I would like to reflect further is that of the different types of sacrifice in the Old Law. Thomas discusses this in the response to the eighth objection to question 102. The first and most perfect kind of sacrifice is, he says, the holocaust, by which the offering is completely consumed so as to show total reverence to God the giver of all. This intense mode of sacrifice typifies those who are at a high level of spiritual attainment. The second kind is the sin-offering, offered to God on account of one's need for forgiveness. This is characteristic of those less-perfect spiritual subjects who find themselves in the state of penitence. And the third type of sacrifice is a peace-offering, presented to God either in thanksgiving or for the well-being of those who offer it. This corresponds to those in a sort of intermediate spiritual state, adept at obeying the commandments but not yet perfected, such as the rich young man in the Gospel account. In question 48 of the *tertia pars*, we see clearly how all three of these modes of sacrifice are fulfilled and perfected in the event of the cross. It is obvious, Thomas says, that the cross constituted a sin-offering, since Jesus explicitly said that he was spilling his blood as a ransom for the many. But precisely in its great charity, the self-offering of Jesus also recapitulated the holocausts and peace-offerings of the Old Law.[8] As such, the cross of the Lord touches and fulfills believers at every stage of spiritual attainment, from vilest sinner, through faithful follower of the law, to saint.

The New Law of the Gospel

Having glanced at the human law in its nesting relation to both the natural law and the eternal law, and having examined in somewhat more detail the structure and finality of the divine law in its Old Testament expression, let us now turn to the culmination of that *ordo* by which God draws his rational creatures to a participation in his life, namely, the New Law of the gospel. Thomas's treatment of the New Law runs from question 106 through question 108 of the *prima secundae*. At the outset of question 106, he gives a pithy definition: "The New Law is chiefly the grace itself of the Holy Spirit, which is given to those who believe in Christ."[9] It is a law because it is a *mensura*, a rational *ordo*, but it differs from the natural law in being utterly supernatural and from the precepts of the Old Law in being interior rather than written. Inscribed in the hearts of believers, the New Law is that living law prophesied by Jeremiah: "Behold the days are coming, says the Lord, when I will make a new covenant with the house of Israel and the house of Judah. It will not be like the covenant I made with their fathers. . . . But this is the covenant

I will make with the house of Israel . . . I will place my law within them, and write it upon their hearts."[10] This grace of the Holy Spirit justifies the believer, setting him right before God and giving him a concrete participation in the supernatural life of God—something that neither the human law nor the figurative form of the divine law could ever accomplish. Why was this interior and supernatural *regula* not offered to the human race from the beginning? One reason, argues Aquinas, is that the perfect properly comes to us not all at once but as the culmination of a lengthy process of preparation. This is in line with both the Pauline insistence that the Old Law was a kind of pedagogue readying us for the New and also Irenaeus's contention that salvation occurs through a gradual evolution, God as it were fitting the human race to himself. But Aquinas offers another explanation, one that is very close in spirit to the speculations of the Reformers in regard to the law. The New Law, he explains, is above all the law of grace, of a free divine gift. "Therefore it was appropriate that man first of all be left to himself under the state of the Old Law, so that through falling into sin, he might realize his weakness, and acknowledge his need of grace."[11] Part of the pedagogy of the Old Law, evidently, was a training in humility and non-self-sufficiency.

Thomas makes another key clarification in responding to the second objection of article 1, question 108. The objection hinges on the tension between law and liberty, and Thomas explains that the grace of the Holy Spirit is like a habit that naturally inclines one to do as he ought. Accordingly, the New Law is perfectly compatible with the easy exercise of virtue, which is tantamount to liberty in the proper sense of the term. And here he contrasts the New Law of love to the Old Law of fear: whereas the former binds freely, the latter accomplished its end through threats of temporal penalties. Though good and from God, the Old Law remained external to the soul of human beings, but the *regula* of the gospel has worked its way into the mind, imagination, desire, and bodily sinews of the believer in such as way that it is a fully interior law.

Now there is one more question to consider before we turn to Thomas's explicit doctrine of the Eucharist—namely, that of the causal process by which the grace of the Holy Spirit becomes operative in the spiritual system of the believer. In accord with his incarnational sensibilities, Aquinas says that the New Law is brought to bear through the sacraments, visible signs of invisible grace. As both embodied and fallen, human beings attain to knowledge and experience of spiritual things through physical signs, and a sacrament is none other than "a sign of a holy thing so far as it makes men holy."[12] What is distinctive in Thomas's doctrine of the sacraments is the claim that these material signs do not simply indicate grace but rather contain it and cause it. In question 62 of the *tertia pars*, he explains that the passion of Christ is the principal cause of the divine life in us but that sacraments function as the instrumental causes of that grace, communicating a power not of themselves but inasmuch as they are moved by Christ: "In this way, none but God can cause grace, since grace is nothing else than a participated likeness of the divine nature. . . . But the instrumental cause works not by the power of its form, but only by the motion whereby it is moved by the principal agent. . . . And it is thus that the sacraments of the New Law cause grace."[13] This implies that the sacraments are the primary means by which the *regula* of the divine life is inserted into the hearts of those who believe in Christ Jesus and therefore that the sacraments are, strictly speaking, the *telos* of the law in both its natural and supernatural manifestations. They are the instruments by which God has deigned to make possible and to order a participation in his life.

The Sacrament of the New Law: The Eucharist

It is against this loamy background of Thomas Aquinas's doctrine of law that we now approach the Eucharist, the sign that Aquinas calls the prime sacrament of the New Law. To show the primacy of the Eucharist, Thomas must demonstrate first its distinctiveness vis-à-vis the figures of the Old Law and second vis-à-vis the other sacraments of grace. We turn to question 75 of the *tertia pars*, which considers "the change of the bread and wine into the Body and Blood of Christ." Article 1 poses the query whether the body of the Lord be in this sacrament "*secundum veritatem, vel solum secundum figuram vel sicut in signo.*" Now practically every word of that question is ambiguous and controversial, including *vel*, but what becomes clear as Thomas's *respondeo* unfolds is that the primary contrast he intends to highlight is that between this sacrament and the various sacrifices and sacraments of the Old Law. It is suitable, he says, that Christ be really present in the Eucharist, due to the perfection of the New Law in relation to the Old. As we have seen, the various sacrifices of the old dispensation were prefigurements of the unsurpassable sacrifice that would take place on the cross of Jesus: "And therefore it was necessary that the sacrifice of the New Law instituted by Christ should have something more, namely, that it should contain Christ himself crucified, not merely in signification or figure, but also in very truth."[14] If Jesus were not substantially present in the Eucharist, that sacrament would not be qualitatively different from the signs and gestures of the Old Covenant. Relatedly, the "real" presence of the Lord in the Eucharist is the greatest sign of his love, for, as Aristotle points out, it is the special feature of friendship that friends live together, and this takes place when Christ shares his very body and blood with those he loves. We recall that the ultimate purpose of the Old Law was to draw people into *amicitia* (friendship) with God. The real bodily presence of Jesus in the Blessed Sacrament is thus the definitive fulfillment of the entelechy of the Old Law.

Now how does Aquinas demonstrate the uniqueness of the Eucharist not only in comparison to the forms and figures of the Old Testament but also in relation to the other sacred signs of the new dispensation? His customary approach is the following. In the sacraments of baptism, confirmation, holy orders, penance, and so on, some physical element—water, oil, the imposition of hands—conveys in a transient way the power of Christ and thereby instrumentally causes grace. But in the sacrament of the Eucharist, it is not merely the power of Christ that is present, but *ipse Christus* (Christ himself), the author of grace. And on this distinction much of the radicality and, frankly, strangeness of Thomas's teaching on the Eucharist hinge. The second objector to article 2 of question 75 expresses the commonsensical view that, in the other sacraments, we don't speak of the matter or substance of oil or water ceasing to be; why doesn't it follow then, given the conformity between the sacraments, that we could speak of bread and wine existing alongside the grace of Christ that operates through them? Forms of this objection echo up and down the Christian centuries, finding most convincing expression, perhaps, in the Eucharistic theology of Martin Luther. Urging a comparison not so much with the other sacraments but with the incarnation itself, Luther maintains that the coming-close of divinity in Jesus did not require any sort of compromise of the Lord's humanity. Why therefore, he wonders, do we insist upon such a competitive construal of the relation of divinity and matter in the sacrament of the altar?

Let us take Luther's objection first. Thomas's *respondeo* to article 2 commences with the blunt assertion that the truth of the sacrament of the Eucharist would be fatally compromised were one to say that the bread and wine coexist with the body and blood of the Lord. Thomas Aquinas was certainly as aware as Luther that the incarnation—the coming together of two natures, divine and human, in one hypostasis—involved no undermining of Jesus's materiality or humanity. He commented incisively and often upon the Chalcedonian formula that the natures coincide in the unity of the person, but without "mixing, mingling, or confusion." Precisely because God is not one being among many, not one competitive worldly nature among others, God *can* indeed enter into this sort of intimate and nonthreatening union with a creaturely nature. Thus, something else must be in play when we speak of the Eucharist. And it is none other than the very *bodiliness* of the Lord's presence. We do not say that Jesus's spirit or personality or form becomes really present in the Eucharist, but precisely his *body* and *blood*. To be sure, we are speaking about his glorified and hence transformed body, but glorification does not involve the evanescence of Christ's flesh into something non-bodily. Though God can become ontologically united to a creature without compromising the integrity of the creature he becomes, two worldly natures cannot similarly coinhere without mutual compromise. And this is why Aquinas insists that the real bodily presence of Jesus in the Eucharist requires the absence of the substances of bread and wine.

The main argument in the *respondeo* of article 2 features, consequently, an analysis of the coming-to-be of a body where it previously was not. This can take place, Aquinas contends, in one of two ways: either through local motion or through the conversion of another thing into itself. Thus, fire can be carried into a room, or it can be newly generated there from preexisting materials. But Christ's body cannot come to be on the altar through local motion, since that would entail his subsequent absence in heaven and his passing visibly through intermediary space. Therefore, Thomas concludes, the body and blood of Christ come to be through the transformation of something preexisting, namely, the bread and wine, which, as it were, cede place to them. Once more, to speak in the Lutheran manner of impanation or companation would be, for Thomas, metaphysically incoherent.

These clarifications help us to understand the response to the objection concerning the other sacraments. Aquinas insists that "Christ himself is not really present in the other sacraments, as in this; and therefore the substance of the matter remains in the other sacraments, but not in this."[15] Christ's power is operative in the other sacred signs, but that divine efficacy is altogether compatible with the full ontological integrity of the instrument through which Christ has chosen to work. But Christ himself (*ipse Christus*) is present in the Eucharist, and such a state of affairs is indeed incompatible with the complete integrity of the instrument by which that presence is borne. The water used at baptism need not undergo a transubstantiation, but the bread and wine utilized at the Eucharist must.

This insistence upon a change at the level of substance leaves us with the famously vexed problem of the ontological status of the accidents, or phenomenal features of the bread and wine, that remain. Aquinas examines the issue in the fifth article of question 75. The first objector poses a problem that was very recently taken up by Germain Grisez: "It seems that the accidents of bread and wine do not remain in this sacrament. For when that which comes first is removed, that which follows is taken away. But substance is naturally before accident. Since then, after the consecration, the substance of the bread does not remain in this sacrament, it seems that its accidents cannot remain."[16] The objection is a serious one, given Aquinas's commitment to the proposition that not even God can effect what is logically incoherent. If an accident qua accident inheres in a subject, then it appears that once the subject has disappeared, it cannot endure, and no appeal to the divine power can render this impossibility possible. Thomas's pithy response indicates that he doesn't consider this state of affairs ontologically incoherent. Invoking the *Liber de causis*, he contends that any effect depends more upon its first cause than upon any intermediary cause. "And therefore by God's power, which is the first cause of all things, it is possible for that which follows to remain, while that which is first is taken away."[17] What becomes clear here is that transubstantiation is not an ordinary natural change that could be effected easily enough by a finite cause; rather, it is something akin to creation, since it involves a change at the most fundamental level of reality. Therefore, it is only the "first cause of all things," operating, as it were, at the full pitch of his causal efficacy who can bring it about. And it is only this appeal to the creative authority of God that can render the anomalous perdurance of the accidents without their proper subject metaphysically possible.

This technical analysis is most important in regard to the topic under discussion here, for it demonstrates how the real presence of Christ in the Eucharist constitutes, at least within this dimensional system, the *telos* of the law. All modes of law—from the most trivial traffic regulations, through the dictates of the natural law, to the regulations of the Old Testament and the soul-enhancing power of the sacraments—conduce toward the deepening of divine-human friendship. The Eucharist—which is grace in person—*is* divine-human friendship and is thus that *regula* to which all other forms of law are ordered and subordinated. The first article of question 79 of the *tertia pars* considers whether the sacrament of the Eucharist confers grace; and Thomas answers that it does so maximally. Since it contains Christ himself in person, the Eucharist must convey to the individual who receives it what the incarnate Christ conveyed to the world, namely, "grace and truth." More to it, since it makes present the *passio Christi*, "the effect which the suffering of Christ produced in the world—grace—this sacrament produces in a human being."[18] And this key sacrament is operative through the physical signs of food and drink and thus has, spiritually, the same effects that nourishment has physically: "sustenance, growth, healing, and delight."[19] Through it, the divine friendship is strengthened and deepened, sin is forgiven, and the joy of intimacy with God is tasted. In a word, the person is, through worthy reception of the Eucharist, maximally reformed, justified, set right.

There is one more step that we have to make. Though it is the fullest expression of law within the created realm of space and time, the Eucharist is not, per se, the limit case of the divine *regula* in relation to human beings. For Aquinas teaches, in line with the patristic tradition, that just as the regulations of the Old Law are subsumed, so to speak, in the dynamics of the New Law, so the Eucharist itself will cede place to a more perfect order, that of heaven. In question 106 of the *prima secundae*, Thomas addresses the issue of the eternal duration of the New Law. In response to the first objector, he offers an admirably laconic summary of his overall position: "There is a threefold state of human beings: the first was under the Old Law, the second under the New Law; the third state takes place not in this life but in heaven. But as the first state is figurative and imperfect in comparison to the state of the Gospel, so this state is figurative and imperfect in comparison to the heavenly condition, at the coming of which, this state will pass away."[20] The laws of the old dispensation merely indicated a grace that they did not contain, whereas the sacraments of the New Law do indeed contain grace and communicate the divine life, but they do so indirectly, since they convey the invisible through the visible. Even the Eucharist—which involves the evacuation of the substances of the bread and wine—nevertheless conveys *ispe Christus* under sensible signs and to that extent is still imperfect. As we saw, Thomas insists that the Eucharist, like all the other sacraments, is *in genere signi*.

The fullness of divine friendship—and hence the absolutely final *telos* of the law—is realized beyond the Eucharist, in the worship that characterizes the heavenly homeland. "In the state of the Blessed, then, nothing in regard to the worship of God will be figurative; there will be nothing but thanksgiving and voice of praise. . . . Hence it is written concerning the city of the Blessed (Rev. 21:22 DRA): 'I saw no temple therein. For the Lord God Almighty is the temple thereof, and the Lamb.'"[21] So much of the Old Law centered on temple worship; the incarnate Christ, whose body is the church, is the new temple from which living water flows; but in heaven there will be no temple, precisely because worship will be identical to life. In other words, one won't celebrate the Eucharistic liturgy in heaven, because heaven is nothing but the perfect praise of the Father through Christ.

And this all implies that there won't be laws in the *patria* because Christ, the very *regula* of God, will be all in all.

10

✠

The Liturgical Self

*An Exploration of Christian Anthropology
in Light of the Liturgy*

The nature of the self cannot really be determined abstractly, since no self finally exists apart from the practices and gestures that constitute it. In order to understand the human person, we must attend to what he or she does and how he or she moves, staying, as Wittgenstein said, "close to the rough ground."[1] To be sure, certain generic features of the human being across time and culture—rationality, the capacity for speech, sociability, and so on—can be identified easily enough, but these don't take us very far. People thickly display what they mean and who they are through their participation in certain distinctive games, movements, and activities. Thus the ancient Greek self came to light especially through the public discourse of the polis and the disciplined conversation of the philosophical community; the contemporary Western self appears perhaps most clearly in the dynamics of the marketplace.[2] So where and how does the distinctively Christian self emerge? Vatican II famously asserted that the liturgy is the "source and summit" of the Christian life, that is, the practice that most clearly defines the uniquely Christian way of being in the world.[3] Therefore it is altogether reasonable to look precisely at the

Eucharistic liturgy to discover a thick description of who the Christian is, and this is the project that I will pursue in the course of this chapter.

The Sign of the Cross

Though it is preceded by the gathering of the people and by a procession of the ministers to the sanctuary, the liturgy proper commences with the sign of the cross and words, "in the name of the Father, and of the Son, and of the Holy Spirit." Immediately we see something of great importance, namely, that the Christian self is claimed, positioned, named by another. From the first moment of the liturgy, the priest, ministers, and people signal that they are not self-disposing, not in control of their lives. They stand, instead, within God, and what they are about to do will be done under the aegis of God. This decentering of the self calls to mind Paul's salutation in his first letter to the Corinthians: "Paul, called to be an apostle of Christ Jesus by the will of God" (1 Cor. 1:1 NABRE). The first thing that Paul says about himself is that his life has been placed in the passive voice: he is called, named, summoned by another. The second thing he specifies is that he is an apostle of Christ Jesus, that is to say, someone sent and commissioned, a messenger of a higher power. Though Paul is writing a letter to the Corinthians, he himself is a letter sent by the author Christ. Emmanuel Levinas argued throughout his career that the distinctive mark of the biblical self is just this radical passivity before God. Abraham heard a voice calling to him, and he responded, "Here I am," and all that Abraham came to be followed from that response.[4] Unlike the Greek heroes and philosophers who determined the course of their lives through action or creative thought, Abraham and his spiritual descendants were determined from the outside, placed in the passive voice.

This positioning by Another puts the Christian self at odds with the modern ego as well. Perhaps *the* characteristic of the Cartesian *cogito* is its sovereignty in regard to the whole of reality outside of itself. For Descartes, both the sensible universe and God are verified only in the measure that they conform to the epistemic demands of the *res cogitans*. And the Cartesian construal of the sovereign self can be found throughout modern philosophy: in Kant's aprioristic epistemology, in Hegel's virtual apotheosizing of the ego, in Nietzsche's will to power, and in Sartre's granting of priority to existence over essence. And despite postmodern attempts to dismantle the modern ego, the Cartesian self has by no means disappeared from the contemporary scene. In its 1992 decision in the matter of *Casey v. Planned Parenthood*, the United States Supreme Court opined that it belongs to the very "heart of liberty" to "define one's own concept of existence, of meaning, of the universe, of the mystery of human life."[5] That breathtaking statement takes us beyond the wildest fantasies of Nietzsche and Sartre, turning the free human subject into a godlike creator of value. This entire tradition of modern anthropology is repudiated when liturgical people gather as named and claimed by God.

But how is this passivity before God not tantamount to dehumanization? How is it not denigrating to human freedom, integrity, and ontological independence? We must recall that the God invoked at the commencement of the liturgy is not a monolith but rather a community of persons, whose coinherence constitutes the divine unity. The Father is Father only in relation to the Son, and the Son is Son only in the measure that he is generated by the Father, and the Holy Spirit is nothing other than the mutual love between the Father and the Son. These "persons" are, in Aquinas's highly paradoxical language, "subsistent relations," established as unique precisely in their being-toward the others. This means that, at the heart of ultimate reality, metaphysical integrity is not opposed to relationality; rather, the absolute and the relative coincide.[6] The Son is fully divine, and yet, as Son, he stands in a relation of receptivity vis-à-vis the Father; and the Father is fully divine and yet, as Father, *is* a relation to the Son; and the Holy Spirit is fully divine and yet, as Spirit, *is* a breathing forth from the Father and Son. In the simpler and more evocative language of the Scripture, God *is* love (see 1 John 4:8). All of this entails that ontological integrity and a total being-toward the other are not mutually exclusive, provided that the relationality is one of love and not domination. And thus, when the liturgical person says that he belongs utterly to the God who is love, he is affirming rather than denying his integrity.

The *Kyrie Eleison*

Just after the sign of the cross and the greeting of the people, the priest invites all the participants in the liturgy (including himself) to call to mind their sins and to beg for the divine mercy: *Kyrie eleison; Christe eleison; Kyrie eleison.* This is another practice that shapes the distinctively Christian self. In the tenth chapter of Mark's Gospel, we find the story of blind Bartimaeus, a beggar who sits outside the walls of Jericho and pleads for the mercy of Jesus. In Mark's Greek, he cries out, *"Uie David Iesou, eleison me"* (Mark 10:47), anticipating the liturgical cry. In the symbolic language of the Bible, blindness is evocative of sin, the inability to see the world aright, due to an alienation from God. And Jericho, the town whose walls were blown down in order to allow the Israelites to take possession of it, suggests the fallen city, the dysfunctional arena of sin—as in Jesus's famous parable in which we hear of a man who went *down* from Jerusalem to Jericho. Moreover, Bartimaeus begs. It is a biblical commonplace that we are unable to save ourselves from sin, since the very powers that we would muster to do so—the mind, the will, and the passions—are precisely what sin has compromised. Our only hope, therefore, is in the divine salvation offered as a gift. Thus blind Bartimaeus, crouching by the walls of Jericho and begging for help, is a *Jederman* figure, a symbol of sinful humanity.

The liturgical person is compelled to assume the attitude of Bartimaeus during the *Kyrie* prayer. An anthropology based upon schemas of perfectibility is thereby explicitly and operationally ruled out. This once more distinguishes the Christian conception of the self from either the classical or modern varieties. It goes without saying that neither the Nietzschean superman nor the Sartrean self-creating existentialist could honestly adopt the stance of Bartimaeus, but it is just as surely the case that the adepts of the classical philosophical schools would be hard pressed to pray the *Kyrie eleison* with any degree of conviction. Both Plato and Aristotle were aware of human weakness, but both felt that it could, through the proper discipline and education, be overcome. Plato's elite manage to escape from the realm of superficial perception through a carefully managed program of physical and philosophical formation, culminating in the introduction to the realm of the forms and, finally, the form of the Good.[7] What blocks this ascent is essentially ignorance, an ordering of the mind toward the realm of the relatively unreal. And Aristotle's disciples endeavor to acquire virtue and hence happiness through education, habituation, and the imitation of ethically upright models.[8] Though he clearly recognized the presence of vice—and even of beastlike forms of human behavior—Aristotle felt that these could be mastered and that full human flourishing was a lively possibility.

Sin, in the Christian sense, is something far more radical and dangerous than either Platonic ignorance or Aristotelian vice, for it involves the unmooring of the self from its properly divine origin and *telos*. Because we are, by nature, supernaturally oriented toward intimacy with God, this disassociation results in the disordering and disintegration of the entire self: body, mind, spirit, and passions. In rebellion against God—and not simply ignorant or vicious—the sinner finds himself powerless, incapable of realizing either his supernatural end or even those natural virtues identified by the classical tradition. There is a high paradox here. The Bible recognizes the supreme dysfunction of sin—beyond anything imagined by Plato or Aristotle—in the same measure that it recognizes simultaneously the supreme calling to friendship with God, which the human being has received. The great American Catholic writer

Flannery O'Connor fully grasped this anthropology of the *Kyrie eleison* and set out, in story after story, to show it, in contrast to the illusory anthropology of complacency and perfectibility so characteristic of both antiquity and modernity. Very often in her fiction, the moment of grace—the call to real divine friendship—coincides with the moment of judgment, that is to say, with the deep realization that one is incapable of achieving salvation.[9] The *Kyrie eleison* produces precisely this dynamic in the depth of the Christian self.

The *Gloria in Excelsis*

One of the most beautiful prayers in the liturgical tradition follows immediately after the *Kyrie*. In a sense, the whole of Christian theology is developed in the course of the *Gloria*, but I will focus only on the opening lines: "Glory to God in the highest and peace to his people on earth." This pithy formula effects a correlation between the praise of God and the building up of the human *communio*. It implies that when human beings honor God above all things—above pleasure, money, material goods, honor, country, political party, culture, and so on—then and only then will authentic peace obtain among them. The clear implication is that the deification of anything other than the true God produces, at best, a dysfunctional, ersatz communion and, at worst, outright conflict. Aristotle argued that a friendship will endure only in the measure that the friends push beyond a mere mutual love for each other and together fall in love with a transcendent third, be it beauty or truth or goodness. Only when they look together to a value greater than themselves will they escape a shared egotism that will, in time, devolve into animosity. The *Gloria* implies the same principle but in radical form, for it speaks of the God who is, himself, nothing other than the fullness of truth, beauty, and goodness. This notion was expressed in plastic form in the rose windows of the great medieval cathedrals. Invariably, the central feature of the rose is a depiction of Christ, and then around that anchoring point are arranged, in harmonious patterns, the remaining images and medallions. The window is, in a sense, a picture of the well-ordered soul and the properly functioning community.[10] When Christ is unambiguously the center of one's life, then all the elements that constitute the self—mind, will, imagination, passion, sexuality—tend to fall into an ordered pattern around it. Similarly, when Christ is the transcendent third, loved in common by a variety of people, then that group becomes an authentic and beautiful *communio*.

We notice a striking contrast between this conception of *communio* and that proposed by the modern political tradition, with its roots in the speculation of

Hobbes and Locke. Inheriting the breakdown of a participation metaphysics bequeathed to him by late-medieval nominalism, Hobbes held that the only real things are absolute individuals, particles in motion. This principle holds true in regard to both voluntary and involuntary movers. Thus, human beings are antagonistic, self-interested individuals, whose desires force them, almost invariably, to bounce into one another conflictually. What holds them together is the artificial expedient of the social contract, an agreement entered into on purely egotistic grounds, out of each participant's concern to avoid violent death. Though this program is softened a bit by Locke, the essential Hobbesian framework remains in place in Locke's political philosophy, which in turn had such an influence on the formation of the modern liberal state both in Europe and America. What results from the social contract is at best a provisional and unstable peace, since it dissociates political *communio* from common praise and grounds it instead in some form of shared self-interest.

The analysis I've been offering is anticipated, of course, in Augustine's critique of Roman political society in *The City of God*. Augustine argued that, despite its claim to be the paragon of justice, the Roman Empire was, in fact, only a community of thieves, precisely because its common life was correlated to the wrong kind of praise.[11] Since the Roman gods and goddesses were nothing but deeply flawed human beings writ large and imagined as immortal, the worship of them simply confirmed the native egotism and self-absorption of the populace. The sheerest sign of this correlation, Augustine felt, was the centrality of violence in the maintenance and expansion of Roman power. From its earliest days, Rome had been continually at war, expressing relentlessly the *libido dominandi* in its relations to both its own citizens and neighboring peoples. It thus stood as the paragon not of right order but of the *civitas terrena*, the earthly city of sin. The only solution, Augustine taught, was the adoption of the Christian way of life, at the center of which stands the worship of the true God, the God of compassion made manifest in the cross and resurrection of Jesus.[12] The peaceful community, gathered together in giving glory to God in the highest, is the political vision implicit in the *Gloria* prayer.

Opening Up the Biblical World

After the *Gloria* and the opening collect of the Mass, the people sit in order to listen to the Word of God. Passages from the Old Testament, the epistles of Paul (usually), and the Gospels are read, and between the first and second readings, a psalm-based response is customarily sung. Following the proclamation of the Gospel, the deacon or priest preaches a homily. Though the entire liturgy is deeply biblical in inspiration, this section of the Mass constitutes a special immersion in the world of Scripture, that is to say, the manner of thought, action, reaction, and behavior characteristic of the great characters of biblical revelation, including and especially that mysterious central figure of God.

When Karl Barth commenced his theological work in the second decade of the twentieth century, he complained that the regnant liberalism of the period resulted in a bland, highly abstract, and philosophical account of both God and the human being. One of Barth's principal sparring partners, Paul Tillich, proposed a description of God as *das Unbedingte*, the Unconditioned Reality, to which Barth responded: "*Das Unbedingte*, that cold monster!" He meant that Tillich's name for God, largely derived from Kant's epistemology, had little biblical resonance and seemed only vaguely related to the dense narratives of the Scripture through which the character of God is delineated. To be fair, Barth had similar problems with the classically Catholic manner of naming God as "necessary being" or "unmoved mover," for he saw in this the same indifference to the particularity of the Bible.

What he proposed in answer to this blandness was a patient and thorough tour of the biblical world, that peculiar space through which move Adam, Noah, Abraham, Jacob, Jeremiah, Ezekiel, Esther, Daniel, Peter, Paul, Andrew, and, most significantly, Jesus. Through our immersion in this environment, we discover who we are and who God is. The term *immersion* is important here inasmuch as it suggests the only way that one can fully learn a foreign language. As any careful linguist knows, an attempt to learn an unfamiliar language through translation is doomed to failure. On Barth's reading, so much of the liberal approach to theology and anthropology amounted to a translation project, a transposing of the biblical language into the categories and intellectual patterns of modernity. And this went a long way toward explaining just why, in his judgment, liberalism was a substantially flawed enterprise.

This Barthian approach informed the highly influential work of George Lindbeck and Hans Frei and the Yale school that grew up around them. In his *On the Nature of Doctrine: Theology in a Post-Liberal Age*, Lindbeck distinguished between an experiential-expressivist and a cultural-linguistic theory of doctrine.[13] According to the first construal, dogmas and doctrines are expressions of some undifferentiated, preverbal religious experience. The theologizing of Schleiermacher, Rahner, and Tillich would be prime examples of this approach. According to the contrasting second interpretation, doctrines are cultural forms, rules of discourse and action, which serve to structure and make possible very particular types of experience. The theological methods of Barth himself and Hans Urs von Balthasar would aptly exemplify this cultural-linguistic model. On the more liberal reading, the biblical stories, poems, histories, and myths are finally literary expressions of certain primordial religious experiences undergone by the heroes of Scripture and, in principle, accessible to present-day interpreters. On the second reading, by contrast the biblical material is a densely textured framework of meaning that serves to ground a distinctive kind of religious sensibility.

It seems to me that the liturgical presentation and exploration of the biblical texts make much more sense on cultural-linguistic grounds than on experiential-expressivist ones. If the scriptural stories are only exemplifications of experiences that can be (and have been) thematized in other ways, then their prominence within the liturgy seems exaggerated, misplaced. From a purely experiential-expressivist perspective, it is not clear why the biblical texts would have a greater authority than, say, particularly evocative passages from Shakespeare, or Cervantes, or Dostoevsky, or even for that matter than sacred books from other religious traditions. In a word, the more liberal reading of the Bible assumes that the religious self is substantially in place prior to and independent of the proclamation of the Scripture. What the liturgy seems to take for granted, on the contrary, is the indispensability of the Bible in the formation of the self; that is to say, in the development of a distinctive manner of thinking, choosing, acting, and reacting, especially in relation to God. The liturgical person discovers who he is in the context of a community that listens to and explains the Bible and acts in accord with it. In this, he stands opposed to those whose identity is shaped by the heroes, ideals, and norms of the environing secular culture and to those whose sense of self is formed by the texts and practices of other religions.

Before we quit this discussion of the scriptural world, I would like to say just a word about the liturgical act that follows immediately upon the conclusion of the homily: the proclamation of the Creed. Having been immersed in the biblical world, the people are then encouraged to declare their commitment in it. They do so by reciting the Nicene Creed, a tightly structured, doctrinal summary of the essentials of the scriptural narrative. I would like to focus only on the opening words of the Creed, the declaration that grounds and conditions everything that follows: *credo in unum Deum* (I believe in one God). The most elemental expression of Old Testament faith is the Shema found in the book of Deuteronomy: "Hear O Israel, the LORD our God is one LORD" (Deut. 6:4). God's unity was, for the ancient Israelites, much more than one divine attribute among many; it was the defining feature of God's way of being. And monotheism was, consequently, much more than an intellectual conviction; it was an existential statement of the highest import. In saying that the God of Israel is the only God, the people were claiming, implicitly, that nothing other than God commands their final loyalty. No country, leader, political party, culture, civilization, moral ideal, or rival god can compete with the one God. The Shema, in all its radicality, is echoed in the opening line of the Creed, and this is why Joseph Ratzinger, later Pope Benedict XVI, commented that *credo in unum Deum* is a properly subversive remark.[14] To hold that nothing in this world is one's ultimate concern is to be constituted as a biblically distinctive self.

The Offertory

After the liturgy of the Word draws to a close, the liturgy of the Eucharist commences. Though Vatican II placed a renewed stress on the liturgy of the Word, it would not be correct to say that the two principal sections of the Mass are coequal in importance. For at the heart of the liturgy of the Eucharist is the realization of the "substantial" presence of Jesus Christ, a presence that is qualitatively different than those realized in the gathering of the people, the person of the priest, or the proclamation of the Scriptures.[15] We might say that the liturgy of the Eucharist focuses and fully expresses what is inchoately present in the first part of the Mass. And thus, in accord with the central argument of this article, the Christian self will be most richly on display in this portion of the liturgy.

Representatives from the congregation bring forth gifts of bread, wine, and water, as well as, customarily, a financial offering. The bread is then presented to God accompanied by the words, "Blessed are you, Lord God of all creation, for through your goodness, we have this bread to offer, which earth has given and human hands have made." Then the wine, mixed with water, is offered with a similar prayer. These words and gestures are rooted in the "Berakah" oration of the ancient Israelite tradition, by which the people thank God for the gift of the created universe. In the context of the Mass, the bread and wine speak beyond themselves and represent the whole of what God has given in making the world. The Berakah signals that biblical, liturgical people believe in the doctrine of creation, a belief that radicalizes and renders absolutely unique their sense of self.

Basic to the biblical revelation is the conviction that God is not a being in, above, or alongside the world, precisely because God is the maker of the entire universe, both heaven and earth. God is properly called the Lord of creation, since he is not ingredient in creation and cannot be measured the way creatures are. He is not caught in the nexus of contingent relationality and hence cannot be, strictly speaking, compared or contrasted to created things.[16] Even as we say that God is *totaliter aliter* (completely other), we must maintain, simultaneously, that he is, in Nicholas of Cusa's phrase, the *non-aliud* (the non-other). In their attempt to express this biblical idea in more philosophical language, Christian theologians began to speak of *creatio ex nihilo* (creation from nothing). They implied thereby that the true God is not like the gods of ancient mythology or philosophy, who fashion the universe out of some preexisting matter, or draw it forth from chaos. For the One who creates all of finitude, there can be nothing that stands over against him, nothing that confronts him as independent. Therefore, he makes the universe *ex nihilo*, which is to say, not from anything preexisting. This crucially important doctrine tells us something about both how God exists and how we exist. Were God a mere fashioner of the world, he would be a being in it, a thing among things. But Aquinas tells us that the creator God is not so much the *ens summum* (the supreme being) as *ipsum esse subsistens* (the sheer act of to-be itself), that which grounds and conditions all creation even as it radically transcends it. And Anselm makes much the same point when he names God as "that than which nothing greater can be thought." Were God a being among beings, like one of the deities of mythology or philosophy, then he plus the rest of the universe would be greater than he alone. But the creator God must exist in such a way that the created world adds nothing to the perfection of his being: God plus the universe is not greater than God alone. And this very strangeness of the divine manner of being is the condition for the possibility of the real independence of the world. Precisely because he is not one being among many, God is not competitive with creation; since he is noncontrastively transcendent, he can let the other be, even as he remains absolutely immanent to it.

And what does this key doctrine tell us about the creaturely mode of being? It tells us that every creature, to the very core of its existence, is received. The "positioning" of the self that we explored in connection with the sign of the cross is intensified here, for we see that it reaches to the roots of creaturely being. Thomas Aquinas comments that creation is not a change, since there is no independent substrate that takes in and perdures through the act of creation. Rather, he argues, every creature *is* a relationship to God: creation is *quaedam relatio ad creatorem cum novitate essendi* (a kind of relationship to the Creator, with freshness of being).[17] This means that there is, quite literally, no place where a creature can stand apart from God; simply to be at all implies a connection of the most intimate sort to the Creator. And now we can return to the Berakah prayer with greater perception. When the priest leads the people in rendering thanks to God for the bread and wine, which symbolize all of created reality, he is expressing and embodying that attitude that should rightly characterize a creature at his best. I am using the more neutral term "creature" to signal the cosmological dimension of this liturgical act. In a certain sense, the Berakah gives voice to the ontological situation of all creation. Since the whole of a creature is received, the whole of his existence should be an act of thanksgiving.

The Law of the Gift

After the offering of the bread and wine, the priest moves into the Eucharistic prayer, which involves the intonation of the preface, the singing of the *Sanctus*, and the consecratory prayer proper. What becomes especially clear as the Mass comes to its high point is the relevance of the law of the gift, a principle centrally on display throughout the Bible and the tradition of the church. The axiom can be stated simply enough: one's being increases and is enhanced in the measure that one gives it away. The Old Testament story of the encounter between the prophet Elijah and the widow of Zarephath expresses the law poetically. When the prophet comes upon the widow, he asks her for something to eat. She informs him that she has precisely enough to make one more meal for herself and her son before they die. At this point, Elijah, with extraordinary chutzpah, says, "Make me a little cake" (1 Kings 17:13). At the limit of her resources, against all reason, she does so—and her flour and oil are replenished, sustaining her throughout a time of famine.

We find the same law reaffirmed throughout the life and preaching of Jesus. In the parable of the prodigal son (Luke 15:11–32), the younger brother demands to have the share of his father's inheritance that is coming to him. Taking the money (significantly, the word *ousia* is used to designate it),[18] he moves into the *chora makra*, perhaps best translated as "the great emptiness." There he quickly squanders what he had taken. Realizing his folly, he comes back home and is greeted with ring, and robe, and fatted calf. The point is clear: as long as he remains in a relationship of receptivity and gratitude vis-à-vis the giving of his father, he has enough; but when he severed that rapport and took for himself what he wanted, his *ousia* (substance) rapidly dissipated. And the older brother lives in his own version of the *chora makra*, isolated from his father in the measure that he attempts to buy his father's affection through a slavish moral effort. What he cannot take in is the father's assurance, "All that is mine is yours" (v. 31). He too would have abundance of life if he could but enter into the loop of grace, accept love as a gift, and, with an answering abandon, return it as a gift. The principle is summed up in Jesus's pithy formula: "The one who would cling to his life will lose it, while the one who gives his life away for my sake shall find it" (AP, see Matt. 10:39; Luke 17:33). And it comes to richest expression when Jesus offers himself to the Father on the cross, returning totally what he had received: "Father, into your hands I commend my spirit" (Luke 23:46 NABRE).

This ethical and spiritual law is rooted in the distinctive metaphysics of creation that we sketched above. Because God is the noncompetitive ground of created reality—and not a supreme being hovering threateningly over it—one's self-offering to God is tantamount to the flourishing of the one who so surrenders. Linked to the divine center, a person can give and give and never find his being exhausted—just the contrary. Were God a being in or above the world, this total self-gift on the part of the creature would be debilitating, ontologically compromising. But given the way that God actually exists, the glory of God, as Irenaeus knew, dovetails with the human creature coming fully to life. It is upon this peculiar ethics and metaphysics that the spiritual efficacy of the liturgy hinges.

Thus, in the liturgical setting, the bread and wine—symbolizing the whole of creation—are offered to God, and they come back to us infinitely enhanced, since they are transformed into the very body and blood of Christ. God takes what we have given him, and since he does not in any sense stand in need of it, he returns that offering to us, elevated in worth. It is as though our gift breaks against the rock of the divine self-sufficiency and redounds to our benefit. This idea of the loop of grace is elegantly expressed in one of the prefaces for weekday Mass: "You have no need of our praise; yet our desire to thank you is itself your gift. Our prayer of thanksgiving adds nothing to your greatness, but makes us grow in grace." It is in this context that we can best understand the sacrificial nature of the Mass. The Father has given his only Son to the world, and the Son has offered himself back to the Father, this mutual "sacrificing" economically expressing the interior life of God, the love that *is* the Holy Spirit. In the liturgy, we join ourselves to the sacrifice of the Son, offering ourselves with him to the Father, and are thereby drawn into the dynamics of the Holy Spirit. There is a passage in Eucharistic prayer number three that invokes the Third Person of the Trinity: "May he make us an everlasting gift to you"—that is to say, may the Spirit draw us into the dynamics of the law of the gift, expressed utterly in the sacrifice of the Son to the Father. Now we see how the decentering of the human self, hinted at in the sign of the cross and intensified in the Berakah prayer, comes to most radical expression. The properly Christian self is one that gives itself away in imitation of the God who is nothing but a community of self-surrendering persons. In regard to Christian identity, therefore, we must learn to speak not so much the language of substance but rather of sheer relationality and other-orientation, the coinherence of love.

Before closing this discussion of the Eucharistic prayer, I would like to say a word about the *Sanctus*, in which the worshiping community joins its song to that of the angels and saints in heaven. It would be a great mistake to dismiss this prayer as a bit of pious decoration. In our discussion of the *Gloria*, we made it plain that the optimal human community is that which is constituted by a shared giving of glory to God in the highest. Just before the prayer of consecration, the Christian community here below—still too marked by sin, rivalry, and violence—consciously joins itself to the *communio* of heaven, the angels and saints who have indeed found their connection through common praise of the true God. The blending of our voices with theirs is therefore a participation even now in the chorus of coinherence, which is the heavenly life. We find an echo of *Sanctus* in the Our Father, the Lord's prayer that immediately follows the Eucharistic prayer proper. When we pray that God's kingdom may come and God's will may be done on earth as in heaven, we are begging that the *ordo* of the angels and saints—the nonviolent society—might set the tone for our struggling society here below.

The Sending

After the people receive the body and blood of the Lord, the priest prays the closing prayer of Mass, blesses the congregation, and then dismisses them with the words, "The Mass is ended; go in peace to love and to serve the Lord." It has been commented that after the words of consecration themselves, these are the most sacred of the liturgy. Throughout the Bible, men and women are sent by God on mission. Abraham, at the age of seventy-five, is told to leave the security of his life in Ur and to set out in search of a promised land; Moses sees the burning bush, hears the voice of Yahweh, and then is sent back to Egypt to lead Israel to freedom; Isaiah experiences a vision of God in the temple and then hears a summons to become God's spokesperson; Peter, James, and John go up the Mount of Transfiguration and then go down again to follow Jesus to Jerusalem; Saul sees the light and hears a voice and then receives a commission to preach the good news to the gentiles. In point of fact, no one in the biblical tradition ever is granted an experience of God without being subsequently sent. Scriptural religion is a religion of mission.

Hans Urs von Balthasar has argued that in a Christian context, the concepts of *mission* and *person* are tightly linked. The person of Jesus—in which divinity and humanity coinhere—is constituted by the mission that he has from his Father.[19] He is, at the deepest ground of his existence, the One who was sent by the Father into godforsakenness for the salvation of the world. Who is Jesus? The question cannot be adequately answered in an abstractly metaphysical or psychological manner, for he is, first and foremost, the One sent. Now the personhood of the Christian is realized in the measure that he or she participates in this mission of the Son. This is why, Balthasar contends, the New Testament hero does not truly know who he is until he is properly commissioned.[20] This relationship is signaled by certain eloquent changes of name: Simon becomes "Peter" when he realizes that his mission is to lead and defend the church; Saul becomes "Paul" when he knows that his task is to evangelize the gentiles. These are not incidental reorientations of practical agendas; they are the moments when Peter and Paul become persons in the Person. Thus, liturgical subjects, sent by the priest out into the world to "love and serve the Lord," receive much more than instructions for action. They receive personhood.

Here we see, for the final time, the "positioning" of the self that takes place throughout the Mass. The Christian subject is neither self-grounding nor self-disposing, but utterly in the hands of the Other who makes him, claims him, and sends him. And the nature of this mission, which is constitutive of the self, is always fundamentally the same, though it finds a myriad of variations. It is the task of carrying the dynamics of the liturgy out into the world. Like the dove sent forth from Noah's ark, the liturgical person is meant to convey to the wider society the form of life realized in the liturgical space. Commissioned by Christ, she now seeks to produce in others a deeper sense of belonging to God and of being a forgiven sinner; a richer participation in the biblical world; a denser appreciation for the implications of the Creed; a fuller immersion into the rhythm of the gift; and a more complete sharing in the mystical body of Christ.

In this great act of giving to the other what one has received from the liturgy, the Christian self is both grounded and expressed.

11

✠

The Eucharist

Sacred Banquet, Sacrifice, Real Presence

In the spring of 2007, I was privileged to be a visiting scholar at the North American College in Rome. While I was there, I had the opportunity, on three occasions, to distribute communion at a Papal Mass in St. Peter's Square. In the typical Italian style, things were a tad disorganized. As I stood at a station, a crowd of people were compelled to reach across a barrier in order to receive the host. I saw hundreds of hands—old and young, dirty and clean, lined and unlined—stretching out to me for the bread of life. When I was forced to move at the prompting of a Swiss Guardsman, I heard people crying out, "*Padre, per favore*" ("Father, please"). Though I had distributed the Eucharist to thousands in the course of my priesthood, I had never before sensed so powerfully that I was offering food to those who were desperately hungry for it. The behavior of those faithful in St. Peter's Square reflected accurately the Catholic conviction that without the Eucharist, we would, in the spiritual sense, starve to death.

I would like to relate another story by way of contrast. Not long ago I was speaking to my sister, who told me that many of her contemporaries were leaving the Catholic Church and joining a local Congregationalist community.

When I asked her why, she replied that the Congregationalist church was perceived as "user-friendly," since it made no moral demands on people and was welcoming, inclusive, and friendly. My first comment was this: "After reading any of the Gospels, do you have the impression that Jesus is simply a welcoming, inclusive, and friendly fellow?" But then I said, "What about the Eucharist? Do they care that they are turning away from Christ's real presence?" She looked at me and said, "I don't think that they would even know what you're talking about." My sister's assessment is, I'm sorry to say, probably fairly accurate, especially in regard to members of her and my generation, who came of age in the immediate postconciliar period. If Vatican II is right in saying that the Eucharist is the "source and summit of the Christian life," and if John Paul II is right in insisting that the church comes from the Eucharist, how we stand in regard to this great sacrament makes all the difference. Are we indifferent to it, or are we starving for it? It is my conviction that if we don't see the Eucharist as indispensable to the spiritual life, it is simply a matter of time before we couldn't care less about it.

What I would like to do in this chapter is lay out the meaning of the Eucharist in terms of three themes: sacred banquet, sacrifice, and real presence. I want to show that the Eucharist is a prime theological *locus*, that is to say, a lens through which the most basic theological themes—creation, sin, redemption, and eschatology—are clearly viewed. And I want to demonstrate thereby that the bread of life and the cup of eternal salvation are essential for the living of the Christian life, and that without them we would starve to death.

Sacred Banquet

There is, arguably, no more evocative and oft-used scriptural image for the good life than the sacred banquet. Imagine the most convivial, life-affirming, joyous meal that you have ever been part of, and you would have some idea, on the biblical reading, of what God intends for his people. God wants us to receive his grace as a gift and then, in joy, to share that gift with those around us, the divine life effectively flowing into and through the community. To understand the full sense of this image, we have to explore the biblical idea of creation. For the scriptural authors, God does not create out of need or through the conquest of rival powers. Rather, he brings forth the created universe simply out of a desire to share his life and through the peaceful pronouncement of his word. The First Vatican Council reaffirmed this perspective when, against the regnant Hegelianism of the time, it said that God created not to perfect himself ontologically but to manifest his glory. One of the prefaces for daily

Mass says, "You have no need of our praise; yet our desire to thank you is itself your gift. Our prayer of thanksgiving adds nothing to your greatness, but makes us grow in grace." This theological truth could be expanded: God has no need of our existence; our being adds nothing to his greatness. St. Anselm signals this paradox in his famous "definition" of God as "that than which nothing greater can be thought." Though it seems straightforward enough, this designation expresses the peculiar fact that God plus the world would not be greater than God alone, for if the world could add anything to God's perfection, then God would not be that than which nothing greater could be thought. A key implication of this doctrine is that God and the world that he makes are not competitors. Since the world can neither add to nor detract from God's perfection, the flourishing of the world in no way denigrates or threatens God. In almost all the mythic and philosophical accounts of the God-world relationship, something like a zero-sum game obtains: the more one attributes to God, the less one can attribute to the universe and vice versa. But the creation reading that we find rooted in the biblical witness and developed throughout the Christian tradition holds just the opposite. In the words of St. Irenaeus, "the glory of God is a human being fully alive." God is glorified precisely through the flourishing of the creation that he has graciously willed into existence. A second implication is that God can give and give and be in no way exhausted, for the world cannot take away from the infinity of the divine being. And this means, by consequence, that God's life, once received by us, can be given and given and in no way diminished. As the story of the widow of Zarephath makes clear, the divine life increases in the measure that it is given away. The sacred banquet is nothing other than the exchange of grace made possible by this ontological structure. God can offer his life to us, without diminishing himself, and he can invite us to a similar self-forgetting generosity.

Against this metaphysical background, we can best understand the motif of the sacred meal. From the very beginning of the biblical narrative, the banquet theme is stressed. Adam and Eve are given practically free rein in the garden, permitted to eat of all the trees but one. This enjoyment of the fruits of Eden was interpreted by the church fathers as an expression of all forms of human flourishing: science, art, friendship, politics, and law. This life was given by a gracious God, received by a grateful humanity, and shared generously. But why was there, amid all of this exuberant giving and receiving, a prohibition? As John Paul II explained so effectively in *Veritatis splendor*, when human beings make themselves the criterion of good and evil, when finite freedom determines right from wrong, the flow of grace is interrupted. When human beings make themselves into God, they undermine the condition for the possibility of the sacred banquet. In the Genesis telling, of course, this is precisely what happened. Having grasped pathetically at divinity, the first humans fell out of right relation to God and, consequently, out of right rapport with one another, the sacred banquet interrupted. Immediately after the original sin, there emerged recrimination, scapegoating, violence, jealousy, murder, and domination. With admirable economy of expression, the first eleven chapters of the book of Genesis tell the whole sad story of sin, the negation of Yahweh's fondest desire for his creation.

One way to read the rest of the biblical narrative, up to and including the story of Jesus, is under the rubric of God's attempt to restore the sacred banquet, the convivial sharing of grace with creation. Thus the liberation of the Israelites from slavery in Egypt is accompanied by the Passover meal, which in turn becomes the defining ritual of the people, to be repeated, at Yahweh's urging, for all generations. And in the eschatological visions of the prophet Isaiah, the sacred meal figures prominently. Isaiah sees Mount Zion, raised above the other mountains, as the true pole of the earth, the magnetic point to which all the tribes of the world are attracted. To that place of right worship, the human race comes and there finds peace: swords are beaten into plowshares and spears into pruning hooks, the lion and the lamb lie down together, and the child sleeps by the cobra's den. The violence, division, and hatred bred by sin are overcome through the proper praise of the true God. This Isaian notion is expressed in the great liturgical prayer of the *Gloria in excelsis*: "Glory to God in the highest and peace to his people on earth." The implication of the prayer is that these states of affairs are in a causal relationship: when God is given highest glory, then peace within the hearts of individuals and among the members of the worshiping community tends to break out. And this holy mountain of peace and praise is also a place where a great banquet takes place, where God provides "juicy, rich meats and pure, choice wines" (AP, see Isa. 25:6). We find something very similar in the book of Proverbs where God's Wisdom is pictured as a woman spreading out for her children a great supper: "She has slaughtered her beasts, she has mixed her wine," and she has said, "Come, eat of my bread and drink of the wine I have mixed" (Prov. 9:2, 5). In Isaiah 55:1–2, we hear the Lord speaking through the prophet: "Everyone who thirsts, / come to the waters; / and he who has no money, / come, buy and eat! / Come, buy wine and milk / without money and without price. / . . . eat what is good, / and delight yourselves in [rich food]." What is being envisioned in these various texts is the restoration of the banquet of gracious fellowship lost through sin.

Since Jesus Christ is, as N. T. Wright suggests, "a portrait of Yahweh sprung to life,"[1] we shouldn't be surprised that Jesus made the realization of the sacred meal central to his mission. In Luke's Gospel, this theme is present from the very beginning, as the Christ child is laid in a manger, the place of eating. In all the Gospels, Jesus's open table fellowship is a central motif. As the Messiah, he was the gatherer of the tribes of Israel, the very embodiment of Isaiah's magnetically holy mountain. Accordingly, he called to the table with him both saints and sinners, both men and women, both the righteous and the unrighteous, both the healthy and the sick. Around the table, where the divisions and stratifications of his society were customarily on display, Jesus cultivated a different kind of community, one based upon forgiveness, compassion, and the love of enemies.

This dimension of Jesus's ministry came to full expression, of course, as he sat down with his disciples for a last meal on the night before his death. The apostles, evocative of the twelve tribes of Israel, stood for the properly gathered nation through whom the rest of the world would be, in time, brought to the Lord. Celebrating the Passover supper, Jesus spoke of a definitive liberation not from physical bondage but from the spiritual enslavement of sin. And then he invited his disciples to feed on him and to drink his blood. He was offering his own divine life as a grace and luring the renewed Israel into receiving it and sharing it. "Take this all of you and eat it; take this, all of you, and drink from it" is what Yahweh had wanted to say to his people from the moment of the original sin. The *autobasileas* (the kingdom in person), Jesus was acting in the very person of Yahweh, remaking his people and restoring the lost integrity of creation precisely through the dynamism of a sacred meal.

The Mass is nothing less than the summing up, the recapitulation, of this entire history. Wherever the Eucharist is celebrated is Isaiah's holy mountain; whenever the Eucharist is celebrated so are the Passover meal and the Last Supper. As we eat and drink the body and blood of the Lord, we overcome the self-assertion of sin and the scattering that it caused; as we commune in the most intimate way with Jesus, we enter into the inexhaustible richness of the divine life.

The Sacrifice

Certainly when my generation was coming of age, we heard a great deal about the Mass as a meal, but the sacrificial dimension of the liturgy was almost completely ignored. The price that we paid for this bifurcation was a compromising of the integrity and spiritual seriousness of the Mass. A basic principle of both the Bible and the great tradition is that communion and sacrifice are linked in a causal way. Precisely because the world has gone wrong, there can be no sacred meal without sacrifice. The fallen world has to be wrenched back, as it were, into shape, and this process is always painful and sacrificial in nature.

We see this juxtaposition of communion and sacrifice specially in regard to the establishment of the covenants between Yahweh and his people. Genesis 12 tells the story of the call of Abram, the summons with which commenced Yahweh's great rescue operation, the process by which he would form a people after his own heart, a people who would, in time, become the means by which the entire human family would return to the Lord. It is by no means accidental that the narrative centers on the response to a divine call. If the fundamental problem was Adam's grasp at godliness, the fundamental solution must involve an act of radical obedience.

But such a transition will be necessarily painful. And hence, the covenant is accompanied by a sacrifice. Just after promising his fidelity, Yahweh instructs Abram to perform a sacrificial ritual: "Bring me a heifer three years old, a [female] goat three years old, a ram three years old, a turtledove, and a young pigeon" (Gen. 15:9). Abram presented all of these animals and cut them in two, laying them out on the altar. Though the practice can seem bizarre to us, the logic of a sacrifice is actually rather straightforward. A person takes a portion of the created order and offers it to God as a sign of his own self-offering, either in atonement for sin or in pledge of fidelity or as a sign of gratitude. By the very violence of the act, he is signaling that this realignment with God must involve a painful reordering of the self. The sacrificial component of the covenant with Abraham becomes clearest in the account of the *Aqedah*, the binding of Isaac. The Scripture says that God tested Abraham's faith by asking him to sacrifice the very son through whom, according to the divine promise, Abraham would become the father of many nations. As the Midrashic commentaries make apparent, this command awakened in Abraham not only a supreme emotional crisis but also a kind of theological crisis. How could the God of the promise be so fundamentally at odds with himself? What was at stake in this moment was the law of the gift and the nature of authentic freedom. Could Abraham accept the fact that, despite all evidence to the contrary, his being would increase in the measure that he would make of it a gift, that his willingness to sacrifice Isaac would, in the highest paradox, guarantee his spiritual progeny? And could Abraham see that his deepest freedom would be found precisely in complete surrender to a truth and goodness that conditioned him? That both of these challenges involved a sacrifice at the most intense level goes without saying.

The same dynamic holds in regard to the covenant cut with Moses. Having drawn the Israelites out of Egypt, Yahweh gave them the law that, under the rubric of the freedom for excellence, was designed to complete their liberation. And to seal this covenant, Yahweh demanded an act of sacrifice. In Exodus 24, we find the description of what Moses and the people did after they had taken in the ten commandments and their attendant legislation. After sacrificing oxen, Moses "took half of the blood and put it in basins, and half of the blood he threw against the altar." Then he took the remaining blood "and threw it upon the people, and said, 'Behold the blood of the covenant which the LORD has made with you in accordance with all these words'" (Exod. 24:6–8). This ritual represented the sharing of life between God and the people, but it also evoked the sacrificial nature of this communion. The lifeblood of the oxen stood for the lifeblood of the Israelite nation, offered to Yahweh as an act of reparation and atonement. We find the same association of covenant and sacrifice in regard to Yahweh's dealings with David the king. The culminating covenantal promise of the Old Testament is that God will place on the throne of David a king who will rule eternally, and this pledge is accompanied by the long centuries of sacrifice in the temple, which was planned by David and built by Solomon his son. At the very heart of that temple liturgy was the ritual of the Day of Atonement, when the high priest would enter the holy of holies. There he would symbolically place the sins of the people onto a scapegoat, which would be sent into the wilderness. Next, he would slaughter a second goat, sprinkling the holy of holies with some of its blood and coming out, as the very embodiment of Yahweh, to sprinkle the people in the remaining blood. By this sacrificial act, he was recalling the Mosaic move that we outlined above, but he was also participating symbolically in Yahweh's own remaking of his fallen and distorted cosmos. In fact, the temple itself, with its strict proportions and harmonies, was meant to invoke the reconstituted universe. What we see, once again, is that the covenant (communion) was ratified and made possible by sacrifice.

Two great prophetic texts must be mentioned in this context. The first is from the prophet Jeremiah: "The days are coming, says the LORD, when I will make a new covenant with the house of Israel and the house of Judah. . . . I will put my law within them, and I will write it upon their hearts; and I will be their God, and they shall be my people" (Jer. 31:31–33). But how will this intimate communion come about? To answer this question, we must consult the mysterious texts of the prophet Isaiah dealing with the suffering servant. Yahweh, Isaiah assures us, has "bared his holy arm" (Isa. 52:10) and will bring salvation to his people; but this vindication will come not through a clever political ruler or through a marauding military hero but through someone "despised and rejected by others, a man of suffering and acquainted with infirmity"; someone who will "bear our infirmities and carry our diseases," and who will be "wounded for our transgressions, crushed for our iniquities"; someone by whose "bruises we will be healed" (AP, see Isa. 53:3–5). In short, it will be through a great act of sacrificial love that God's victory over the dysfunction of the world will come. The communion that Jeremiah predicted will come at the cost of sacrifice that Isaiah described.

Only against this rich and loamy biblical background can the sacrificial nature of Jesus's work be understood. Though it runs altogether counter to the academic consensus of the present day, Jesus came to die, compelled by a divine mandate (*dei*) to offer himself in sacrifice. This terrible necessity of the cross can be seen in the utterly stark and unsentimental depiction of the Christmas scene on the facade of Chartres Cathedral. We see the figure of Mary, staring into the middle distance, and next to her is a depiction of the child Jesus lying on the cold slab of an altar. The point is simple and harsh: he was born in order to die. Jesus's task was to journey into sin and dysfunction and, as it were, to wrench them back into shape, offering himself as a victim for the redemption of the world. From the beginning, he is a warrior doing battle with the false kings Caesar Augustus and Herod. At the commencement of his public ministry, he does battle with the spiritual power who reigns over all the Augustuses and Herods of the world, the scatterer (*ho diabolos*) and the accuser (*ho Satanas*). Just before the confrontation with the devil, he stood in the muddy waters of the Jordan, shoulder to shoulder with sinners, seeking the baptism of repentance offered by John, and the language that he used to justify his behavior was redolent of sacrifice and covenant: "Let it be so now; for thus it is fitting for us to fulfil all righteousness" (Matt. 3:15) He would make things right precisely by entering into solidarity with the sin and disorder of the world. And so he sat down to celebrate with Matthew and his disreputable friends; he came to the home of the notorious sinner Zacchaeus; he called to him the blind Bartimaeus; he reached out in mercy to the woman caught in adultery; and he cajoled the woman at the well from concupiscent desire to the waters of eternal life. In all of this, he assumed a sacrificial stance, becoming conformed to Isaiah's image of the suffering servant, bearing the sins of many in order to bring about the communion that Yahweh desires.

This sacrificial ministry reached its climax on the cross. What we see in the various passion narratives is Jesus's confrontation with the manifold power of sin. Betrayal, denial, stupidity, cowardice, institutional corruption, injustice, arrogance, jealousy, cruelty, violence, and utter indifference to the pain of others—all of it comes at him, surrounds him, finally doing him to death. And what was his response? "Father, forgive them, for they know not what they do" (Luke 23:34). He met the darkness of a dysfunctional world with the grace of the divine forgiveness, fighting it not on its own terms or with its own weapons, but on Yahweh's terms and with the weapons of the Spirit. And on the third day afterward, he rose from the dead and returned to those who had abandoned, betrayed, and denied him, and he uttered a word of peace, *shalom*. He took on the power of sin and took it away by swallowing it up in the infinite ocean of the divine mercy. He allowed the evil of the fallen world to spend itself on him and became thereby the sacrificial Lamb of God. Appearing in the upper room and speaking that *shalom*, Jesus was the high priest coming forth from the holy of holies, bearing peace to the world. That was how the author of the letter to the Hebrews summed up Jesus's sacrificial mission.

All of this was anticipated, with enormous clarity and spiritual power, by what Jesus did the night before he died. Taking the bread, he said, "This is my body, which will be given up for you," and taking the cup, he said, "This is the cup of my blood, the blood of the new and everlasting covenant, which will be shed for you and for all so that sins may be forgiven." None of his listeners on that awful night could have missed the dual reference, first to Jeremiah's prediction of a new covenant that Yahweh would make with his people, writing the law on their hearts, and second to Isaiah's prediction that this salvation would be effected through the sacrifice of a suffering servant. Jesus's words and gestures that night provided the hermeneutical matrix for his words and gestures the next day. He would effect the new covenant precisely by shedding his blood as a sacrificial victim.

What, therefore, is the Eucharist but the making present in a sacramental mode of this sacrificial event? It is the manifestation in our time of the sacrifice that made possible the communion that we share in the divine grace.

Real Presence

By now probably everyone knows the story of Flannery O'Connor's dinner party with the writer Mary McCarthy. At the time of their encounter, O'Connor was at the beginning of her career and was very much the junior party in the conversation. In fact, she felt like "a dog who had been trained to say a few words but, overcome with inadequacy, had forgotten what he was going to say." Trying to engage the Catholic O'Connor, Mary McCarthy, who had been brought up a Catholic but had wandered away from the church, said that she thought the Eucharist was quite a powerful symbol. Flannery O'Connor replied, "Well, if it's only a symbol, then I say to hell with it." And with that she gave marvelously blunt expression to the Catholic conviction that Christ is really present in the Eucharist.[2]

The biblical grounds for this conviction are multiple, but perhaps the clearest warrant can be found in the sixth chapter of the Gospel of John, in the bread of life discourse that Jesus pronounced at the synagogue at Capernaum. When Christ spoke of his flesh as the living bread come down from heaven and urged his listeners to eat of it in order to attain everlasting life, many in his audience balked. "How can this man give us his flesh to eat?" (v. 52). Their reticence has to be understood against the background of the strong Old Testament prohibition against the consuming of animal flesh along with the blood. To suggest that a man's flesh should be eaten would have struck Jesus's audience as not only revolting but theologically repugnant as well. Given, therefore, every opportunity to explain his language in more metaphorical terms, to soften its literalism—as he did for example when the phrase "born again" was countered by Nicodemus's objections—Jesus instead intensified his statement. "Unless you eat the flesh of the Son of Man and drink his blood, you have no life in you" (v. 53). As every commentator indicates, the Greek term behind the word "eat" is not the customary *phagein* but rather *trogein*, a word used to designate the way that animals eat. Something like "gnaw" or "munch" would carry the sense of it in English. Thus if they were bothered by the gross realism of his language, Jesus endeavored to bother them further. And in case they missed the point, he insisted, "My flesh is food indeed, and my blood is drink indeed" (v. 55). So dismayed were they by this uncompromising language that many in the crowd left him, a reaction that would be hard to understand if they were taking his words in a merely metaphorical or symbolic sense. But Jesus did not pander to them. Instead, he asked his intimate disciples whether they would leave him too, anticipating, it seems, the decisive and divisive role that the Eucharistic doctrine would play in the ensuing history of the church.

Though none of the church fathers wrote a treatise exclusively on the Eucharistic mystery, there are numerous references to the sacrament sprinkled throughout their writings. One of the most basic motifs is that of the Eucharist as "food for eternal life." Origen, Chrysostom, Irenaeus, Ambrose, and Augustine all comment that the body and blood of Jesus are the means by which the believer becomes adapted to the heavenly mode of existence, quite literally "eternalized." Once again, it would be very difficult to make sense of such language if the fathers were construing the Eucharistic presence in a straightforwardly symbolic manner, for no contrivance of ours, however powerful or evocative, could possibly carry such a supernaturalizing virtue. In fact, the fathers, both east and west, typically relied upon the intensely organic language of John and Paul when articulating the Eucharistic mystery. They saw it as a real *koinonia* and participation in the life of Jesus, a means of living in the Lord.

In the eleventh century, in the Western church, the question of the real presence emerged with special force, due to the speculations of Berengarius of Tours. This philosophically minded monk made the commonsensical observation that, since the body of Jesus exists now in a glorified state in heaven, the "body" spoken of in the Eucharistic context must be a symbolic representation of that heavenly reality. Though intellectually attractive and clear, Berengarius's theory inspired in some prominent theologians a strong negative response, and the church was compelled to intervene in the controversy. It eventually condemned Berengarius's approach as crucially inadequate to the dense reality of Christ's presence in the Eucharist. In the wake of this contretemps, some theologians (and eventually the magisterium) began to use language borrowed from the natural philosophy of Aristotle, namely, the categories of substance and accident. The chief advantage of this usage was that it allowed one to speak of the objective reality of the Eucharistic presence without falling into a crude physicalism or literalism. In 1215, the Fourth Lateran Council used the term *transubstantiation*, though it did so in a subordinate clause and without providing anything even approaching a definition of the word.

It is in the writings of the great thirteenth-century Dominican master Thomas Aquinas that the doctrine of transubstantiation received its richest articulation. It is important to note that the Eucharist was central to the spiritual life of St. Thomas. He would both celebrate and assist at a second Mass every day, and it was said that he rarely got through the liturgy without weeping, so conscious was he of his participation in Christ's passion. His socius, Reginald of Piperno, reported that when Aquinas was wrestling with a particularly thorny intellectual problem, he would retire to the chapel and pray, frequently resting his head on the tabernacle where the Blessed Sacrament reposed.

Thomas's most concentrated treatment of the Eucharist takes place in questions 73–83 of the third part of the *Summa theologiae*; in question 75, he broaches directly the issues of real presence and transubstantiation. He comments that figurative or merely symbolic language is inadequate in regard to Christ's Eucharistic presence precisely because there must be *aliquid plus* (something more) in the Eucharist than in the rituals and signs of the Old Covenant. If the Eucharistic bread and wine are but symbols of holy realities, then they are no more powerful or evocative than the Passover meal, the Jerusalem temple, or the paschal lamb of sacrifice. He also observes that the "real" presence of Jesus in the Eucharist is a function of Christ's friendship with his people, for there is no higher sign of intimacy than the desire to be with one's friends. Such intimacy would hardly be signaled by a mere figurative presence.

Now how does Thomas endeavor to explain this distinctiveness? He does so through recourse to the inherited language of substance and accident. Though much of the sacramental theology of the twentieth century dismissed Thomas's usage of reputedly "naive" Aristotelian physics, this critique is, in fact, wide of the mark. By employing this terminology, Aquinas was by no means tying the church's doctrine to a particular scientific or philosophical theory; rather, he was using the intellectual argot of the day to articulate an essential truth concerning that doctrine. A very fair rendering of "substance and accident" would be, simply, "reality and appearance." Practically every major philosophy, both ancient and modern, makes a distinction between these two categories, for though reality and appearance customarily cohere, there are numerous cases when they decidedly do not. When I was a child, I was sitting in the backseat of the car as we moved through the countryside one clear summer night, and I noticed that the moon was traveling along with us, making its way through the branches of the trees that lined the road. When I remarked this to my father, he replied, "No, it just looks that way." When you gaze up into the starry sky, you see what, to all appearances, are the myriad stars and planets. But any astronomer will tell you that you are, in point of fact, looking into the distant past, for the light from those bodies has had to pass through oceans of time before reaching your eye. Or you meet someone who makes a very bad first impression, and you remark to a friend that that person is arrogant and self-preoccupied. But your friend, who knows the person in question much better, says, "I know he seems that way, but he really isn't." In all three cases, appearance is deceptive, and the testimony of an authority is required to reveal the deepest truth.

Thomas Aquinas says that, in the Eucharistic transformation, the deepest reality of the bread and wine is changed into the body and blood of Christ, even as the appearances of bread and wine remain unchanged. The same divine power that brings reality into existence from nothing is capable of effecting this unique transfiguration. How can the accidents of bread and wine exist apart from their proper substances? The creative cause of the whole of the universe can suspend secondary causality when it suits his purpose. Pope Benedict XVI, in an essay written in the 1970s, said that transubstantiation is the act by which the Creator grasps the bread and wine by the very roots of their being and transforms them into pure signs, that is to say, into pure bearers of the presence of Jesus, so that they no longer speak of themselves or refer to themselves, but only to Christ.[3] How is this change brought about? Echoing Aquinas, the Council of Trent said, "*Vi verborum*," by the power of the words of consecration, which are nothing other than the words of Jesus.

And this simple observation gives us a most important key to understanding the real presence. In his *How to Do Things with Words*, the twentieth-century philosopher of language J. L. Austin observed that language has much more than a descriptive purpose, for at times it can be used to change and affect reality. If a properly deputed officer of the law says to you, "You're under arrest," you are, whether you like it or not, whether the officer's judgment was sound or not, in fact under arrest. His words have changed reality. Or if a National League umpire shouts "You're out" as Anthony Rizzo slides into third base, the unfortunate Cub is, whether he likes it or not, in point of fact out. An umpire's words can, quite literally, change the course of a game. Now consider the case of the divine word. God's word is not simply descriptive but is rather, in the most powerful sense of the term, creative. God says, "Let there be light," and there is light; God says, "Let us make man in our own image and after our likeness," and so it happened. The prophet Isaiah reminds us that the divine *dabar* (word) goes forth and does not return without accomplishing the purpose for which it was sent. Now Jesus is not one interesting religious figure among many, not merely a sage or prophet, but rather, as St. John put it, the Word made flesh, Yahweh's *Dabar* in person. Therefore, what Jesus says, is. When he said, "Little girl, get up," she got up; when he said, "Lazarus, come out," the dead man came out; when he said, "My son, your sins are forgiven," they were indeed forgiven. The night before he died, Jesus took bread and gave thanks, and then he said, "Take this all of you and eat it; this is my body." In a similar way, after the meal, he took a cup filled with wine and said, "Take this, all of you, and drink from it; this is the cup of my blood." The divine word, which creates the universe, can change reality in the most fundamental way. *Vi verborum*, by the power of the words, the bread and wine become the body and blood of Christ. The Eucharist—along with creation itself—is the most concentrated instance of a divine word event, and it is for this reason that the church has always insisted on the dense reality of what happens in the Eucharistic change.

Conclusion

The three themes that I have considered in this chapter—sacred banquet, sacrifice, and real presence—are tightly linked. As we have been insisting, given the fact of the fallenness of the world, there can be no communion without sacrifice and no sacred banquet without the shedding of blood. But if these two facts are presented to us now in merely a symbolic way, then their power is attenuated. The doctrine of the real presence signals the transformative efficacy of the sacrificial meal, and it thereby guarantees that our participation in it amounts to an authentic Christification. When these three dimensions are seen in their proper coinherence, then the Eucharist is fully appreciated as the source and summit of the Christian life, that spiritual food without which we would starve to death.

PART 4

A NEW
EVANGELIZATION

12

✠

Why Bernard Lonergan Matters for Pastoral People

Bernard Lonergan, SJ, was one of the theological masterminds of the last century. He had a thoroughgoing understanding of the classical Catholic tradition—especially the thought of Thomas Aquinas—and he combined that knowledge with a profound grasp of modern mathematics, logic, and science. His books *Insight* and *Method in Theology* have emerged as benchmarks in the areas of speculative theology and theological method, respectively. Through the work of a number of his gifted disciples—including David Tracy, David Burrell, Matthew Lamb, and Michael Novak—Lonergan continues to exert a significant influence on the contemporary theological scene. But could the thought of this extremely complex and abstract theologian possibly affect the work and ministry of those engaged in the pastoral enterprise? I believe that this question can be answered with a resounding yes. And one does not have to dig around in obscure corners of Lonergan's writings in order to find something of pastoral relevance. On the contrary, a motif that stands at the heart of both *Insight* and *Method in Theology*—namely, the dynamics by which the well-functioning mind knows—is of immediate relevance to preachers, pastors, and spiritual directors. It is this practical implication of Lonergan's epistemology that I would like to explore in this chapter.

As an academician, Lonergan specialized in questions of method (the means of hunting down the truth), but we must not forget that he was a Jesuit and hence schooled, through Ignatius's spiritual exercises, in the discernment of spirits (the means of hunting down the will and movement of God). Lonergan intuited, of course, that the two are deeply related, precisely because God is the ground of truth and the ultimate goal of the seeking mind. Thus, whether one is a theoretical physicist in search of a unified field theory, a quarterback struggling to read a defense, or a spiritual director looking for clues in the soul of a directee, one is using his or her God-given and ultimately God-directed mind.

What constitutes a good mind? What makes it go off the rails? Are there disciplines and exercises that foster the proper use of the intellectual faculties? Lonergan answered these questions by articulating a method that can be expressed in terms of four imperatives: (1) be attentive, (2) be intelligent, (3) be reasonable, and (4) be responsible.[1] Before examining each in detail, we should notice that the imperative form implies that the mind tends easily to deviate from the ideal: we wouldn't tell a child, "Be good," unless we knew that he was quite apt to become bad. To put it in properly religious terms, Lonergan knew that the mind, though rooted in God, is fallen and hence stands in need of constant conversion.

Learning to Pray

Now, to the imperatives. By "attention," Lonergan means something very simple and, in practice, very elusive: seeing what is there to be seen, really taking in the light, colors, shapes, objects, sounds, textures, and movements that surround one. It means to perceive not myopically, selectively, or superficially but clearly, wholly, and accurately. As a young man, my uncle worked in army intelligence. As part of his training, he was asked to look into a room for twenty seconds and then describe, as completely as possible, after the door was closed, everything that he saw. It was, he told us, a remarkably difficult exercise. We need to hear the first Lonerganian imperative because most of us are not very adept at simple observation; we don't know how to see. Many scientists fail, not because they lack speculative intelligence or vivid imagination or the requisite laboratory equipment, but because they get their data wrong; they don't *look*. Many psychologists fall short, not because they lack education, intelligence, or sympathy, but because they miss the clues that are right in front of them, in their patient's mood, affect, behavior, or style of dress. It is said that when Spanish caravels arrived off the coast of certain

Caribbean islands in the late fifteenth century, the native people simply didn't see them. This was not because their visual apparatus was malfunctioning but because they simply did not have a frame of reference for taking in this new sight. Without an intelligible context, they filtered out this particular datum of experience. We too can perceive selectively, sometimes choosing not to see what doesn't correspond to our *a priori* categories of what is reasonable or acceptable. And so, once more, we must hear the command: be attentive.

How does all of this apply in the religious or spiritual context? Thomas Aquinas said that God is in all things "by essence, presence, and power . . . and most intimately so."[2] If Aquinas is right, God should not be understood as a supreme being standing at a distant remove from the world but rather as a power implicated in every aspect of the creation, which he, at the same time, transcends. This means that the spiritually alert perceiver must *see* God everywhere, finding traces of his presence in all things and all places. She must realize that nothing escapes the press of God, that everything is saturated with the divine. St. Bonaventure's *Itinerarium mentis in Deum* includes a lyrical section on the practice of opening one's eyes and seeing the presence of God in the simplest physical objects: a flower, the grass, a bird winging by. Thus the preacher must attend to every event in the life of his parish, every happening on the national and international scene, every movement in his interiority as a vessel of God's presence; and the spiritual director must take in each detail of his directee's life and experience as a potential sign of the sacred. As in regard to ordinary acts of perception, there are many blocks to spiritual seeing: laziness, willful indifference, selectivity, and so on, and these must be resisted. Many of the spiritual masters have commented that prayer is not so much an escape from the ordinary as a heightened attention to the depth dimension of the everyday and the commonplace, an act of real seeing. The Lonerganian command "be attentive" might therefore be translated for spiritual people as "pray."

See the Biblical Patterns

The second epistemological imperative is "be intelligent." By this Lonergan means the seeing of patterns, or what in more classical philosophical parlance are called "forms." This grasping of intelligible structure, this seizing of the matrix of meaning that gives coherence and order to what we perceive, is the "insight" that Lonergan makes the special subject of his masterwork. Some people are extremely attentive, taking in thoroughly even the tiniest details of what goes on around them, but they don't *understand* their experience;

they don't "get" it. Intelligent perception corresponds to the aha moment, the sudden turning-on of the light, the eureka-inducing grasp of meaning. One of the best ways to understand what Lonergan means by "intelligence" is to analyze a joke. A jest is made up of any number of elements—characters, descriptions of events, dialogue, the looks and vocal nuances of the jokester, and so on—but none of these particulars, not even their sum total, *is* the joke. The essence of the jest is the form that connects and renders meaning-ful all of its component parts; to "get" it is to have insight into this form, and the sign that one has successfully perceived the pattern is a delighted burst of laughter. Some people can take in every aspect of a joke, but the light doesn't go on and their laughter is, at best, forced: in biblical terms, they have ears but they haven't heard; in Lonerganian terms, they have been attentive but unintelligent.

In a scientific context, intelligence undergirds the forming of hypotheses or plausible explanations for a phenomenon. An observer has correctly perceived the data associated with the aurora borealis, and now he proposes a likely scenario, a causal pattern that might explain the remarkable event. Both the primitive mythologist who opined that the northern lights are manifestations of the gods' anger and the contemporary astronomer who guesses that they are epiphenomena of sun spots are exercising intelligence, the seeing of forms. At the beginning of the *Metaphysics*, Aristotle remarks that "philosophy com-mences in wonder," which is to say, the desire to understand. This intellectual passion, which prompts the relentless posing of the characteristically philo-sophical question "Why?" is what Lonergan means by *intelligence*. Toward the end of his life, Ludwig Wittgenstein retreated to a lonely Irish cottage to think through what he took to be the thorniest problem in philosophy. While he wrestled with this difficulty, he would wander the moors and the seacoast, muttering to himself, sometimes gesturing wildly with his cane, frowning in concentration—and alarming his neighbors! He described the problem that so bedeviled him as follows: how do we manage to see something *as* something? He was wondering, in a word, about the dynamics of the second Lonerganian imperative.

How does this second move of the mind play itself out in the spiritual con-text? Having taken in the world around her with great attentiveness, convinced that God is present in all things, the intelligent believer now seeks to discern the sacred patterns, to know precisely what God is up to. In this process of understanding, she utilizes the interpretive lenses provided by the Bible and the theological tradition, gaining insight by aligning her experience to the Great Story of divine revelation. Guided by the patterns of creation, exodus, prophecy, vocation, sin and grace, incarnation, death and resurrection, and second coming, she seeks analogies and correspondences to her own story. Thus, as Jacob labored under the tyranny of Laban, she and her colleagues are oppressed by an unfair employer; as Yahweh dealt with Israel during its wandering in the desert, so God is dealing with her in her depression and loneliness; as Jeremiah was summoned to speak the divine word despite his youth and inexperience, so she feels a vocation to mediate God's demand to her family, despite her feelings of unworthiness; as Peter was forgiven for his betrayal, so she is forgiven for her infidelity; as Jesus rose from the dead through the power of the Spirit, so she manages to conquer a besetting fear of death. Picasso once remarked that if there were a key to his artistic genius it would be the capacity to see visual analogies: the shape of that pear is like the contour of a guitar, which is evocative of the curves on a woman's body. Indeed, a Picasso composition is usually an artful juxtaposition of such formal family resemblances. So the intelligent Christian is one who has an analogical religious imagination, the capacity to appreciate the resemblances between the biblical patterns and the patterns of her experience.

Just as the scientist or philosopher or quarterback is trained to see through a long process of apprenticeship to the masters in his respective field, so the religious person must be trained through a steady immersion in the universe of the Bible. This is why the discerner of intelligible Christian forms must become acquainted with the Scriptures themselves as well as with that whole collectivity of interpretive guides that constitute the Catholic tradition: icons; the liturgy; the poetry of Dante; the *Summae* of Aquinas; the sermons of Newman; the Sistine Ceiling; Chartres Cathedral; the councils of Nicaea, Chalcedon, Trent, and Vatican II; the lives of the saints; and, above all, the Eucharist. The Bible and tradition are the privileged means by which the Catholic community learns the practice of intelligent discernment of the patterns of grace. Paul reminded us long ago that faith—a keen intelligence in regard to the unseen things of God—comes from hearing, that is to say, from an immersion in a world of meaning that we do not create. One of the real threats to theological intelligence is a tendency—sadly prevalent in the years after the Second Vatican Council—to bracket the objectivity and density of the interpretive tradition in favor of subjective religious experience. This approach is analogous to inviting a boy onto a baseball diamond and telling him to play, but without placing the moves of baseball in his body or the rules and tradition of baseball in his mind. Innocent of that objective "world," the child will never become either an insightful perceiver of the forms of the game or a particularly adept practitioner of it. Similarly lost will be the Christian left to her unstructured spiritual experience. So a pastoral translation of Lonergan's second imperative might be "see the biblical patterns."

Discern the Spirits

The third Lonerganian imperative is "be reasonable." This is the hard-edged and decisive epistemological move of judgment, the determination of truth. Once we have attended to the data before us and have had a number of intriguing insights as to their formal structure, we have to make a decision. We have to determine which of our many bright ideas is the one right idea. All hypotheses are, almost by definition, interesting, but only one of them is truly adequate to the case and the evidence. At the level of intelligence, playfulness and imagination are altogether in order, since sometimes the most outrageous hypothesis is in fact the correct one; but when seeking to make a judgment, one has to be clear, hard, and censorious. Many people who are sufficiently attentive and wonderfully intelligent balk at being reasonable, since they don't want to make the tough choice that leaves certain opinions behind. It is no accident that *decision* is derived from the Latin term that means cutting (*secare*).

In the sciences, experimentation represents this third move of the mind. Once the hypotheses are on the table, the researcher must find some means to discriminate among them; accordingly he constructs a series of experiments designed to test them and, ideally, to eliminate all but one of them. By careful questioning of his client and discerning assessment of the answers he receives, the psychologist tests his various guesses and determines that his patient is suffering from obsessive compulsive disorder and not repressed guilt feelings. A similar dynamic obtains in philosophy. Through spirited conversation, intense meditation, wide-ranging reading, and constant testing against experience, a philosopher decides that, of all the intriguing metaphysical options on offer—from Plato's to Whitehead's—Aquinas's is truest. Here we see another reason that this third step is so difficult: it involves one in disagreements, sometimes terrible ones, with colleagues, friends, potential benefactors, and so on. To say, for instance, that Aquinas's metaphysical account is true is implicitly to criticize those who have staked their lives and careers on an entirely different decision. It is indeed much easier to remain at the level of intelligence, playfully entertaining the various intellectual options, maintaining oneself in an attitude of bemused detachment. But the third imperative forbids this; it tells us to make up our minds.

Preachers, teachers of the faith, and spiritual directors have to move through this third phase as well. They have been religiously attentive to all things, they have applied a whole series of biblical grids seeking to understand how their story relates to the Great Story, and now they must determine what precisely God is saying and how precisely God is luring them. A preacher who is content to display the Christian form in a generic or abstract way is an ineffective preacher. Martin Luther King Jr. in Montgomery, John Paul II in Poland, and Oscar Romero in El Salvador were, through their proclamation of the Word, helping their people to be religiously reasonable, to know concretely which decision to make. Similarly, a spiritual counselor, satisfied with exploring options with his directee, is functioning inadequately. He must help his client through the thorny thickets of judgment. Monitoring and encouraging the third step is essential to the work that I do in a seminary context. The men that I deal with on a regular basis are trying, in a very conscious way, to discover how God is calling them. Is it priesthood or not? It can't be both, and they know it. A judgment, a decision, in either direction painful, has to be made, and they know that too. But what seminarians do in a particularly focused way is what all responsible Christians must do.

And this is the rub. How do we make this all-important judgment that touches not simply on what we are to do but on who we are to be? How do we know? As we saw, scientists proceed in their work by way of controlled experimentation, carefully eliminating guesses and causal explanations until they arrive at the most persuasive hypothesis. There is, I think, something similar operative in the arena of religious judgment. The discerning and reasonable disciple of Jesus can also employ a process of elimination, gradually setting aside various inadequate patterns until he finds the one that fits. Thus, when determining what God wants me to do, I can certainly rule out a form of life that runs contrary to the central narratives and symbols of revelation, say, a life centered on sensuality, self-absorption, or violence. More pointedly, I can eliminate a pattern that is inconsistent with the fundamental pattern of Jesus's life; somehow I know that whatever form my vocation takes, it will be essentially Christoform. Thus, for example, a style of life that is predicated on the assumption that there is no resurrection after death or that enemies should not be loved would be necessarily inadequate. But having negated these rather obviously problematic hypotheses, how do I proceed in the face of a variety of christologically viable options?

Here the discernment must become more refined. One of the best guides is in the fifth chapter of Paul's letter to the Galatians. Jesus had said that a tree is known by its fruits, and Paul makes this very specific. He tells us that the fruits of the Holy Spirit are "love, joy, peace, patience, kindness, goodness, faithfulness, gentleness, self-control" (Gal. 5:22–23), implying that the Spirit's presence in one's life can be read from its radiance in these soul-expanding qualities. All of Paul's "fruit of the Holy Spirit" are marks of an outward-looking, expansive *magna anima* (great soul), which stands in contradistinction to the *pusilla anima* (the cramped soul) of the sinner. Thus love is willing the good of the other as other; joy is self-diffusive; patience bears with the troublesome; kindness makes the other gentle; self-control restricts the havoc that the ego can cause, and so on. Which vocation, which form of life, ought to be mine? The one that awakens and sustains in me these attributes; the one that makes great my soul. So priesthood and married life are both good; both clearly correspond to biblical forms and patterns; and both have been suggested to me by my playful and perceptive religious intelligence. But only one of them can be right for me. Therefore, I must "try both on" in the theater of my mind and imagination; I must, as far as possible, practice each one—and then I must determine which one produces in me more love, joy, peace, patience, kindness, and so on. And then I have to follow the third Lonerganian imperative and decide. Thus, the pastoral translation of "be reasonable" might be "discern the spirits."

Do the Truth in Love

The final epistemological imperative is "be responsible." Once we have been attentive, intelligent, and reasonable, we must, finally, accept the full implications of the true judgment that we have made. Now we must adjust our lives in light of the truth that we have discovered, no matter how uncomfortable that adjustment might be. Lonergan knew well that many people fail precisely at this point: they have followed the process admirably and have made a correct judgment, but they just cannot bring themselves to act on it. Thus, politicians decide that backing a particular bill is morally objectionable, but they do so anyway out of a desire to be reelected; or a researcher discovers a truth that may save lives, but he doesn't publish his findings for fear of losing his funding; or a seminarian determines that he should be a priest, but opts out because he is intimidated by the demands of the lifestyle or cowed by the disapproval of his family. I have, over the years, known people who are absolutely fascinated by Catholicism but never become Catholics. They can cite chapter and verse from Aquinas, they can aptly quote Chesterton, they know the history and lore of the liturgy, they idolize the pope, they admire the objectivity of Catholic morality, and they think the world of Mother Teresa—but they cannot or will not actually practice Catholicism. They lack the courage of their convictions, or to put it in formal Lonerganian terms, they are irresponsible.

We have seen that all the imperatives have a moral overtone, since all are a summons to a type of conversion, but here especially we perceive the ethical implication of Lonergan's epistemology. A good Thomist (and hence an anti-Cartesian), Lonergan knew that the mind is not radically separated from the body, desire, and the passions. Instead, all of these faculties wrap around one another in a tight coinherence. Therefore, when the intellect comes to truth, this conviction must radiate outward to inform the will and to direct the body—which is why the spiritual incoherency of knowing the truth and not acting on it threatens to shake a person apart. One reason that the play *A Man for All Seasons* is so compelling is that it paints such a vividly realistic portrait of one man who maintains his intellectual and moral integrity, amid a bevy of figures casually losing theirs.

Religious people take this last step by realizing, as the Gospel of John implies, that the truth is something that is *done*. No figure in the Bible ever has an experience of God—a glimpse of God's truth—without being sent on mission, without being given something concrete to do. Isaiah sees the manifestation of the divine presence in the temple and then hears, "Whom shall I send?" (Isa. 6:8). Moses spies the burning bush, learns the most sacred name of God, and then is commissioned to liberate God's people Israel. Elijah attends to the tiny whispering voice of the Almighty and then is given a whole list of tasks to fulfill. Paul encounters the risen Jesus and is immediately sent as an apostle to the nations. The truth of God belongs not just in our heads but in our hearts, hands, viscera, and feet. Dorothy Day once commented that everything a baptized person does should be directly or indirectly related to the corporal and spiritual works of mercy. What she meant was that the intellectual convictions associated with being a baptized Christian—believing in one God, the Father almighty, and in Jesus Christ his only Son, our Lord, and in the Holy Spirit, the Lord and giver of life, and in the one, holy, catholic, and apostolic church—look like something in practice. They look like feeding the hungry, clothing the naked, visiting the imprisoned, counseling the doubtful, praying for the living and the dead, and so on. It is insufficient for a responsible Christian to hold to truths that don't show up in his body and actions.

As I write these words, the American church is embroiled in the controversy about refusing communion to those politicians who actively support abortion rights. My own judgment, which is neither here nor there, is that such a refusal would be, in most cases, imprudent, but I want to say just a word in favor of those who advocate it. It is irresponsible, on Lonerganian grounds, to hold the truth that abortion constitutes the taking of an innocent human life and then proceed to do nothing about it, to allow a truth of such importance to dawn in the light of intelligibility and then not to act in accord with it. People of good will can and do disagree about the advisability of a particular strategy, but I applaud those who at least see the indispensable need for some sort of strategy, and I am impatient with those who are content to sit blandly on the sidelines, their intellectual convictions utterly unrelated to their wills and bodies. When we stop at the level of judgment, we are ignoring the final imperative "be responsible." If we were to translate this fourth demand into more explicitly biblical terms, we might say "do the truth in love."

Conclusion

Lonergan makes a distinction between the need for certitude and the quest for understanding. The need to be apodictically certain is the mark of many of the philosophies of modernity. Descartes's frantic sweeping away of received traditions, ideas, and even ordinary sense experience in an attempt to discover an absolutely firm foundation for philosophy is the paradigm. This compulsive desire struck Lonergan as neurotic. To it he contrasted the quest that we have been tracking throughout this chapter, namely, the search for understanding guided by the four great epistemological imperatives. This rigorous journey of intellectual discovery is conditioned not by the neediness of the ego but rather by that sense of wonder of which Aristotle spoke. It does not involve the gathering of reality around the ego but the dissolving of the ego in rapture at the density and complexity of the real. In both academic and pastoral people, on both the right and the left, I have often sensed the ghost of Descartes. The signs are an intellectuality that is angry, desirous of incontrovertible certitude, and finally afraid. I believe that Bernard Lonergan's epistemology is not only pastorally very useful but also an antidote to this troublesome Cartesianism.

Thus, in the hopes of opening and expanding their minds, Lonergan instructs all preachers, pastors, teachers, and ministers to be prayerfully attentive, biblically intelligent, discerningly reasonable, and, for God's sake and the sake of the people they serve, spiritually responsible.

13

---✠---

Announcing the Lordship of Jesus Christ

The Evangelical Task within Contemporary Culture

If I may be permitted to begin with something of a commonplace, it is not altogether accurate to say that the church has a mission to evangelize, for the church *is* a mission to evangelize. In its theology, formal structure, practices, internal organization, sacraments, liturgy, and preaching, the church is above all God's means of announcing the lordship of Jesus Christ. Therefore, to speak of evangelization as though it were one ecclesial preoccupation among many is already to have misconstrued the question, to have given away the game. It is my conviction that although considerable lip service has been paid to evangelization in the years after the Second Vatican Council, we have, in point of fact, proven to be rather remarkably inept at it, and this ineptitude has flowed from a serious misunderstanding of its nature and centrality. What I would like to do in the course of this chapter is to explore the evangelical art of proclamation, especially in its relation to the contemporary postmodern culture.

The Evangelical Bottom Line

Evangelization—the proclamation of the good news, the gospel, the *euange-lion*—has to do with the resurrection of Jesus Christ from the dead. On every page of the New Testament, one can discern an excitement born of something utterly novel and unexpected: that Jesus of Nazareth, who had died on a cross and was buried, was, through the power of God, raised bodily from death. Everything else in Christian life flows from and is related to this event, and it was this message of resurrection that provided the content for the kerygmatic preaching of the first evangelists. Before we say anything about the practicalities of evangelization, before we explore concrete strategies and methods, we must be clear and straight in regard to the resurrection. Without this foundation, the entire evangelical enterprise—indeed Christianity itself—collapses. In my judgment, the fundamental problem in regard to evangelization in the years since the Second Vatican Council has been a tendency among theologians, teachers, and preachers to soft-pedal the resurrection, to demythologize and domesticate it, turning it into either a harmless and generic universal symbol or an expression of the convictions of the believing community. Once we tame the resurrection, we undercut the enthusiasm necessary for proclamation, and we turn the evangel into something neither particularly good nor particularly new.

In his extremely influential 1974 study *Jesus: An Experiment in Christol-ogy*, Edward Schillebeeckx offered the following demythologizing interpreta-tion of the resurrection. After the tragic death of Jesus, Peter and the other disciples had an experience of grace that amounted to a radical conversion or enlightenment. Though they had abandoned Jesus in his darkest moment, they nevertheless felt forgiven by him after his death, and they translated this conviction into the symbolic language of resurrection from the dead and ecstatic vision. Originally, Schillebeeckx argues, this "resurrection faith" had nothing to do with the empty tomb or with reports of seeing Jesus in any objective way. A mistake that we make is to misconstrue the highly symbolic speech of the biblical authors in a naive and literalistic manner. "We suffer from the crude . . . realism of what 'appearances of Jesus' came to be in the later tradition, through unfamiliarity with the distinctive character of the Jewish-biblical way of speaking."[1] Resurrection, Schillebeeckx assures us, "has nothing to do with bodies" and everything to do with the experience of the first believers.

We find something very similar in Roger Haight's controversial 1999 text *Jesus: Symbol of God*. Haight maintains that the objective referent to the language of resurrection is the disciples' memory of the earthly ministry and teaching of Jesus. Through God's grace, they came to realize, after Jesus's

death, that the way of life taught and exemplified by him was indeed revela-
tory of God's own values and rule. This deep and saving conviction came later
to be expressed in the suggestive language of appearances and bodily resurrection.[2] Where does resurrection faith come from? "It arises out of a basic
faith in God as mediated by Jesus, and a lingering commitment to the person
of Jesus as the one in whom the disciples encountered God."[3] In somewhat
cruder, but for all that more telling, language, James Carroll makes the same
argument. He opines that the dejected followers of Jesus sat, after his death,
in a memory circle and recalled his marvelous words and deeds and thereby
became convinced that his cause goes on. To this conviction they gave poetic
expression through tales of the empty tomb and resurrection appearances.

Now within the confines of this chapter, I can scarcely effect an adequate
engagement with these various texts, but suffice it to say that were this hermeneutical approach correct, the language of resurrection from the dead could
be applied, with equal validity, to practically any great religious or spiritual
figure in history. Didn't the followers of the Buddha fondly remember him
and his cause after his death? Couldn't the disciples of Confucius have sat in a
memory circle and recalled how he had radically changed their lives? Couldn't
the friends of Zoroaster have felt forgiven by him after he had passed from
the scene? Indeed, couldn't the members of an Abraham Lincoln society
manage to generate many of the convictions and feelings about Lincoln that
Schillebeeckx and company claim the apostles generated about Jesus? And
would any of these demythologizing explanations begin to make sense of
that excitement I spoke of at the outset, that sense of novelty, surprise, and
eschatological breakthrough that runs right through the four Gospels, through
every one of the epistles, to the book of Revelation? Can we really imagine
St. Paul arriving in Corinth with the earth-shaking message that a dead man
was found to be quite inspiring? Can we really imagine St. Peter enduring his
upside-down crucifixion because he and the other disciples had "felt forgiven"?

More to it, these painfully reductive readings of the resurrection stories
actually betray a thin and unsophisticated grasp of the biblical authors. Here
the magisterial work of the New Testament scholar N. T. Wright is particularly illuminating.[4] Wright says that the composers of the New Testament
were aware of a whole range of options in regard to the status of those who
had died. From their Jewish heritage, they knew of the shadowy realm of
Sheol and the sad figures that dwell therein. They knew further that people
could return from Sheol in ghostly form (think of the prophet Samuel called
up from the dead by the witch of Endor in the first book of Samuel). They
even had a sense of reincarnation, evident in widespread convictions about
the return of Elijah in advance of the Messiah or in the popular report that

Jesus himself was John the Baptist or one of the prophets returned from death. By the first century, an increasingly common view among Jews was that the righteous dead would, at the close of the age, return in their bodies at the general resurrection. From the Hellenistic and Roman cultural matrix, furthermore, the New Testament authors would have inherited the Platonic theory that the soul at death escapes from the body as from a prison in order to move into a higher spiritual arena. They also were aware of a perspective, combining both Greek and Hebrew elements, according to which the souls of the dead abide for a time with God in a quasi-disembodied state while they await the general resurrection at the eschaton. This view is on clear display in the famous passage from the book of Wisdom, which says, "The souls of the just are in the hand of God and no torment shall touch them" (3:1 NAB). Finally, they knew all about hallucinations, illusions, and projections (though they wouldn't have used those terms), as is clear from the first reactions of the disciples upon hearing the reports of Jesus's post-resurrection appearances.

The point is that they used none of these categories when speaking of the resurrection of Jesus. They didn't say that Jesus had gone to Sheol and was languishing there; nor did they claim that he had returned from that realm à la Samuel. They certainly did not think that Jesus's soul had escaped from his body or that he was vaguely "with God" like any other of the righteous dead. They did not think that the general resurrection of the dead had taken place. And most certainly, they did not think that the resurrection was a symbolic way of talking about something that had happened to them. Again and again, they emphasize how discouraged, worn down, and confused they were after the crucifixion. That this dejected band would spontaneously generate the faith that would send them careering around the world with the message of resurrection strains credulity, to say the very least. What is undeniably clear is that something had happened to Jesus, something so strange that those who witnessed it had no category apt to describe it. Perhaps we would get closest to it if we were to say that what was expected of all the righteous dead at the eschaton—namely, bodily resurrection—had come true in time for this one man, Jesus of Nazareth, the same Jesus whom they knew, with whom they had shared meals and fellowship. This Jesus, who had died and had been buried, appeared alive to them, bodily present, though transformed, no longer conditioned by the limitations of space and time. This is what rendered them speechless at first and then, especially after the event of Pentecost, prepared to go the ends of the earth, enduring every hardship even to the point of martyrdom, in order to proclaim the good news. I'm emphasizing this point—even at the risk of belaboring it—because I feel that it has always been the indispensable ground for effective evangelization.

Now, from the fact of the resurrection flowed another astonishing claim: Jesus is who he said he was. Though it is all the vogue now in academic circles to say that Jesus died because he befriended the marginalized or upset the social conventions of his time or threatened the power arrangements in ancient Palestine, none of this has much relation to reality. Jesus was put to death because he claimed to be God. That Jesus upset the status quo of his society is true, but it is not the reason that he was put to death. The Jewish authorities moved against him because of his (to them) blasphemous claim to act and speak in the very person of God, and the Romans went along because he was perceived, as a consequence, to be a disturber of the peace. What impressed the first Christians to a life-changing degree was that the resurrection validated the extraordinary claims of Jesus about himself. Wolfhart Pannenberg argued for years that the historical fact of the resurrection placed a sort of divine seal on the preresurrection words and actions of Jesus, legitimating and confirming them.

But what precisely were these claims? In the fifth chapter of the Gospel of Matthew, we find this statement of Jesus: "You have heard that it was said, 'You shall love your neighbor and hate your enemy.' But I say to you, love your enemies and pray for those who persecute you" (vv. 43–44). The content of this saying—the teaching dealing with enemy love—is extraordinary enough, but what is most astounding is the placing into question of the Torah, almost casually effected by the rhetorical framework of "you have heard it said, but I say." The speaker is clearly insinuating that he has the authority to trump the Torah, the inspired word of God. Who could possibly make such a claim coherently except the one who is, himself, the author of the Torah? Before healing the paralytic, Jesus says matter-of-factly, "My son, your sins are forgiven." Shocked, the Pharisees respond, "Who is this that speaks blasphemies? Who can forgive sins but God only?" (see Luke 5:20–21). They were quite right, of course, which is the whole point. If you had hurt me, I could, with some legitimacy, offer you my personal forgiveness of your offense; but if someone else had harmed you, I could scarcely offer *that person* my forgiveness for his sin. The only way that such a statement could be anything but blasphemous would be if I were the one who is offended in every sin. And this is what the Pharisees correctly intuited. In Luke's Gospel, Jesus makes the jaw-dropping announcement, "If any one comes to me and does not hate his own father and mother and wife and children and brothers and sisters . . . he cannot be my disciple" (14:26). At the limit, we could imagine a religious leader or founder saying something like, "You must love God more than your very life," or perhaps, "You should reverence my ideas more than you do your mother and father"; but to insinuate that the religious spokesman himself must be loved above even the greatest values in this world is to imply that the person of the spokesman is itself the highest Good. In all three Synoptic Gospels, Jesus ecstatically declares, "Heaven and earth will pass away, but my words will not pass away" (Luke 21:33). Who could coherently utter such a statement except the one who is himself the incarnation of the eternal Word of God?

It will not do, by the way, to say that the so-called high christological language affirming Jesus's divinity is found exclusively in the relatively late Gospel of John. Every passage that I've cited so far is taken from one of the Synoptics. What John does, it seems to me, is to make explicit and ontologically precise what was implicit in the witness of the Synoptics. Hence, we find in the Johannine prologue the unambiguous assertion that the Word, which is God, became flesh in Jesus. Further, we hear Jesus say, "Before Abraham was, I am" (8:58), connecting thereby his own existence with the "I am" of Exodus 3:14. And we overhear him at the Last Supper discourse telling Philip, "He who has seen me, has seen the Father" (14:9). My point is that none of this language is out of step with what we find in the Synoptic accounts; it is the same fundamental idea being expressed in terms of a different and more philosophically explicit symbol system. Nor will it do to say that all of this language was simply placed in the mouth of Jesus by later generations of believers, for that only postpones the problem and renders more puzzling the enigma. Why would committed monotheists, without the slightest provocation, suddenly place on the lips of the hero, whom they were proposing to the world, the most outrageous and indefensible sentiments?

Having considered these statements of Jesus, there is, of course, a coherent option that remains, namely, that he was mad, an insane and dangerous blasphemer. Let's face it, mental health institutions are filled with people who think they are God. And indeed, this is precisely what Jesus's enemies thought and precisely why they hounded him to his death. Either he is who he says he is (in which case we are obliged to give our whole lives to him, making him Lord of every aspect of our personality and every dimension of our society) or he is a madman (in which case we should be against him). What does not remain, as C. S. Lewis saw so clearly, is the bland middle position that, though he isn't divine, he is a good, kindly, and wise ethical teacher. If he isn't who he says he is, then he isn't admirable at all; instead, he is guilty of making the most insane and outrageous claims of any major figure in world history. The classical apologetic tradition expresses this dichotomy in the pithy adage *aut Deus, aut malus homo*—either he is God or he's a bad man. Thus Jesus compels a choice, a decision, in a manner that no other religious founder does. The Buddha could claim that he had found a way that he wanted to share with his followers, but Jesus said, "I *am* the way." Muhammad could say that, through him, the final divine truth had been communicated to the world, but Jesus said, "I *am* the truth." Confucius could maintain that he had discovered a new and uplifting form of life, but Jesus said, "I *am* the life" (see John 14:6). And thus, as he himself stated, "Either you are with me or you are against me" (see Matt. 12:30; Luke 11:23). No other founder forces that choice as baldly as Jesus does.

Now just as a number of contemporary theologians have undermined the reality of the resurrection, so an army of theologians in the modern period have questioned or watered down the divinity of Jesus, turning Christ into one interesting religious figure among many. In a word, they have taken the middle option that C. S. Lewis (following the inner logic of the New Testament witness) proscribed, and in so doing, they have contributed mightily to the undermining of the evangelical project. In the massively influential rationalist Christology offered by Immanuel Kant in his *Religion within the Limits of Reason Alone*, Jesus is reduced to the level of an inspired ethical teacher and example. Kant goes so far as to suggest that the real historicity of Jesus is fundamentally irrelevant to his essential function as an imagined archetype of the moral life. An American variant of this Kantian approach can be seen in the work of Thomas Jefferson, who issued a version of the New Testament from which all reference to the supernatural—including the divinity of Jesus—had been carefully expunged. And we see a similar reductionism in the Christology of Friedrich Schleiermacher, the founder of modern liberal Protestantism. In his *Glaubenslehre*, Schleiermacher held that Jesus experienced a perfectly realized "God-consciousness" and bequeathed to his followers a participation in that blessed awareness. Because his human spiritual consciousness was utterly filled with a knowledge of God, the tradition referred to Jesus as "divine." Schleiermacher's most ardent twentieth-century disciple was the German Lutheran Paul Tillich. Tillich held that Jesus experienced to an unsurpassed degree the breakthrough of the unconditioned reality of God, so that he became the bearer of a new being. It was this total determination of Jesus's life by the power of God that Peter recognized when he confessed, "You are the Christ." Karl Rahner developed a Catholic version of the Schleiermacherian understanding of Jesus, holding that Christology is a fully developed anthropology. By this he meant that Jesus realized utterly the transcendental orientation to God that is constitutive of the human mind and will in general. In the Christologies emerging from the Jesus Seminar, we find a sort of neo-Kantianism. On this reading, Jesus is also an ethical teacher and example, but the ethical ideals have become those of early twenty-first-century liberalism: inclusivity, feminism, nondomination, and friendship to those on the margins. John Dominic Crossan—the best known of the Jesus Seminar figures—teaches that the essential message of Jesus was one of resistance to the domination system of the Roman establishment.

Now it is most important not to jump to the conclusion that all of these various theologians are saying the same thing about Jesus; they clearly are not. But what these liberal theologies do indeed have in common is a tendency to render Jesus something like a "super-saint," someone quantitatively but not qualitatively different from other deeply holy people. Indeed, if we were to press the issue, what in fact would render, say, Francis of Assisi or Mother Teresa of Calcutta less sterling Kantian moral exemplars than Jesus? Why would Jesus be a more effective or important challenger of oppressive social structures than, say, Martin Luther King Jr. or Mohandas Gandhi? In what sense would we be obliged to say that Jesus's spiritual consciousness was more perfect or intense than, say, John of the Cross's or, for that matter, the Buddha's? In one of his trenchant critiques of Rahner's theology, Hans Urs von Balthasar remarked that if one were to follow strictly the lines of Rahner's Christology, there would be nothing essential to distinguish Jesus from Mary, that is to say, from the greatest of the saints. At the Council of Ephesus in 431, the church anathematized Nestorianism, the view that Jesus is a human person who enjoys a particularly rich relationship with the person of God. One could say that those Christologies that proceeded from a Kantian or Schleiermacherian provenance are basically reworkings of the Nestorian mistake. For our purposes, the problem is this: if Jesus is nothing more than a super-saint, if he is not qualitatively different from any number of inspiring spiritual figures, why should the proclamation of his life and message be a particularly compelling obligation? In point of fact, one of the most telling marks of liberal Christology is its lack of missionary and evangelical enthusiasm. For instance, in the years after the Council, when Catholic theology came increasingly under the influence of Rahner, Catholic missionaries seemed much less interested in proclaiming the lordship of Jesus than in working for social justice and validating the culture of the people whom they were sent to evangelize.

The evangelical bottom line, it seems to me, is the claim that Jesus rose from the dead and that, therefore, he is who he said he was: the Son of God. When those two facts are brought forward unambiguously, we find generated the excitement, the spark, the enthusiasm for sharing the good news.

The Gospel as a Message of Freedom and Humanism

The theological liberalism that I have been describing and criticizing did not emerge in a cultural vacuum. One of the principal causes of the liberal shift was a desire to make the faith more credible to an increasingly skeptical modern audience. Thus, liberal theologians, for the past two hundred years, have been repeating, with certain variations, the speeches that Schleiermacher gave to the cultured despisers of religion at the beginning of the nineteenth century. But a second major cause of this transition was the modern preoccupation with personal liberty. If the resurrection and divinity of Jesus are hard for the contemporary mind to take in, they are, perhaps, even harder for the contemporary will to accept. If, as I have been arguing, the proper practical conclusion to draw from the essential Christian message is that Jesus must be the total Lord of one's life, then it's not surprising that freedom-loving moderns would prefer either to reject that message outright or to water it down in the ways that we have been tracing. In this section, I would like to address this second concern more carefully. It is my conviction that human freedom is, paradoxically enough, fully realized not when the lordship of Jesus is questioned or compromised but precisely when it is robustly emphasized. And I am therefore further convinced that a full-bodied evangelical proclamation is in fact the condition for the possibility of realizing the flourishing and freedom for which the philosophers of modernity longed.

Let me place this assertion in a wide biblical framework. The Genesis image of Adam and Eve, at play in the garden of Eden, tasting from all the trees but one, poetically expresses the humanism at the heart of the Bible. God wants his human creatures to be fully alive, and the ranginess of Adam and Eve in paradise evokes all the modes of human accomplishment: politics, art, music, literature, social organization, sports, philosophy, and so on. But why are they prohibited from eating of the tree of the knowledge of good and evil? We know, from the text itself, how not to interpret that prohibition, for we are given the serpent's hermeneutic: God, out of jealousy, wants to prevent his creatures from accomplishing all that they can. But God in fact is not our rival; our being neither adds to nor subtracts from his perfection. The prohibition obtains because human flourishing will be undermined precisely in the measure that human beings arrogate to themselves the properly divine prerogative of determining good and evil. When our freedom to choose is anchored to the objective truth that God establishes, then it finds authentic realization, but when it ranges outside of that divine norming, it comes into conflict with itself. The proper exercise of the will—the coordination of freedom and truth—is symbolized in the image of Adam and God walking together as friends in the cool of the evening; and the self-destruction of freedom is evoked in the expulsion of Adam and Eve from paradise. The rest of the biblical narrative is the story of God's attempt to lure his human creatures back into friendship with him. Through the law and the prophets, through the example of the patriarchs, in all the vagaries of Israelite history, in the longing of the psalmist and wisdom figures, the God of Eden is trying to re-coordinate human freedom and divine truth. This story reaches its climax in the event of the incarnation, for Jesus is, in his own person, this reconciliation, this friendship between divinity and humanity.

Now precisely *how* do divinity and humanity coinhere in Jesus? In their classic christological formula, the fathers of the Council of Chalcedon in 451 said that in Christ two natures, divine and human, come together in a personal union, but "without mixing, mingling, or confusion," that is to say, noncompetitively. In becoming a creature, God neither ceases to be God nor compromises the integrity of the creature he becomes. This demonstrates that God is not a being in the world, one thing among many, but rather the sheer act of to-be itself. But it also demonstrates that God's proximity is not a threat to our well-being, just the opposite, and for our purposes this is decisive. In point of fact, the closer the noncompetitive God comes to us, the more we are realized in our humanity. Thus, the incarnation grounds the deepest sort of humanism. This principle came to special clarity during the monothelite controversy of the eighth century. Certain theologians had maintained that in Jesus there is only one divine will, which had, more or less, supplanted his human freedom. Following its Chalcedonian instincts, the church said that there are in fact two wills—human and divine—in Jesus, working in a coordinated harmony. This shows, once again, that authentic human freedom is realized precisely through a submission to the promptings of the divine freedom. In summing up his existentialism, Jean-Paul Sartre said that if God exists, we cannot be free. Christian humanism, with its roots sunk deep in the doctrine of the incarnation, gives the lie to this construal of human liberty. Sartre could never begin to make sense of the paradoxical Pauline claims "For freedom Christ has set us free" (Gal. 5:1), and "I am a slave of Christ Jesus" (Rom. 1:1 NABRE); but for those tutored in the dynamics of the incarnation, Paul's statements are mutually implicative, not mutually exclusive.

The contemporary Dominican moral theologian Servais Pinckaers has illuminated this paradox through his distinction between two very different conceptions of freedom, one that we might call "Sartrean" and the other "Pauline." He calls them "the freedom of indifference" and "the freedom for excellence."[5] The former, which came for a variety of reasons to dominate the modern consciousness, is freedom as choice, a sort of indifference in the face of contraries, the capacity to decide without internal or external compulsion. This sort of liberty is, to say the least, in a tensive relationship to the objectively good and true, for they can only limit the capacity for self-determination. The freedom for excellence, however, the notion of liberty that held sway during the classical and medieval Christian period, is not primarily choice but rather the conditioning of desire so that the achievement of the good becomes first possible and then effortless. This is, for example, the freedom to speak English fluently and creatively, which comes only after a long tutelage to a series of masters and submission to myriad rules and regulations. Or it is the freedom to play basketball fluidly and successfully, responding appropriately to the ever-evolving exigencies of the game, a liberty that comes only after years of ordered discipline. This freedom for excellence is thus positively related to the objectively good and true, for it finds in them its own fulfillment and raison d'être. Thus, Sartre was quite right in seeing God as the principal threat to human flourishing, precisely because Sartre was operating from a typically modern freedom of indifference framework; and Paul was equally right in seeing submission to Christ as the gateway to real liberty, because he was seeing things through the lens of the freedom for excellence. Essential to evangelization is this message of freedom, rightly construed.

The proclamation of the lordship of Jesus Christ risen from the dead is in line with the Irenaean dictum *Gloria Dei homo vivens*, the glory of God is a human being fully alive, and is thus conducive to the deepest humanism. I believe that one of the obstacles to effective evangelization in recent years is a kind of embarrassment, born of the stubbornly modern reading of religion as oppressive. Something that all the false modern humanisms—Enlightenment rationalism, Marxist Communism, European Fascism, militant secularism—have in common is a hatred of religion, more specifically of Christianity. The Enlightenment philosophers saw it as obscurantist and oppressive; Marx thought it was the "opium of the people"; Hitler and his colleagues persecuted it viciously; and contemporary secularists construe it as a block to progress. One of the signal accomplishments of John Paul II was to show, both theoretically and practically, how these *soi-disant* humanisms have actually conduced to a violation of human dignity and freedom, and furthermore to demonstrate how there is no ideology or philosophy in history that is more favorable to the human person than the robust Christianity whose central tenet is the divinization of man. We should go about the humanizing task of declaring the lordship of Jesus with some of John Paul's confidence and panache, and stop pandering to the objections of the failed ideologies of modernity.

To this point, I have placed a great stress on the resurrection and the incarnation. As I bring this section to a close, I want to say a word about the crucifixion, for no account of Christian evangelization would be adequate without a consideration of the cross. Didn't Paul in fact say, "For I decided to know nothing among you except Jesus Christ and him crucified"? The crucified Lord Jesus is, in a sense, a display of the two modes of freedom that we have been describing. In one of his earliest kerygmatic sermons, St. Peter said, "you killed the Author of life" (see Acts 3:15). He could have just as well said "we." It is a commonplace of the Gospels that everyone, in one way or another, contributed to the death of Jesus: Jewish authorities, Romans, Jesus's own followers, the mobs of Jerusalem, and so on. The tragedy is that the ultimate good—God incarnate—appeared, and we responded not with exultation but with murderous violence. This makes plain the full perversity of the freedom of indifference, this terrible capacity to say no, even when presented with that which would bring us greatest life. One of the essential features of evangelical proclamation is an honest naming of sin. Whenever we are tempted to say collectively "I'm OK and you're OK," whenever the culture is drawn toward self-complacency, Christian evangelists need to hold up the cross of Jesus. The crucifixion of the Author of Life is God's judgment on the world and the fullest expression of the divine anger at sin. We should not, by the way, shy away from this thoroughly biblical language, for it is simply another way of speaking of the divine love, God's passionate desire to set things right.

But the cross is also a display of freedom, rightly construed. Freedom of indifference is liberty from external constraint so as to find liberty for self-expression; but the freedom for excellence is liberty from attachments and distractions in order to find liberty for following the will of God. Thomas Aquinas said that the key to happiness, to full human flourishing, is learning to despise what Jesus despised on the cross and to love what he loved on the cross. What Jesus eschewed on the cross were all of those worldly goods—pleasure, wealth, esteem of others, material things—that can distract us from attaching ourselves to the ultimate good. And this gave him the consummate freedom to love the one good worth loving above all others: the will of the Father. Thus, though it is the highest of paradoxes, the image of Jesus pinioned to the cross, in the agonies of death, is a picture of true freedom and richest humanism.

The Indispensability of the Church

To this point in the discussion, an energetic, bright evangelical Protestant might find him or herself in total agreement with the program I have been laying out. Over against a regnant theological liberalism, an evangelical would enthusiastically affirm a robust sense of the resurrection and divinity of the Lord, as well as the liberating and humanizing potential of the good news.

So what is it that makes evangelization—the proclamation of Jesus risen from the dead—distinctively Catholic? The short answer, it seems to me, is the indispensability of the church. In saying that, we right away confront a major cultural prejudice. As I have been implying in various ways, America is a culture very much formed by modernity and Protestantism. One of the marks of that particular intellectual matrix is a preference for the individual and an accompanying suspicion of institutions—evident in both Luther's fierce polemics against the corruption of the church and in the checks-and-balances structure of the modern political state. It is not for nothing that a favorite narrative motif in both the high and popular culture of America is that of the heroic individual facing down the oppressive institution. Thus it is, to say the least, challenging in our cultural context to announce that one's relationship with Jesus Christ is properly and ordinarily mediated by a church, especially one that, today, seems so flawed.

The first point to make is this: the church, on a Catholic reading, is not primarily an institution. Rather, it is the mystical body of Jesus, an organism composed of interconnected and interdependent cells, molecules, and organs. It is the field of force established by the dying and rising of Jesus and the sending of the Holy Spirit, the new way of being that Christ came to establish, the *communio* that imitates and participates in the *communio* of the Trinity. John Henry Newman said that the fundamental principle of Catholicism is the incarnation, God's entry into flesh. The ongoing fleshly presence of Christ down through the ages is the church, a truth suggested in Paul's master metaphor of the body. On a Protestant reading, the church is a collectivity of like-minded people, the banding together for mutual support of those who have been justified, and it is not therefore, in itself, essential for salvation. But the same cannot be said of the church according to Catholic theology. Instead, it is the indispensable means by which one is grafted onto Jesus Christ. Thus, we are not evangelized—and then brought into the church; rather, we are evangelized by and into the church. We are not saved first and then integrated into a church of our choosing; we are saved through the church that is an extension of Christ's power. This Catholic ecclesiology is, if you will, more Aristotelian than Platonic, for it holds that the soul (the grace of Jesus) does not exist in radical separation from the body. Just as one does not know me apart from my body, so one does not know Christ apart from the body of which he is the head. Catholic theology sees this tight link between Jesus and his body signaled in the account of the conversion of St. Paul. When Saul was knocked to the ground while journeying to Damascus to harass the Christian community there, he heard a voice saying, "Saul, Saul, why are you persecuting me?" (Acts 9:4 NABRE).

We can specify this general notion in a number of ways. First, the church is that place where our minds are formed according to Jesus Christ. The French philosopher Pierre Hadot has reminded us that, in the ancient context, philosophy was not so much an academic subject as a form of life, a *bios*. When a student came to Plato's academy, for instance, he was not so much instructed in Platonic theory as introduced into a way of being, which included distinctive patterns of speech, action, and practice. This same assumption undergirds the earliest Christians. When Augustine speaks, in his *Confessions*, of passing from Manichaeism to Platonism and finally to Christianity, he does not mean simply that he entertained a number of different intellectual positions; he implies that his whole life underwent a series of conversions. When the young Gregory Thaumaturgos approached Origen in the hopes of learning the Christian philosophy, the Egyptian master told him, "First you must become our friend; then you must live our life, and finally you will understand our teaching." The clear implication is that the church—which is to say, that place where one lives in Jesus Christ—is necessary for an adequate evangelical knowledge of the Lord.

Now this body, like all complex organisms, is necessarily ordered in a hierarchical way. No animal body would survive for a moment unless it were structured according to something like command and obedience. Were the brain compromised, the entire nervous system, which depends upon it, would collapse; were the heart disabled, the intricate play of cause and effect in the circulatory system would come undone. And the same is true of a political or social organism. If the people were prevented from voting on a regular basis for their representatives, a democratic republic would cease to exist, or if the manager were consistently ignored, the baseball team qua team would come apart. It is the Catholic conviction that Christ himself chose the Twelve, evocative of the re-gathered tribes of Israel, to be the governors and teachers of his church, to be, in a word, the ordering element within the mystical body. In the account of the Sermon on the Mount in Matthew's Gospel, Jesus sits down and teaches the disciples directly and, through them, the crowds; in Luke's rendering of the feeding of the five thousand, similarly, Jesus hands the loaves to the disciples who in turn give them to the people. And it is to the eleven apostles that the risen Jesus gives the command to evangelize the nations. It is clear that the body of Christ is not an amorphous, egalitarian collectivity but rather a structured society, governed and ordered hierarchically. To be fully in Christ's body, therefore, is to be integrated into the complex system of an apostolic *ordo*. And this is why it is insufficient evangelically simply to proclaim Christ without at the same time inviting people to participate in the structured life of the church.

The lifeblood of the ecclesial body, moreover, is what the tradition has termed *grace*, and the ordinary means by which that grace becomes available are the sacraments, visible signs of an invisible power. The divine life of Jesus is always, therefore, either directly or indirectly, mediated through the sacraments. Again, it is not as though one is incorporated into Christ and then chooses to celebrate that incorporation through a number of evocative symbols; rather, that very incorporation (how appropriate the word is) is effected through the bodily signs of the sacraments. John Henry Newman took this objective sacramental efficacy to be one of the guiding principles of the Oxford Movement, and later in his career, he articulated it as one of the nine principles of a healthy Catholicism. Thomas Aquinas consistently relates the sacraments to the concept of law or *ordo*. Just as, in the Old Testament context, one was ordered to God through a variety of cultic, moral, and judicial precepts, so, after the incarnation, one is properly and really related to God through the sacraments by which the divine life is infused.

Now the chief sacrament of the new law is the Eucharist, for though the other sacraments contain the "power" of Christ, the Eucharist contains, in the language of Aquinas, *ipse Christus*, "Christ himself," in person. Under the signs of bread and wine, Jesus becomes really present to us as food and drink, and therefore the Eucharist is what, in John Paul II's phrase, makes the church (*ecclesia de eucharistia*). And this is why the Eucharist is so central to evangelization. This centrality is already stated in the sixth chapter of John's Gospel. After laying out in no uncertain terms the dense reality of his presence in the Eucharist ("my flesh is food indeed and my blood is drink indeed"), Jesus faces the consternation of the crowd ("how can this man give us his flesh to eat?"). When many abandon him because of this "hard saying," he turns somewhat plaintively to the apostles and asks, "Will you also go away?" To which Peter responds, "Lord, to whom shall we go? You have the words of eternal life" (see vv. 51–68) Staying with Jesus, participating in his life—which is the *telos* of evangelization—is closely tied, in short, to the Eucharist. The tight relationship between evangelization and Eucharist also becomes clear in the account of the appearance on the road to Emmaus. As they move away from Jerusalem, which is to say, away from the place of Jesus's cross and resurrection, the two disciples speak of the Lord in an inadequate way. Though they are cognizant of all the relevant facts—he was a prophet mighty in word and deed; he was put to death by the leaders of the people; he embodied the Messianic hopes of the nation; he was reported to be risen from the dead—they did not see the pattern. As Jesus explains the Scripture to them, the facts begin to coalesce into a form ("Did not our hearts burn within us?" [Luke 24:32]), but it is only in the breaking of the bread that they "get" him. They are, in a word, not sufficiently evangelized by the empirical data before them or even by the breaking open of the Scriptures; they are evangelized fully only through the Eucharist. The Eucharist alone provides the hermeneutical lens through which the data of Jesus's life and work can be legitimately read. And finally, enlightened by that vision, they know where to go and what to do. Despite the lateness of the hour and the dangers of the road, they race back to Jerusalem, back to the city of the paschal mystery and become, themselves, evangelizers: "Then they told what had happened on the road, and how he was known to them in the breaking of the bread" (Luke 24:35). Proclamation, interpretation, incorporation, and mission all flow from and return to the Eucharist.

There is one more clarification I would like to make under this rubric of the indispensability of the church to the evangelical project. The Catholic Church is a kind of treasure house of beautiful things, for it is a deep Catholic conviction that God is accessed through beauty. One of the most powerful literary accounts of conversion is Evelyn Waugh's masterpiece *Brideshead Revisited*. Waugh, playing a bit with Paul's metaphors of *bride* and *headship*, uses the great manor house Brideshead as a symbol of Christ's body, the church. The narrator of the story, Charles Ryder, whose conversion is the *telos* of the entire novel, is first attracted by the extraordinary beauty of Brideshead: "To walk through its corridors and rooms," he says, "was an aesthetic education." So it is to walk through the artistic and architectural and literary traditions of the Catholic Church. Meditating upon the sermons of John Chrysostom, the mosaics at Ravenna, *The Confessions* of Augustine, Giotto's Arena Chapel, Dante's *Commedia*, Bonaventure's *Itinerarium*, Aquinas's "*Pange Lingua*," the cathedral of Chartres, Michelangelo's Sistine Ceiling and Last Judgment, Teresa of Avila's *Interior Castle*, John of the Cross's *Ascent of Mount Carmel*, Bernini's Colonnade and Baldachino at St. Peter's, Newman's *Parochial and Plain Sermons*, Thomas Merton's *Seven Storey Mountain*, and the *Catholic Worker* columns of Dorothy Day—to take all of that in is to have an aesthetic education that conduces toward a contemplation of the Beauty from which these beautiful things come and to which they point. It is a deeply Catholic conviction that we are evangelized truly only in relation to the beautiful—and therefore in relation to the church.

Conclusion

I'll conclude with a few simple reflections on the communication between the gospel and the culture. From the time of Schleiermacher on, the dominant method employed by theological liberalism has been, to use Paul Tillich's term, "correlational." On this reading, the task of the theologian or evangelist is to analyze the present cultural situation as a set of questions and then to place those interrogations in correlation to the "answers" that emerge from the Bible and the theological tradition. The great virtue of this approach, it seems, is its evenhandedness and openness, its willingness to take into consideration not only the content of revelation but also the legitimate concerns and longings of the culture to be evangelized. Karl Barth, one of the most trenchant critics of Schleiermacher's style of theologizing, made the incisive observation that the method of correlation would work perfectly well in paradise or in heaven but not in the actual world. This is the case because, in those blessed states, we would be able to formulate the right questions, those that do indeed correspond to the answers that God wants to give. But in our fallen condition, we tend, Barth thought, to pose precisely the wrong kinds of questions and hence to interpret the answers provided by revelation in a distorted way. Barth's greatest Catholic disciple, Hans Urs von Balthasar, commented that the method of correlation—best exemplified in Catholic circles by Karl Rahner—involves the positioning of theological answers by existential questions. Just as the questions posed by Socrates clearly govern and orient the conversation within the Platonic dialogues, so, on correlationalist grounds, the questions emerging from contemporary culture condition and interpret the answers of the Bible. But this, for Balthasar, is to get things backward, for it is precisely the novelty and surprise of revelation that ought to teach the culture to ask new questions.

Contemporary theologian Bruce Marshall has presented one of the most thoroughgoing criticisms of the correlationalist method in his book *Trinity and Truth*.[6] Marshall takes as a point of departure the maximalist claims made about Jesus Christ in the first chapter of the letter to the Colossians: "He [Christ] is the image of the invisible God . . . for in him all things were created, in heaven and on earth, visible and invisible . . . all things were created through him and for him. He is before all things, and in him all things hold together" (Col. 1:15–17). This extraordinary text, which finds a clear echo in the prologue to John's Gospel, insinuates that Jesus Christ is himself the ordering and creating principle that stands behind all of finite reality. As such, Marshall argues, it is incoherent to assume, as correlationalists must, that there is a secular, philosophical, or cultural realm that stands outside of or over against Christ and to which his revelation must be coordinated. What we call the "natural" or the "secular" is in fact already his, and the evangelical task is therefore not so much to correlate as to render explicit what is implicit. In a word, the Christ presented in the first chapter of Colossians can never be positioned by something outside of himself; rather, he always has ontological and epistemic priority.

In his *Essay on the Development of Christian Doctrine*, John Henry Newman identified one of the signs of a healthy Christianity as "the power of assimilation."[7] By this he meant the church's capacity to take in whatever elements of a given culture are compatible with the truth of the gospel and, concomitantly, the power to resist those influences that are inimical to that truth. A properly functioning church is like a robust organism that can draw into itself what it can and throw off what it must. In light of the critiques outlined above, I would suggest that assimilation is a far better model for evangelization than correlation. An assimilationist theologian would take with utter seriousness the questions, concerns, achievements, and preoccupations of the surrounding culture, but he or she would never allow those elements to drive the conversation or to position the data of revelation. Rather, he or she would endeavor to draw the culture, as far as possible, into the world opened up by the gospel, adapting and critiquing appropriately.

It is my conviction that much of the evangelization work that has been done since the Second Vatican Council has been correlationalist in style. I might suggest that it is high time to switch to an assimilationist model so that the resurrection and divinity of Jesus, the humanism implicit in the incarnation, and participation in the mystical body of the church might always be the controlling and positioning elements in our preaching, teaching, and dialogue with culture.

14

✠

From Correlation
to Assimilation

A New Model for the
Church-Culture Dialogue

All my life I've heard spirited advocacy for the dialogue between the church
and the wider culture, but this call has come almost exclusively from the
church and not from the culture. Putting the church and the world in conversation has tended to mean that Catholicism must make itself intelligible
to politicians, artists, scientists, and social theorists precisely by utilizing the
language and conceptual forms of secular politics, art, science, and social
theory. Rarely if ever have I heard of representatives of the culture eager to
submit their manner of thinking and behavior to the discipline of the church
or to make themselves intelligible to religious people. It is this one-way quality of the conversation that is, I submit to you, problematic. John Milbank,
one of the most incisive ecclesial commentators on the scene today, has said
that the pathos of modern theology is its false humility, by which he means
its Schleiermacherian tendency to seek the favor of its cultured despisers by
mimicking their styles of thought and expression.[1] As Karl Barth indicated

some fifty years ago, the sophisticated critics of Christianity have proven remarkably unresponsive to the overtures of Schleiermacher and his numerous
disciples.[2] What I have called "beige Catholicism," a Catholicism that is too
culturally accommodating, excessively apologetic, shifting and unsure in its
identity, is the fruit of this false humility and this largely one-way conversation.[3]

What I would like to do in the course of this chapter is, first, to explore
more fully the theoretical roots of beige Catholicism in typically modern
experiential, expressivist, and correlational models of theology and, next, to
propose, with the help of John Henry Newman, an assimilationist approach
to the church-culture dialogue. Then, in the light of this method, I would like
to show how an assimilating church might respond to three positive and three
negative features of the American political culture.

Beige Catholicism

The Christian church's willingness to engage the secular culture finds its
origins in Paul's address to Greek intellectuals on the Areopagus in Athens
sometime in the 50s of the first century, and in Justin Martyr's decision, in
the mid-second century, to place Christian "philosophy" in conversation with
the regnant Platonism of the time. At its best, Christianity has resisted the
temptation to ask, with Tertullian, "What has Athens to do with Jerusalem?"
or to speak, with Martin Luther, of "that whore reason." No Christian thinker
better exemplified the practice of ecclesial-cultural conversation than Thomas
Aquinas, who affected a still stunning adaptation of Aristotelian language to
evangelical purposes. But during the modern period, Christian theologians
began to engage the culture in a new and distinctive manner, allowing themselves to be positioned by the concerns and demands of the secular world. It is
to this *way* of establishing the rapport between gospel and culture that I object.

What was its provenance? Given the enormously negative impact of the
wars of religion that had devastated post-Reformation Europe, many modern thinkers began to speculate about a form of religiosity that was, in its
universality, both rational and nonviolent. It was, they concluded, the very
particularity of positive religion and its authoritative interpretation that caused
such trouble. Thus, for example, Catholics claimed that the Eucharist involves the real presence of the Lord, whereas most Protestants claimed that
it is an evocative symbol—and since there was no way, finally, to adjudicate
the dispute, violence was the only recourse. (It is fascinating, by the way, to
read many of the Western reactions to the events of September 11 and to see
these same modern concerns about revealed religion and violence coming

to the fore.) And so we see in Descartes, Spinoza, Locke, Kant, Jefferson, Hegel, and Emerson, to name just a few, the modern desire to set aside the peculiarities of positive religion and embrace a universal religion of reason. Thomas Jefferson literally taking a straight razor to the pages of the New Testament, endeavoring to extricate from it all those passages that smack of the supernatural, is a particularly apt illustration of the process.

But the clearest exemplar of the modern religious style was, as we've suggested, Friedrich Schleiermacher, the father of modern liberal Protestantism. Religion, for Schleiermacher, is not ethics or metaphysics or aesthetics, or even revelation, but rather a mysticism grounded in what he called "the feeling of absolute dependency."[4] This feeling, which is in principle open to all, provides the criterion by which the elements of positive religion—dogma, doctrine, liturgy, practice—can and should be judged. Along more or less Cartesian lines, Schleiermacher suggests that the objective and particular be brought before the bar of the subjective and universal for adjudication: experience measures doctrine, rather than the inverse. The radicality and thoroughness of Schleiermacher's revolution can be seen in his marginalization of the doctrine of the Trinity to an appendix of his magnum opus, the *Glaubenslehre*. The dogma that generations of Christian theologians took to be central to the faith is not discussed in the body of Schleiermacher's work, since its contents did not correspond, he thought, in any direct way to the feeling of absolute dependency. Schleiermacher's fondest hope was that this experience-based and purified version of Christianity would prove attractive, both intellectually and morally, to the enlightened critics of classical religion.

The mainstream of modern theological liberalism has raced down the Schleiermacher autobahn. Thus Rudolf Otto grounds authentic religion in our sense of the *mysterium tremendum et fascinans*; Paul Tillich roots it in "ultimate concern"; Karl Rahner sees it in the experience of standing in the presence of "absolute mystery"; and David Tracy anchors it in certain "limit experiences" that both challenge and provoke us.[5] In all these cases, some sort of universal religious sensibility becomes the norm for reading and judging the tradition of revelation. In much of liberalism, this basic move is broadened out so as to include the two categories of "the world" or "the situation" on the one hand and "revelation" on the other. And thus the fundamental project becomes the effecting of a correlation (Tillich's term) between the two realms.

Now problems with this method abound, but I will draw attention to what I consider its fundamental flaw: in the measure that theological liberalism allows revelation to be positioned by something outside of itself, it runs counter to the structuring logic of the New Testament.[6] In Colossians 1, we find this breathtakingly maximalist claim about Jesus Christ: "In him all things were created, in heaven and on earth, visible and invisible . . . all things were created through him and for him. He is before all things, and in him all things hold together" (Col. 1:16–17). And in the prologue to the Johannine Gospel, we hear that the Logos made flesh in Jesus Christ is that through which all things are made, that apart from him, nothing comes to be. But these claims imply that Jesus Christ is the reasonability that positions, explains, and situates everything within finite creation. Nature, humanity, politics, art, science, culture, the planets and stars, things visible and invisible—all of it comes from him and centers on him. But this means, in turn, that Jesus cannot be positioned or explained from any point of vantage external to him. Both Karl Barth and Hans Urs von Balthasar complained that the principle problem with modern theology is that it permits Christ to be situated under the more general heading of "religion" or "religious experience," whereas such a move is directly repugnant to the incarnational logic of Colossians and the prologue to John. For those who navigate the Schleiermacher autobahn, experience becomes the measure of Christ, but the Jesus of Colossians and the Gospel of John must be the measure of experience—as he is of everything else.[7] A similar difficulty emerges when we analyze the various correlational methods of contemporary theological liberalism. In Tillich's version for instance, culture, the situation, and experience raise the questions to which the theologian attempts to coordinate the "answers" of the biblical tradition. But as any reader of the Platonic dialogues realizes, the one who poses the questions always determines the flow and nature of the conversation. More to it, the questioner provides the context in which the answer qua answer appears. Once again, this correlational style requires that a dimension of finite reality positions the Logos by which and for which the whole of finite reality is made. It is none other than this dominance of the environing culture over revelation that produces beige Catholicism.

Now does this critique of modern correlationalism and experientialism in theology mean that the Christian church is doomed to a sectarian retreat from dialogue with the contemporary culture? The nearly universal tendency to answer that question affirmatively is testament to the pervasive influence of the liberal model. In point of fact, as we saw earlier, numerous Christian thinkers—Paul, Justin, Origen, Augustine, and Aquinas, to name just a few— conversed very creatively with the wider society, but they did so in accord with the Christocentric logic of revelation and not in accord with liberal assumptions. I would like to explicate the nature of this approach more thoroughly by drawing attention to the thought of John Henry Newman, a theologian who was, simultaneously, deeply invested in the dialogue with the culture of his time and, in his own words, a lifelong opponent of "the spirit of liberalism in religion."[8] In his *Essay on the Development of Christian Doctrine*,

Newman argued that one of the marks of a healthy and properly developing church is "the power of assimilation," that is to say, its ability to adapt to its environment, taking in what it can and resisting what it must.[9] A robust organism draws into itself and adapts to its purposes certain features of its world, and it throws off other elements that would compromise or threaten its essential structure. Newman observes shrewdly that an unhealthy animal will, soon enough, be itself assimilated by the stronger animals around it.

In light of these observations, might I suggest a theological relationship to the culture that is assimilationist rather than correlationist? The church ought to reach out to the world but never allow the world (as the postconciliar slogan had it) to set the agenda for the church. The body of Christ ought to move confidently within the environment around it, adapting to itself whatever is good, true, and beautiful and expelling whatever is alien to its form of life, using all the time its own organic structure as criterion and norm. Something I'd like especially to stress is this: a beige, culturally accommodating Catholicism is incapable of both proper resistance to and proper absorption of the wider world. The willingness of the Vatican II fathers to turn to modern society in a missionary spirit was born of their serene confidence in the essential doctrinal and moral integrity of the church. In his remarks on the right interpretation of Vatican II, Benedict XVI observed that the purpose of the council was not to make the church more like the world but rather to make the world more like the church. Accordingly, he interprets John XXIII's famous trope of the opening of the windows as expressive of the church's desire to let the wisdom, truth, and spiritual vitality of the church out, for the sake of transforming the society. Balthasar meant much the same when he spoke in the 1950s of "razing the bastions" of a church still crouching too defensively behind its own walls. To be sure, the Vatican II fathers called for and implemented changes in the church, but these changes had a missionary and evangelical purpose; they were meant to render the church more capable of drawing the *logoi* of the world into the Logos of Jesus Christ, to assimilate rather than correlate. Sadly, after the council, this turning toward the modern society was interpreted, in far too many quarters, as a turning into modern society, assimilation devolving into accommodation. What I have called beige Catholicism is the result of this hermeneutical mistake.

The Assimilating Church and the American Culture: The Negative Dimension

What I would like to do in this next section is to engage in a reading of our American culture from the standpoint of the assimilating church, showing

how the community gathered around Jesus Christ ought to relate to the positive and negative elements within that culture. I am consciously turning away
from the dominant liberal model of analyzing "the situation" in order to put
it into correlation with the "answers" coming from the tradition; instead, I
will endeavor to show precisely why the church must resist certain features
of the culture and precisely how it can adapt others to itself.

Let us turn first to the relatively negative side of the ledger. There is, within
the American political culture, a strong strain of Hobbesianism, mediated
to it largely by John Locke by way of Thomas Jefferson. Thomas Hobbes's
political philosophy is intelligible only against the background of certain
shifts in metaphysics and epistemology at the dawn of the modern period.
Under the influence of the nominalism of William of Occam and the univocal
conception of being formulated by Duns Scotus, early modern thinkers tended
to see the universe as composed of isolated individuals, particles in motion.[10]
This conception had a clear social implication. Whereas for Thomas Aquinas
the human being is by nature a political animal, that is to say, connected to
everyone else in the civil society by ontological and not merely conventional
bonds, for Thomas Hobbes the human is by nature nonpolitical, self-interested,
moved by basic passions for self-preservation. This is why Hobbes's state of
nature is the state of war, productive of a life that is "solitary, nasty, brutish,
and short." Political organization, on Hobbes's reading, comes about through
an artificially contrived social contract in which people reluctantly surrender
some of their rights in order to maintain some modicum of peace. Because of
this reductive understanding of government, the ethical and spiritual purpose
of politics is set aside. The purpose of the state is the adjudication of disputes
among the citizens and, ultimately, the protection of each against the violent
attacks of others. In the classical context, the raison d'être of government was
the encouragement of moral excellence, whereas in the Hobbesian framework,
it is the maintenance of order.

In his political philosophy, John Locke softened and modified Hobbes's
social contract theory but kept its most fundamental features, including and
especially the artificiality of the political arrangement and the severe trunca-
tion of the sense of the common good. Jefferson gives voice to the Hobbes-
Locke perspective when he speaks in the Declaration of Independence of
the right to pursue happiness as one sees fit. Most Western philosophers,
from the classical period through the high Middle Ages, considered the
determination of the objective nature of happiness the central philosophical question, and they furthermore held that the purpose of politics is to
conduce, at least to some degree, to the attainment of happiness. In accord with his distinctively modern assumptions, Jefferson relativizes and

subjectivizes the meaning of happiness and effectively dissociates it from the work of government.

Within the confines of this brief chapter, I can but gesture toward some of the negative consequences of this fundamentally Hobbesian conception of politics. First, we notice the individualism and litigiousness of our society. When the common good remains unexplored and unarticulated, and when the government's purpose is reduced to that of the adjudication of disputes, we do tend to lose our corporate social identity and a shared sense of moral direction. Further, when we no longer understand ourselves to be ontological siblings, connected to one another by the deepest metaphysical bonds, we do indeed devolve into a collectivity of individuals clamoring for rights and special prerogatives. The Hobbesianism of our society can be seen as well, as Robert Kraynak points out, in the flattening and coarsening of our popular culture.[11] When self-expression becomes the supreme value, aesthetic standards are either overlooked or aggressively marginalized. But the Hobbesian influence shows itself perhaps most tragically in the government's unwillingness to intervene firmly when clear moral values are under attack in the society. Two decisions of the United States Supreme Court are especially illuminating in this regard. In *Roe v. Wade*, the court famously found a right to privacy buried in the provisions of the Constitution and on that basis allowed for practically unlimited access to abortion throughout the United States. But the court's resolution of the matter of *Casey v. Planned Parenthood* is even more sobering and disturbing. Expanding on the principle of privacy, the justices decided that it belongs to the very nature of individual liberty to determine the meaning of one's own life, indeed the meaning of existence and the universe![12] It would be hard to imagine a more radical expression of Hobbesian relativism and individualism.

Another negative feature of the American culture—with certain roots in Hobbes—is our typically modern understanding of freedom as choice. The Dominican scholar Servais Pinckaers has drawn a simple but illuminating distinction between this conception of liberty and the idea of freedom that held sway in the classical and Christian periods. The former he calls "the freedom of indifference" and the latter "the freedom for excellence."[13] On the modern reading, freedom is the capacity to hover above the yes and the no and to make a determination in one direction or the other, without any coercion either interior or exterior. In this context, law, discipline, and virtue are in an extremely tensive relationship with freedom, since they represent limitation on the range of choice. Now freedom for excellence is not primarily independent choice but rather the disciplining of desire so as to make the achievement of the good first possible and then effortless. A person becomes a free speaker of the English language not so much by cultivating his power to choose but rather by submitting himself to a whole series of rules, disciplines, and masters. When those directives are sufficiently internalized, that person becomes capable of expressing in English whatever he wants: he becomes free in his speech. Or a person emerges as a free player of golf not in the measure that she swings the club according to her personal whim but inasmuch as she submits herself to a strict and densely objective nexus of rules, practices, directives, and restrictions. In this process, she becomes capable of responding well and creatively to the ever-shifting demands of the game of golf. Given this notion of freedom, liberty is by no means opposed to the law but rather finds itself in relation to the law. For the advocates of the freedom for excellence, self-expression is far less important than the ordering of the self in the direction of the good. John Paul II was one of the most eloquent defenders of freedom in the second half of the twentieth century, but throughout his pontificate, he insisted upon the correlation between liberty and truth.[14] On a freedom of indifference reading, this juxtaposition is puzzling at best; but on a freedom for excellence interpretation, it is coherent. There is probably no word that stirs the American heart more than *freedom*, no value that is more prized than liberty. But the mainstream of American culture interprets that term along modern lines, construing it as spontaneous personal choice and self-determination. This is, of course, repugnant to a biblical tradition that identifies the seizing of the prerogative to determine the nature of good and evil for oneself as the originating sin. One might say that the transition from the freedom for excellence to the freedom of indifference is tantamount to the fall.

A third negative feature of the American culture that must be resisted by the assimilating church is the privatization of religion. Stanley Hauerwas has commented that the modern political states forged with religion a sort of peace treaty, the central stipulation of which was that the state would tolerate religious practice as long as it remained essentially a private matter.[15] Richard John Neuhaus's "naked public square," that is to say, a political arena from which religious ideas and values have been aggressively excluded, is the fruit of this privatization. But authentic Christianity can never be privatized, precisely because it speaks of the creator God who grounds and rules all things. For biblical people, God is not one being among many—as in pagan, Deist, or nominalist conceptions—but rather the creator and ground of all finite things, *ipsum esse subsistens* rather than *ens summum*, in the language of Thomas Aquinas. But this means that all areas of life—the public and the private, the social and the individual, the natural and the conventional—belong to God and are related to God, much as the elements that make up the rose window are connected to the center. In point of fact, a thoroughly secular realm, an arena of life untouched by the sacred, is made possible only by an unbiblical reading of God. Accordingly, the church cannot be one element among many within the society, a collectivity of persons blandly cultivating a private set of convictions; instead, it should be that institution that names the ways that God impinges on every aspect of existence and then encourages participation in the work of God. To be sure, the Christian church enters into these realms nonviolently and using only the power of persuasion—but it certainly doesn't absent itself from them in a stance of false humility.

In regard to these three negative features—Hobbesian individualism, a modern conception of freedom as choice, and the privatization of religion—a robust church should assume the stance that Augustine assumed vis-à-vis the corrupt society of ancient Rome, namely, one of honest and unambiguous opposition. Augustine attempted, in the *City of God*, neither correlation with nor accommodation to what he took to be the ersatz justice and peace of the Roman Empire. Instead, he named the sins of Roman social order and proposed an alternative, what he called the *civitas Dei*, an order predicated upon the worship of the true God.[16] However, to remain within a purely reactive framework would be simplistic and counterproductive, for the assimilating church is also eager to take in and take up what it can from the culture. It is to a consideration of this task that we now turn.

The Assimilating Church: The Positive Dimension

Thomas Aquinas is today probably the most revered and authoritative voice within the Catholic intellectual tradition. It is therefore easy to forget that, in his own time, he was anything but universally admired. In fact, his innovative synthesis of Aristotelian metaphysics and biblical revelation inspired a number of vocal opponents, one of whom famously commented that Thomas was diluting the wine of the gospel with the water of a pagan philosopher. To this critique, Thomas deftly responded, "No, rather I am transforming water into wine." That retort of Aquinas beautifully expresses what Newman meant by the church's assimilation of positive features of its environment: it does not simply absorb them; it elevates and perfects them, in accord with the great Catholic principle *gratia supponit et perfecit naturam*. As I've already hinted at, one problem with a beige Catholicism is that it is incapable of defending itself against truly hostile features of the wider culture, but a second and perhaps even more dangerous problem is that it remains incapable of appropriately transfiguring the positive dimensions of that same culture.

A first, particularly good example of this process of elevating assimilation is the manner in which John Paul II embraced the human rights tradition of the Western democracies, especially the United States, becoming by the end of the twentieth century its most passionate advocate on the world stage. Now at first blush this seems odd, given the rather harsh criticism of the Hobbes-Locke-Jefferson articulation of human rights that was offered in the previous section. A distinction is in order. For the modern political tradition, human rights flow ultimately from desire. Hobbes felt that we have a right to life and the avoidance of violent death, precisely because those are the things that we most passionately, indeed inevitably, want. Locke expressed the same idea with admirable laconicism: we have a right to those things that we cannot not desire, namely, life and its essential supports of liberty and property. Jefferson took in this Lockean understanding, only replacing property with the pursuit of happiness.

But John Paul II understood human rights within a different framework. As a biblical person, he saw them as grounded not so much in the power of subjective desire as in the facts of creation and redemption. Freely created by God and mercifully redeemed by Jesus Christ, every individual, no matter the background, education, skill level, ethnic origin, and so on, is a subject of inviolable dignity and worth. And from this identity flow rights and a claim to justice. For Thomas Aquinas, whom John Paul follows here carefully, justice is the act of rendering to each what is due, and what is due to each person is respect, love, protection, freedom, and the basic necessities of life. Thus, when John Paul spoke glowingly and sincerely of the human-rights tradition in our country, he was claiming ideas that were still too redolent of Hobbes and elevating them into a new, evangelical framework. He was creatively assimilating a key feature of the secular culture into the organic life of the church.

A second most important positive dimension of our political culture is our experiment in civilized pluralism. When John Paul II came to Chicago in 1978, he celebrated Mass on the lakefront, preaching to a typically American crowd drawn from numerous races, backgrounds, and religious persuasions. In the course of his homily, he commented positively on the American national motto *e pluribus unum*, observing that it is an echo of the church's call to draw the many nations of the world into unity around Christ. The biblical theologian N. T. Wright has said that Jesus's proclamation of the kingdom of God was in continuity with the ancient hope that the tribes of Israel would one day be gathered and that through a renewed Israel, the tribes of the world would be gathered into unity around the right worship of God.[17] He further argued that the church understands itself, in accord with Paul's musings in Romans 9–11, to be the new Israel, which is to say, the instrument through which God has chosen to unite the myriad languages, peoples, and cultures of the world into one body of interdependent cells, molecules, and organs. What John Paul was recognizing was the manner in which the American motto expressed a kind of participation in and anticipation of this full eschatological drawing of the many into one. And what he implied, therefore, is that an assimilation of the American political practice of ordered unity in diversity would be a desideratum.

But what precisely is the nature of this practice? John Courtney Murray argued throughout his career that the separation of church and state and the granting of full religious liberty should be construed as "articles of peace," that is to say, ways of fostering civil conversation and practical cooperation among those who entertain varying religious and philosophical perspectives.[18] Neither should be read as religious indifferentism or as an invitation to the privatization of the faith and the stripping bare of the public square. Rather, they are the means by which those who disagree most radically can nevertheless find a sort of practical unity. And in this, the articles of peace are grounded in the instincts of the natural law, which are, on Aquinas's own reading, a participation in the fullness of the eternal law that was made manifest in revelation. Perhaps this is why the fathers of Vatican II were willing, in *Dignitatis humanae*, to "baptize" the distinctively modern practice of separating church and state and recognizing religious liberty as a fundamental right. And perhaps this is why both Murray and John Paul II were willing to appreciate *e pluribus unum* as a real though imperfect echo of the church's own voice.

I would like to indicate a link between Murray's articulation of American liberalism and that of Jeffrey Stout. In his *Democracy and Tradition*, Stout contends that a healthy, American-style pluralism is not ideologically opposed to the presence of religion in the public conversation. Rather, it is, as Murray suggested, simply a means of adjudicating disputes in a civil manner among people with radically different conceptions of the whole.[19] Such nonideological liberalism is not opposed to the respectful and thoughtful injection of religious convictions into political discourse. As prime examples of this style of religious speech in the public square, Stout offers the second inaugural address of Abraham Lincoln and the "I Have a Dream" speech of Martin Luther King Jr.[20] Addressing the nation in a political discourse as the Civil War was coming to a close, Lincoln spoke in the cadences of an Old Testament prophet, using explicitly biblical language and referencing the punishment, providence, and mercy of God. And King, speaking in a public forum on an issue of pressing political significance (and standing on the steps of the Lincoln Memorial), drew massively on the moral and spiritual heritage of his Christian tradition. Neither Lincoln nor King should be read as blurring the distinction between church and state or as attempting to impose a sectarian vision on the nation. Rather, each creatively and nonaggressively introduced his most deeply felt religious convictions into the public forum. One could argue that Mario Cuomo's famous distinction between personal conviction and public performance represents a ham-handed resolution of what Lincoln and King handled so deftly. In fact, Cuomo's sharp dichotomization seems more in line with the ideological brand of liberalism urged by John Rawls or Jürgen Habermas, whereby religion as such must be excluded from properly public forms of political speech. It seems to me that kind of American pluralism advocated by Murray and Stout is what the church can and should assimilate to itself.

A third positive element in the American political culture is the idea of a limited government carefully structured through a system of checks and balances. G. K. Chesterton commented that the single greatest contribution of Christianity to the West was the doctrine of original sin: the deep conviction that there is something wrong with us at a level so elemental that we cannot, even in principle, fix it on our own. Both classical and modern philosophy come together in advocating a version of human perfectibility. Plato and Aristotle thought that we could reach full flourishing through growth in knowledge and virtue, and Marx and Hegel thought that we could achieve the same end through institutional change and social progress. Against both stands biblical Christianity. A constant theme of the Scriptures is that, left to their own devices, human beings tend to go bad. Even the heroes of the Bible—Abraham, Jacob, Moses, Isaiah, Elijah—are riven with flaws and stand constantly in need of divine grace. Moreover, there is no literature anywhere in the world that is so consistently critical of government and governors than is the Bible. When the people of Israel ask for a king, the prophet Samuel warns them, "These will be the ways of the king who will reign over you: he will take your sons and appoint them to his chariots and to be his horsemen, and to run before his chariots. . . . He will take your daughters to be perfumers and cooks and bakers. He will take the best of your fields and vineyards and olive orchards and give them to his servants. . . . He will take the tenth of your flocks, and you shall be his slaves" (1 Sam. 8:11–17). How perennial sounds that description; how it seems to flow from today's headlines! When the people persist in asking for kings so that they might be like the other nations, Yahweh proceeds to give them, beginning with Saul, a line of some of the most dysfunctional, stupid, murderous, and idolatrous leaders in human history. Even David, the best of the Israelite kings, is an adulterer and a murderer. It is as though Yahweh were saying, "I warned you about these kings!"

Men and women formed by these biblical stories and by the doctrine of original sin will be profoundly skeptical of government and its officers, and they will embody their suspicion institutionally in a number of ways. Thus our founders determined that political leaders would be subject regularly to the scrutiny of the electorate and that they would, even while exercising power, be watched, checked, and questioned by many others, both inside and outside the government. Congress watches the president, and the president checks Congress; the judiciary watches both of them, and appointments to the judiciary flow from Congress and the president. And everyone is critiqued by a skeptical and free press, which is, in turn, disciplined through the dynamics of the market. This is a system born of the experience of being tyrannized, and it is one with which Samuel the prophet would be rather sympathetic.

But even more fundamentally, the idea of a limited government is grounded in the biblical sense that law and justice do not flow finally from the government but from God. That law and political institutions are "under God" was a conviction of both the emancipation movement in the nineteenth century and the civil rights movement of the twentieth. Martin Luther King Jr. could write his letter from the Birmingham City Jail, urging civil disobedience, precisely because he knew that unjust laws and cruel social practices can and should be challenged through appeal to an authority higher than the government. Interestingly, King, in that very letter, appealed to Thomas Aquinas, who taught the legitimacy of resistance to tyrants and to unjust law.[21] Thomas's permission of civil disobedience was rooted in his understanding of positive law as a declension of the natural law, which is itself a declension of the eternal law, which is identical to the divine mind. In the final analysis, the simplest traffic regulation, if just and good, is expressive of God's providential care for his world, and the most respected and venerable social practice, if unjust, runs counter to God's purposes. The great Catholic tradition knows that when the connection between the positive law and the natural law is severed, totalitarianism, of either the left or right, follows. Therefore, this rich American instinct that government should be limited and disciplined both from without and from within is something that the church can very much assimilate to itself and adapt to its purposes.

Conclusion

As I suggested at the outset, the question is not *whether* the church ought to engage in a dialogue with the wider culture but rather *how*. To deny the legitimacy of that conversation altogether is to revert into sectarianism, and as Henri de Lubac reminded us long ago, the church of Jesus Christ can never be a sect. Even when it consisted entirely of Mary and John at the foot of the cross, it was universal in form and purpose. I have tried to argue that the Schleiermacherian style of interfacing with the culture—massively influential for the past two hundred years—is both practically ineffective and theologically questionable. And I have proposed the model of an assimilating church that is neither defensive nor acquiescent, capable of both holding off what it must and taking in what it can.

This approach, I hold, mimics the style of the greatest theologians of culture in the Catholic tradition—Origen, Augustine, Aquinas, Newman, Balthasar—and is congruent with the style and substance of the Vatican II documents. St. Paul told us that in Christ's light we should test every spirit, rejecting what is bad and retaining what is good; he also instructed us to bring every thought captive to Christ. The method that I've advocated honors those Pauline directives.

15

━━━━━✠━━━━━

To Evangelize the Culture

What does it mean to evangelize? I submit that to evangelize is to announce the good news (*euangelion*) that Jesus Christ is risen from the dead. The first evangelists—Peter, Paul, James, Philip—had comparatively little to say about the teachings and actions of Jesus, but they couldn't stop talking about his resurrection from the dead. So insistent on this theme was St. Paul that his sophisticated audience on the Areopagus in Athens thought he was declaring a new god called *anastasis* (resurrection). Now the resurrection carries with it many implications, but the most significant of its ramifications is its confirmation of Jesus's staggering claims in regard to his own person. Despite many superficial suggestions to the contrary in both the wider culture and the subculture of the theological academy, Jesus did not claim to be simply one religious figure among many, not one more in a long line of prophets or "symbols of God."

The Jesus portrayed in the Gospels consistently spoke and acted in the very person of Yahweh, the God of Israel. To his disciples he said, "Whoever loves father or mother more than me is not worthy of me, and whoever loves son or daughter more than me is not worthy of me" (Matt. 10:37 NABRE). One could easily enough imagine a spiritual teacher saying that his followers should love God more than the highest goods in this world—but himself? To the paralyzed man, Jesus said, "Child, your sins are forgiven" (Mark 2:5).

Again, we could certainly imagine a spiritual teacher telling people to forgive those who had harmed them, but who is this man who arrogates to himself the prerogative of actively forgiving the sins of someone's entire life? As the bystanders understandably observe, "Why does this man speak thus? It is blasphemy! Who can forgive sins but God alone?" (Mark 2:7). Defending his disciples against the charge of picking grain on the Sabbath, Jesus reminds his interlocutors that priests serving in the temple can, under certain circumstances, violate the Sabbath and still remain innocent; then he adds with breathtaking laconicism, "I tell you, something greater than the temple is here" (Matt. 12:6). The Jerusalem temple was, for first-century Jews, the dwelling place of Yahweh on earth and hence the most sacred place imaginable. The only one who could reasonably claim to be "greater" than the temple would be the one who was worshiped in the temple. In a number of places in the Sermon on the Mount, Jesus states, "You have heard it said . . . but I say . . ." This almost casual dismissal of the Torah, the revelation given by Yahweh to Moses himself and hence the court of final appeal to any pious Jew, would have overwhelmed any first-century Jew. Once more, the only one who could legitimately overrule the Torah with such insouciance would be the one who was himself the author of the Torah.

I have purposely chosen passages exclusively from the Synoptic Gospels in order to hold off the claim that the divinity of Jesus is affirmed only in the much later Johannine Gospel. In point of fact, John expresses explicitly and directly—"The Word became flesh," "I and the Father are one," "He who sees me sees the Father," and so on—the same truth that the Synoptics stated more implicitly and according to a different symbolic system.

As C. S. Lewis and others have noted, these extraordinary claims could be explained as expressions of Jesus's madness or religious megalomania; obviously, many who claim their own divinity can be found, even today, in hospitals for the mentally ill. And though political considerations were undoubtedly at play, the principal reason Jesus was put to death was precisely his blasphemous identification with the God of Israel. The one over whose cross was placed a sign declaring him the King of the Jews was being presented as a pathetically deluded character.

But all such explanations evanesce before the event of the resurrection, Jesus's return from death as the "first fruits" of those who had fallen asleep. The first Christians came to understand this mighty act of God as the ratification of Jesus's stunning claim to be Yahweh moving among his people. And this is why they called him *Kyrios* (Lord), a Greek rendering of the Hebrew *Adonai*, the term used to refer to the Holy One whose proper name, YHWH, could not and should not be pronounced. *Iesous Kyrios* (Jesus is Lord), a phrase often on the lips and under the pens of the first evangelists, is one of the pithiest and most evocative kerygmatic formulas of the early church. To be sure, *Kyrios* had a Roman as well as a Hebrew overtone, for a watchword of that time and place was *Kaiser Kyrios* (Caesar is Lord), a declaration of one's ultimate political and cultural allegiance. The edgy, subversive, dangerous quality of announcing the lordship of Jesus explains why many of the first Christians—Peter and Paul most famously—spent a fair amount of time in jail and were eventually put to death. If I might conjoin the Hebrew and the Roman senses of the kerygmatic declaration, the first evangelists were insisting that Jesus of Nazareth is God and hence the figure to whom final allegiance is due in the political, cultural, and religious spheres. Everything, they were saying, belongs to him; everything comes from him, leads to him, and finds its fulfillment in him. Listen to the extravagant language used by Paul in Colossians: "He [Christ] is the image of the invisible God, the firstborn of all creation. For in him were created all things in heaven and on earth, the visible and the invisible. . . . He is before all things, and in him all things hold together" (Col. 1:15–17 NABRE). We find much the same idea in Philippians: "Because of this, God greatly exalted him and bestowed on him the name that is above every name, that at the name of Jesus every knee should bend, of those in heaven and on earth and under the earth, and every tongue confess that Jesus Christ is Lord [*Kyrios*], to the glory of God the Father" (Phil. 2:9–11 NABRE).

To evangelize, then, is to proclaim precisely this lordship of the risen Jesus. And if Paul is right in saying that every tongue must confess Jesus's lordship and every knee must bend in acknowledgment of it, evangelization cannot be a privatized affair. It has to take place publicly and boldly (though nonviolently, lest in the very act of declaring the crucified savior we undermine him). And it must be directed to every individual and to every institution of culture.

Culture, of course, is a famously slippery word, capable of being defined in any number of ways. I might propose, for our purposes, the following definition: a culture is that whole congeries of practices, beliefs, convictions, and institutions by which a people finds and expresses its collective identity. Now every culture develops out of three transcendental drives: toward the good, the true, and the beautiful. Thus, political, legal, and juridical systems are, at least in principle, ordered by the quest for the just or the morally good. Newspapers, universities, schools, the sciences, the internet, and so on are, again at least ideally, ordered to the pursuit of the true. And literature, theater, dance, music, painting, sculpture, television, and film are ordered, at their best, to the production of the beautiful. What undergirds all of these cultural forms is some entelechy toward the unconditioned, that is to say, the absolute good, the total truth, and perfect beauty. As I have been suggesting, cultures, like individuals, are fallen, and to that degree they deviate from a trajectory toward their proper fulfillment; however, according to their own nature, they maintain an orientation toward the unconditioned, under one of its three principal modalities.

Therefore, what does it mean to evangelize a culture? It is to declare to the representatives and practitioners of the various cultural forms that Jesus Christ is their Lord, and that their work and efforts belong finally to him and find their surest fulfillment in him. There is, accordingly, something imperial but not imperious about this move. The church, as John Paul II never tired of repeating, only proposes, never imposes. Nevertheless, the evangelization of the culture is an ingredient in the overall commission to bring "all things under the feet of Christ" and to assure that "every knee" bends at the sounding of his name. To demonstrate what this looks like concretely and how it does not amount to a sort of religious suppression of culture will be the burden of the rest of this chapter.

The Icon of the Invisible God

In order to grasp how the submission of the culture to Jesus is tantamount not to a compromising of cultural integrity but precisely to its elevation, it is necessary clearly to understand the peculiar nature of the God of whom Jesus is the visible representation. According to the great tradition—stretching from the third chapter of the book of Exodus, through Augustine and Aquinas, to contemporary thinkers such as Rahner, Balthasar, and Ratzinger—God is not one being among many but rather the sheer act of to-be itself, *ipsum esse* in Aquinas's Latin formula. This means that God does not stand over against the beings of the world in a competitive attitude, as though he were jockeying for position with them on the same ontological plane. Rather, precisely as radically transcendent to the creaturely mode of existence, he can function as the ground of the being of created things. Augustine caught this paradox in his neat observation that God is simultaneously *intimior intimo meo et superior summo meo*. God, in a word, is not *a* being but rather the unconditioned act of being, and therefore, finite things do not compete with him; rather, they exist through and in him. Thomas says that God is "in all things by essence, presence, and power," but this divine inherence, far from crushing the creature, is the condition for the possibility of the creature's existence and ontological integrity. This is the conceptual framework for the familiar adage *gratia supponit et perfecit naturam*, for God enhances rather than compromises the created order to which he comes close.

Since God is the sheer act of to-be itself, he must possess the three great transcendental properties of being—namely, goodness, truth, and beauty—precisely in their unconditioned form. As Augustine argued, God is not a true thing among many, not one more item that the inquiring mind discovers; instead, God is the Truth itself, the illumination by which all true things are seen by the mind. In a similar way, God is not one more good thing to which the will is attracted; rather, God is the unconditioned Good that in turn conditions the will when it goes about its work of seeking good things. And finally, God is not the supreme instance of the category of beauty but rather the Beautiful itself, by which all beautiful things are assessed. Paul Tillich is very much in the Augustinian spirit when he says that God is the great *Prius* of all thought, action, and striving. This is why God is the ground of culture, that collection of practices, convictions, and institutions centering on the transcendental properties of being.

Now Jesus is described by Paul as "the icon of the invisible God" (author's translation, see Col. 1:15), which is to say, the human face of the unconditioned reality. It must follow, therefore, that in Jesus the divine truth, the divine goodness, and the divine beauty take visible form and become sacramentally present within the world. For this reason, the church has, from the beginning, presented Jesus as the ground and lure of culture. The mainstream of the Catholic intellectual tradition has consistently resisted the sectarian impulses of a Tertullian ("What has Athens to do with Jerusalem?") and has embraced the broad-minded, culturally engaged theologies of Irenaeus, Origen, Augustine, Thomas Aquinas, and John Henry Newman. It has realized that the Logos made flesh must have an important relationship to the various *logoi spermatikoi* (to use the patristic term) that appear within the cultural sphere.

Let us take these transcendental qualities one at a time. If God is the unconditioned Truth, and Jesus is God's visible icon, then we should not be surprised that the New Testament writers often employ the category of truth in order to make clear the meaning of Jesus. Thus St. John insists, as we've seen, that Jesus is the Logos made flesh, and John's Jesus says of himself, "I am the truth" (14:6). He is not one more prophet or philosopher who speaks true things about God; he is the embodiment of the divine mind itself, the manifestation of the pattern by which God has fashioned all things. In Luke's account of the journey to Emmaus, the still-hidden Christ applies the hermeneutic that enables his dejected disciples to understand the whole of Scripture and hence the whole of God's purpose. And that interpretive key is none other than his own suffering and death, his willingness to go to the limits of godforsakenness in order to save those who had wandered from the divine love. In the light of this truth, the disciples begin to understand the Bible in its totality, and their hearts "burn within them" (Luke 24:32). This metaphor is evocative of the moment of recognition, when the many disparate elements come together according to a form or pattern, what Lonergan called "insight" and Wittgenstein termed "seeing something *as* something." The point is that divine love—the radical being-for-the-other that is the very nature of God—is the "truth," the pattern that informs reality at the deepest level. Any individual or cultural institution ordered to the truth, is ordered, finally, to this.

Now let us consider the second of the transcendentals. If God is unconditioned Goodness, and if Jesus is the icon of the invisible God, then we should not be surprised that the authors of the New Testament often utilize the language and symbolism associated with justice when speaking of Jesus. Law and covenant are, obviously, massively important themes throughout the Old Testament. Again and again, Yahweh pledges fidelity to his people and invites Israel into a life of holiness, disciplined by the moral, juridical, and ceremonial precepts of the law. He "cuts" covenants with them and makes a blood bond with them, first through Noah and Abraham and then through Moses and David. Throughout the history of salvation, the great prophets—from Amos and Hosea to Isaiah, Jeremiah, and Ezekiel—call Israel back to fidelity to the covenant, to meet the divine love with an answering love. The covenants with Israel are not contracts—exchanges of goods and services—but more like a marriage, a mutual giving of hearts: "I will be your God and you will be my people."

The first Christians understood Jesus to be the fulfillment of the law and the perfection of the covenant, for in his own person divinity and humanity came together. In Jesus, therefore, faithful Yahweh finally met faithful Israel, and a perfect justice thereby appeared in the world. Just as he is "the truth," in the unconditioned sense, so he is, definitively, "the way" and "the life," the *Halakah* by which humanity walks according to the divine purpose. The central petition of the Our Father—thy kingdom come, thy will be done, on earth as it is in heaven—is really a prayer that the justice that obtains in Jesus's own person might become normative throughout creation. Here we can appreciate why St. Paul referred to Jesus as "the new Adam." Prior to the fall, Adam walked in easy fellowship with Yahweh, his powers and aspirations aligned to God's will. For the ancient rabbinic interpreters, this made Adam the first priest ("adoring" God, literally "mouth to mouth" with him) and the first scientist ("cataloging" [*kata logon*] the animals, naming them according to the intelligibility placed in them by the Creator). Jesus, the visible icon of the unconditioned justice of God is hence the one who establishes, on Paul's reading, *dikaiosyne* (justice or righteousness). That this takes place "apart from the law" is, as Paul insists, not a judgment on the law but a function of Jesus having brought the law to fulfillment in his own person. What these first Christians saw in Jesus was a human love that answered the divine love so faithfully that it allowed grace to flood into the world. In the consistent obedience of Christ, especially in his obedience unto death on the cross, they saw the visible icon of unconditioned justice. And this is why any person and any cultural institution ordered toward justice is ordered finally toward Christ.

Now we turn to the third of the transcendentals, the beautiful. If God is the unconditioned act of Beauty itself, and Jesus is the icon of the invisible God, then it is only natural that the New Testament would present Christ as supremely beautiful. The event of the transfiguration, during which the splendor of Jesus shone through his ordinary appearance, is the most obvious example of this sort of presentation. However, the whole of Jesus's life—including and especially his crucifixion—can be read under the rubric of the beautiful. In order to see this, it would be helpful to attend to Thomas Aquinas's classical characterization of beauty as the coming together of *integritas* (wholeness), *consonantia* (harmony), and *claritas* (radiance). Whether we are describing a beautiful day, a beautiful face, or a beautiful golf swing, we are noticing, if Aquinas is right, the coming together of those three essential elements.

A beautiful object or picture or idea is marked, first, by unity or integrity. Despite all its complexity, it hangs together as one. Kierkegaard commented that a saint (a radiantly beautiful person) is someone whose life is about one thing.[1] In the *Portrait of the Artist as a Young Man*, Stephen Daedalus (the author's alter ego) endeavors to explain the Thomistic doctrine of beauty to a colleague. He draws his friend's attention to a simple basket and comments that the condition for the possibility of seeing the thing's beauty is the apprehension of it as one, as distinct from the rest of the universe of physical objects. Next, the beautiful object or person is marked by harmony, by the consonance of its parts, by a certain logic that obtains in the arrangement of its various elements. One notices *consonantia* in beautiful golf swings, say, those of Ernie Els or Rory McIlroy. All the twists, angles, turns, and leveraging that go into that notoriously difficult athletic move come together, in the swings of those gentlemen, in a remarkably elegant manner, so that nothing is wasted and nothing is extraneous to the fundamental purpose of the effort. And finally, the beautiful possesses *claritas* or radiance. A relatively naive reading of this term renders "bright and shining colors," and this can indeed be found in some texts of Aquinas, but Jacques Maritain and many others have observed that a more profound interpretation points to the *claritas* of what the scholastics called "form." The beautiful is that which discloses, in a paradigmatic manner, what the thing or event or person ought to be. Upon watching the swing of a McIlroy, one is moved to exclaim, "Now *that's* a golf swing!" After touring Chartres Cathedral, one might be forgiven for thinking, "*That* is what a Gothic cathedral should look like." In both cases, the observer is struck by the splendor or radiance of the form.

In light of these clarifications, we can begin to see why Jesus's entire way of being in the world should be characterized as beautiful. Jesus was one. What is true of Kierkegaard's saint is *a fortiori* the case in regard to Jesus; his life was utterly focused on one thing, namely, doing the will of his Father. We could express this truth in more abstract metaphysical language by speaking of the irreducible unity of Jesus's person, the divine Word that is nothing but a reflection of the being of the Father. But Jesus's *integritas* was accompanied by a uniquely powerful *consonantia*, for grounded in the unity of his person were two natures, divine and human, which came together in a harmony of mind, will, and purpose. The two natures maintained their integrity, coming together, as the Council of Chalcedon put it, "without mixing, mingling, or confusion," yet they found utter harmony in the measure that they both were instantiated in the one divine person. The Gospel accounts of Jesus's words and deeds might be construed as the narrative presentation of precisely this *consonantia* between the two natures. Indeed, the drama of Jesus's life—from his childhood, through his public life and preaching, all the way to the cross—is identical to the artful interplay of divine will and human will, divine mind and human mind. And finally, the splendor of both divinity and humanity shone forth in him, for Jesus was the archetypal human (witnessed to ironically by Pilate's "*ecce homo*") and the full manifestation of divinity within history (as indicated by the apostle Thomas's ecstatic "my Lord and my God" [John 20:28]). In him, therefore, both the form of man and the form of God became luminous. And once more, the essential quality of this beautiful display was love, for the characteristic mark of the *consonantia* between divinity and humanity in Jesus was a mutual surrendering, a giving away for the other. In Christ, the divine love for us ("God so loved the world that he gave his only Son" [John 3:16 NABRE]) met in a splendid harmony the human love for God ("I have come to do the will of my Father in heaven"[AP, see John 6:38]), and thus unconditioned beauty appeared. This is why any cultural institution dedicated to the production of the beautiful is ordered, finally, to Christ.

Engaging the Culture

With this analysis in mind, let us turn now to a consideration of some concrete ways in which Christ can be proposed as the proper fulfillment of the culture according to its three transcendental trajectories. Let us look, however briefly, at Jesus's relationship to the sciences, to politics, and to the arts.

Especially in the North American context, the quest for truth is typically associated with the endeavor of scientists. We have come, with good reason, to reverence the sciences for their practical effectiveness as well as for their clarity and exactitude. And we have benefited enormously from their attendant technologies, which have gone a long way toward realizing Descartes's dream, at the very dawn of modernity, that humans might come to "master nature." Sadly, part of the mythology associated with the emergence of modernity is that science and religion are implacable enemies and that the physical sciences emerged only after a long twilight struggle against superstition and the claims of faith. Robert Sokolowski has suggested that the constant reiteration of this myth up to the present day has something of the quality of a ritual retelling or rehearsal, as though moderns have to continually remind themselves of the painful process by which they were born intellectually. Hypatia, Giordano Bruno, and especially Galileo have become the patron saints of critical reason persecuted by intolerant religion. The great battle between "science" and biblical fundamentalism in America in the early years of the twentieth century—culminating in the "Monkey Trial"—is read as a continuation of the primal struggle between obscurantism and enlightenment. Watch Bill Maher's terrible film *Religulous* in order to see a crude contemporary retelling of the myth.

But all of this is tragic. Though there have undoubtedly been dreadful missteps on both sides, science and authentic faith ought never to be construed as enemies—just the contrary. Despite the persistence of the modern myth of origins, the physical sciences were born precisely out of an intellectual matrix conditioned by the faith. One might wonder why the sciences in their modern form emerged when and where they did, that is to say, in the European civilization of the seventeenth century, and not in the cultural contexts of, say, India, China, or the Middle East. Peter Hodgson and many others have argued that the condition for the possibility of the rise of the experimental sciences was a pair of fundamental assumptions, both theological in nature. In order for the sciences to flourish, intellectuals had to see the world as, first, nondivine, and second, intelligible. As long as the universe itself is construed as sacred—as is the case in most forms of animism, pantheism, and nature mysticism—it is the object not of experimentation and rational analysis but of worship. And before any scientific work can get under way, scientists must presume the intelligibility of what they seek to investigate. Psychology rests upon the assumption that the psyche has an intelligible form, biology on the assumption that life is understandable, physics on the assumption that there is a law-like quality to the microcosmic and macrocosmic structures of the universe, and so on. This universal intelligibility is not so much discovered by scientists but rather intuited by them. Now both of these requisite presumptions should be seen as corollaries of the doctrine of creation, and this is why I said they are theological in nature. If God has made the world, then the world is not God; and if the Creator is intelligent, then his work is stamped, necessarily and universally, by intelligibility. The contention of Hodgson and others is that an intellectual culture shaped by the doctrine of creation provided a particularly healthy breeding ground for the sciences.

Moreover, many of the first great practitioners of modern science—Descartes, Pascal, Copernicus, Brahe, Kepler, Newton, and so on—were devoutly religious men and were keen to show correspondences between their empirical discoveries and their faith. And they all learned their mathematics, astronomy, and physics in church-sponsored universities. After the founding period, many prominent scientists saw no contradiction between their empirical research and their faith. One thinks of Gregor Mendel, the founder of modern genetics and an Augustinian friar; of Georges Lemaître, formulator of the Big Bang theory of cosmic origins and a Catholic priest; and today of John Polkinghorne, Cambridge particle physicist and Anglican priest, and of George Coyne, Jesuit priest and astrophysicist. The myth of the "war" between science and religion was largely an invention of anti-Catholic polemicists of the nineteenth century, but it was sadly confirmed in our country by the emergence of biblical fundamentalism in the early twentieth century. The best of the Catholic tradition, relying on nuanced, nonliteralistic patristic and medieval strategies for reading the Scriptures, managed, for the most part, to avoid this phony conflict. This is why the Galileo case, in all its ambiguity, should be read as a tragic anomaly rather than as paradigmatic of the church's relation to science. Those who honor the Logos made flesh have absolutely no interest in blocking, hindering, or questioning the legitimate exercise of reason in any of its forms—just the contrary.

As I take the next step, I realize I am moving into highly speculative territory. But I believe there are intriguing hints in a good deal of contemporary science that the Logos that informs all reality is, as Christians would expect, marked by a kind of being-with or being-for. Classical physics and astronomy were predicated on the assumption that reality is made up of separately existing objects, relating to one another extrinsically within the great theater of space. But post-Einsteinian physics—and now quantum theory even more radically—tend to see not so much "things" as patterns of interaction, overlapping fields of energy. What Charles Williams called "coinherence," the interpenetration of all dimensions of reality, seems to obtain at the most fundamental levels of being. The EPR experiment and Bell's theorem both indicate that certain subatomic particles, having been at one time in contact, continue to be marked by one another, even after they have been separated by enormous amounts of space. Does this action at a distance, or nonlocal causality, in fact suggest that a kind of coinherence or *Mitsein* obtains across the fields of reality? And might this line of thought be a fruitful entrée for those who hold that the intelligibility that informs all created being is precisely an intelligibility of love?

Now let us turn to a consideration of the cultural trajectory in the direction of justice. As we argued above, all our legal, juridical, and political institutions, at least ideally, are ordered toward the achievement of justice. They operate under the aegis of justice in its unconditioned form, which is another way of saying that they are under God. There is a myth concerning the origins of the modern political state, which curiously mirrors the myth of the emergence of the modern sciences. Many in the West would blithely assume that democratic political reforms emerged after a terrible struggle with the traditional monarch favored by the church. Again, it is instructive to consult the ruminations of both popular and academic authors in the nineteenth century to witness the launching of this myth. But like its scientific counterpart, it is woefully inadequate to the facts.

I would argue that many of the indispensable features of the modern democracies are derived from biblical religion. In order to see this, I would invite you to journey in imagination to a stuffy room in a Philadelphia boarding house in the summer of 1776, where a young Virginia lawyer is composing a rather important document. In the prologue to the Declaration of Independence, Thomas Jefferson wrote, "We hold these truths to be self-evident, that all men are created equal." We've heard or read those words so often that we rarely advert to their peculiarity. Are all people equal? If so, how? Common sense tells us that human beings are radically unequal in beauty, intelligence, courage, virtue, kindness, physical strength, and so on. And if we consult the history of political philosophy, we find that most of the great political theorists of premodern times took it as self-evident that men were not equal. Indeed, Plato, Aristotle, and Cicero considered the recognition of this inequality as requisite to the establishment of a right social order. Think of Plato's account of the three types of people—gold, silver, and bronze—or of Aristotle's sharp distinction between the relatively few aristocrats capable of public life and the vast unwashed destined by nature to remain in the private realm.

So what led Jefferson to say that the equality of all people is not obviously false but self-evidently true? I believe that the clue is found in a single word of Jefferson's formula that our eyes and minds barely take in, namely, the word *created*. Despite our numerous and massive inequalities, we are all equally children of God, created out of love and destined for eternal life. Take the fact of creation out of consideration, and it becomes extremely difficult to defend the proposition that we are all equal. And let us follow the momentum of Jefferson's theologic: "They are endowed by their creator with certain inalienable rights, among these are life, liberty, and the pursuit of happiness." Once more, even a casual consultation of the history of political theory discloses that this claim is anything but universally admitted. Neither Plato nor Aristotle would have thought it correct to ascribe to all people within the city inalienable rights. Rather, both would hold that the privileged aristocracy, the moral and intellectual elite, alone enjoy certain prerogatives. Again, what prompted Jefferson's confident assertion? It was his keen sense—however attenuated by Enlightenment Deism—that a creator God had granted to each of his rational creatures a dignity, which no person or state institution could legitimately undermine. In point of fact, the structures of government exist for no other reason than to protect this God-granted dignity. And here we see something of central importance, namely, that the justice that properly preoccupies the representatives of a Jeffersonian democracy is a type of love, a willing the good of the other as other. All the juridical and political institutions that rest upon the suppositions of the Declaration of Independence are conditioned, finally, by this focused desire that each member of the polity flourish.

If one is tempted to question the validity of this analysis, I might invite that person to consider the example of the great totalitarianisms of the last century: Hitler's Germany, Stalin's Soviet Union, Mao's China, Pol Pot's Cambodia, to name only the most brutal. What the world witnessed in each of those political arrangements was a systematic negation of God and hence a setting-aside of both equality and rights—followed by morally disastrous but utterly predictable results.

Another important religious feature of modern political arrangements is the rule of law, which is to say, the conscious placing of all members of the society, including the governors, under the authority of a law that transcends their individual wills. Grounded in the prophetic tradition of the Bible, Thomas Aquinas teaches that legitimate positive law rests in the moral law, which in turn is conditioned by the eternal law, which is identical to the divine mind itself. When that nesting relationship is forgotten, law in short order becomes an instrument of manipulation, a tool in the hands of the powerful. In his conversation with Pontius Pilate, Jesus reminds the Roman governor that he would have no authority unless it were granted to him "from above." In other words, he suggests none too subtly that Pilate's power is not a function of the governor's will, but is rather granted to him by a transcendent authority. The justice of God, which is unconditioned love, is the aegis under which any and all governmental authority is appropriately exercised. And this is precisely why the rule of law provides, indirectly, an opening to the one who seeks to proclaim Christ to the political culture.

Let us look, finally, at the cultural trajectory in the direction of the beautiful. There was, for centuries, a tight correlation between the Catholic Church and the arts. One has only to think of Gregorian chant, the great French cathedrals, Dante, Palestrina, Giotto, Raphael, Michelangelo, Matthias Grünewald, Mozart, and so on to see the immensely fruitful quality of this relationship. The church readily used the arts for evangelical purposes, and the artists allowed religion to carry them to the heights of creative expressiveness. Would Grünewald's artistry have been fully realized apart from the unsurpassably sublime subject matter of the crucifixion of the Son of God? The rapport between art and the church was considered natural, because God was construed as the supreme artist, and artists as participants in the divine creativity.

Thomas Aquinas utilizes the trope of God the artist frequently and in a number of contexts. In his discussion of the Trinitarian persons, he says that *species* (beauty) should be attributed to the Son, since the Son is the archetype by which God the Father fashioned the universe. The Father makes the world by consulting, as it were, the beautiful forms implicitly ingredient in the Word, much as an artist makes an artifact by consulting a beautiful ideal that he holds in his mind. And since God's creation is *ex nihilo*, there is literally no limit to the extent of the Son's influence over creation, and this means that whatever exists, precisely in the measure that it exists, is beautiful. What the artist seeks to do, on Thomas's reading, is to imitate the beautiful forms that she finds in God's creation and thereby bring more beauty into being. And this is why artistry is inescapably intellectual in nature; it is *recta ratio factibilium* (right reason in regard to things to be made), a kind of contemplative seeing that gives rise to making. James Joyce, who was profoundly shaped by Scholasticism as a young man, expresses the artist's task in a rather Thomistic vein, commenting that the artist is a reporter of epiphanies, privileged moments of manifestation. He is not so much an inventor as an imitator of the beautiful, as becomes clear in Joyce's recounting, in *A Portrait of the Artist*, of his experience of seeing the girl silhouetted against the sea, a scene that consciously echoes Dante's meeting with Beatrice in the *Vita Nuova*.

But much of this began to unravel in the modern period. An even relatively adequate exploration of the causes for this dissolution would take us well beyond the bounds of this chapter, but suffice it to say that the participation metaphysics that undergirded the approach outlined above commenced to evanesce as God, more and more, was seen as a distant first cause and not as the very ground of the being of the universe. In time, this abstracted and detached God came to be seen by many intellectuals as effectively unnecessary—"I have no need of that hypothesis," in Laplace's famous formula—and eventually an outright atheism came to seem plausible. This shift in ontology carried enormous implications for aesthetics, for as the world appeared less and less the work of a transcendent artist, art became more and more a matter of self-expression rather than imitation. Once the objective referent disappeared, subjective purpose and need became paramount in the mind of the artist. In many ways, the history of modern art can be read as the steady march toward abstract expressionism, that is to say, toward the complete setting-aside of objective form and the embrace of a pure, subjectively conditioned creativity. The result of this transition was (and is) an explosion of art that is wildly inventive—often subversively so—but frankly not very beautiful, and concomitantly, a tendency on the part of many artists to perceive the church—the guardian of form—as the enemy of art, censorious and unappreciative.

The evangelization of the arts can happen only when we recover a more classical notion of nature as the repository of formal beauty, the work of a transcendent Artist, and of art itself as *recta ratio factibilium*, a rightly ordered reason that contemplates the objective form and makes beautiful things in accord with that contemplation. Once those moves are made, the evangelist can propose Jesus—the harmonious coming-together of divinity and humanity—as the most sublimely beautiful form, and he can endeavor to show that any and all forms within nature are finally a participation in that primordial beauty. And he can encourage artists to return with energy and enthusiasm to the community, which has, up and down the ages, most faithfully preserved the idea of the supernatural Artist.

Conclusion

Allow me to conclude this chapter with a few remarks of biblical inspiration. The great story of Noah's ark in the book of Genesis was interpreted by the church fathers as a sort of icon of the church. During a time of crisis, Noah and his family, along with a microcosm of God's good creation, hunkered down; the moment the flood waters receded, Noah opened the windows and doors of the ship in order to flood the world with the life he had preserved. So the church through the ages is a place of refuge, where something of God's good order is preserved while flood waters of sin surge all around. But the ultimate purpose of church people is not to hunker down behind walls but rather to flood the world with the ideas and practices that they have cultivated. This is,

I suggest, a provocative image for the evangelization of the culture. Christians must vigorously resist the modern prejudice that favors a privatized religion. The faith that speaks of the Logos by which all things were created cannot, even in principle, be privatized. The church must come out from behind its walls—nonviolently, to be sure—with confidence and panache in order to share its life everywhere and with everyone.

One of the last images in the Bible, at the close of the book of Revelation, is of the descent of the heavenly Jerusalem. The visionary sees the great city illumined by the light of the Lamb, adorned with jewels and filled with streets of gold. He notices that there is no temple in the new Jerusalem, certainly a curious state of affairs given the prominence of the temple in the earthly Jerusalem. But we are meant to see that there is no need for a temple precisely because the city in its entirety has become a temple, a place where God is properly praised. This is an image of the evangelized culture in which the arts, the sciences, politics, sports, finance, and law are all ordered to Jesus Christ, the icon of the invisible God, the human face of the unconditioned good, true, and beautiful.

Notes

Foreword

1. Rainer Maria Rilke, "Evening" in *Selected Poems*, trans. C. F. MacIntyre (Berkeley: University of California Press, 1968) © 1968 by C. F. MacIntyre. Used with permission.

2. Henri de Lubac SJ, *The Drama of Atheist Humanism*, trans. Edith M. Riley, Anne Englund Nash, and Mark Sebanc (San Francisco: Ignatius, 1995), 24.

Chapter 1 Augustine's Questions

1. John Caputo, "What Do I Love When I Love My God? Deconstruction and Radical Orthodoxy," in *Questioning God*, ed. John Caputo (Bloomington: Indiana University Press, 2001), 291–92.

2. Augustine, *Confessions*, trans. Maria Boulding (Hyde Park, NY: New City Press, 1997), 159.

3. Joseph Campbell, *The Power of Myth* (New York: Doubleday, 1988), 213.

4. Ibid., 230–31.

5. Augustine, *Confessions*, 160.

6. Ibid., 164.

7. Ibid., 169.

8. Ibid., 173.

9. Robert Sokolowski, *The God of Faith and Reason: Foundations of Christian Theology* (Notre Dame, IN: University of Notre Dame Press, 1982), 35–36.

10. Augustine, *The Trinity*, trans. Edmund Hill, OP (Hyde Park, NY: New City Press, 1991), 189.

11. Ibid., 191.

12. Ibid.

13. Ibid., 192.

14. Ibid., 196.

15. Joseph Ratzinger, *Introduction to Christianity* (San Francisco: Ignatius, 1990), 129.

16. See John Milbank, *Theology and Social Theory: Beyond Secular Reason* (Oxford: Blackwell, 1990), 389–90.

17. Augustine, *The City of God against the Pagans*, ed. R. W. Dyson (Cambridge: Cambridge University Press, 1998), 61.

18. Ibid., 225.

19. Milbank, *Theology and Social Theory*, 391.

20. Augustine, *City of God*, 634–38.

21. John Henry Newman, *An Essay on the Development of Christian Doctrine* (Westminster, MD: Christian Classics, 1968), 336–37.

44

Chapter 2 Thomas Aquinas and Why the Atheists Are Right

1. Christopher Hitchens, *God Is Not Great: How Religion Poisons Everything* (New York: Twelve Books, 2007), 66–67.

2. Richard Dawkins, *The God Delusion* (New York: Mariner, 2006), 80.

3. Ibid., 82.

4. Hitchens, *God Is Not Great*, 249.

5. Thomas Aquinas, *Summa theologiae* Ia, q. 3, prol.

6. Kathryn Tanner, *Jesus, Humanity, and the Trinity* (Minneapolis: Fortress, 2001), 12.

7. Thomas Aquinas, *De potentia Dei*, q. 3, art. 3, in *Quaestiones disputatae* (Turin: Marietti, 1965).

8. Aquinas, *Summa theologiae* Ia, q. 8, art. 3.

Chapter 3 The Metaphysics of Coinherence

1. Peter Brown, *The Rise of Western Christendom* (Oxford: Blackwell, 2003), 372–73.

2. Charles Williams, *Essential Writings in Spirituality and Theology*, ed. Charles Hefling (Cambridge: Cawley, 1993), 146–50.

3. Robert Barron, *The Strangest Way: Walking the Christian Path* (Maryknoll, NY: Orbis, 2002), 36–40.

4. G. K. Chesterton, *The Everlasting Man*, in *G. K. Chesterton: Collected Works*, vol. 2 (San Francisco: Ignatius, 1986), 302.

5. Robert Sokolowski, *The God of Faith and Reason: Foundations of Christian Theology* (Notre Dame, IN: University of Notre Dame Press, 1982), 35–37.

6. Kathryn Tanner, *Jesus, Humanity, and the Trinity* (Minneapolis: Fortress, 2001), 12.

7. "*Hic solus verus Deus bonitate sua et omnipotenti virtute non ad augendam suam beatitudinem, nec ad acquirendam, sed ad manifestandam perfectionem suam per bona . . . liberrimo consilio . . . de nihilo condidit creaturam.*" Decretals of the First Vatican Council, *Dei Filius* 1, in *Decrees of the Ecumenical Councils*, vol. 2, ed. Norman Tanner, SJ (Washington, DC: Georgetown University Press, 1990), 805.

8. Robert Louis Wilken, *The Spirit of Early Christian Thought: Seeking the Face of God* (New Haven: Yale University Press, 2003), 146–50.

9. Thomas Aquinas, *De potentia Dei*, q. 3, art. 3, ad 3, in *Quaestiones disputatae* (Turin: Marietti, 1965), 2:43.

10. Ibid.

11. John Milbank, *Theology and Social Theory: Beyond Secular Reason* (Oxford: Blackwell, 1990), 391.

12. James Alison, *The Joy of Being Wrong: Original Sin through Easter Eyes* (New York: Crossroad, 1998), 190.

13. Thomas Merton, *Conjectures of a Guilty Bystander* (New York: Doubleday, 1989), 156–57.

14. Ibid., 157.

15. Joseph Ratzinger, *Introduction to Christianity* (San Francisco: Ignatius, 1990), 106.

16. John Polkinghorne, *Faith, Science, and Understanding* (New Haven: Yale University Press, 2000), 46–47.

17. Bernard Lonergan, *Method in Theology* (Toronto: University of Toronto Press, 1971), 42–44.

18. John Henry Newman, *An Essay on the Development of Christian Doctrine* (Westminster, MD: Christian Classics, 1968), 33–38.

19. Karl Rahner, *Hearers of the Word* (New York: Herder and Herder, 1969), 42.

20. See Fergus Kerr, *After Aquinas: Versions of Thomism* (Oxford: Blackwell, 2002), 30.

21. James William McClendon, *Systematic Theology: Ethics* (Nashville: Abingdon, 1986), 43.

22. Pierre Hadot, *What Is Ancient Philosophy?* (Cambridge, MA: Harvard University Press, 2002), 55–56.

23. Stanley Hauerwas, *Sanctify Them in the Truth: Holiness Exemplified* (Nashville: Abingdon, 1998), 26.

24. Colin E. Gunton, *The One, the Three and the Many: God, Creation, and the Culture of Modernity* (Cambridge: Cambridge University Press, 1993), 28–35.

25. Jean-Paul Sartre, *L'existentialisme est un humanisme* (Paris: Editions de Nagel, 1970), 21.

26. Casey v. Planned Parenthood of Southeastern Pennsylvania, 112 Sup. Ct. 2791 at 2807.

27. See Servais Pinckaers, OP, *The Sources of Christian Ethics* (Washington, DC: Catholic University of America Press, 1995), 229.

Chapter 4 The Trinity on Display in the Economy of Salvation

1. Irenaeus of Lyons, *Adversus haereses*, trans. Eric Osborn, 4.19.13.

2. Irenaeus of Lyons, *Adversus haereses* 4.20.1

3. Irenaeus of Lyons, *Demonstration of the Apostolic Preaching*, trans. Armitage Robinson, 9.

4. Irenaeus of Lyons, *Adversus haereses* 4.14.1.

5. Eric Osborn, *Irenaeus of Lyons* (Cambridge: Cambridge University Press, 2005), 27.

6. Irenaeus of Lyons, *Adversus haereses* 2.6.1.

7. Irenaeus of Lyons, *Adversus haereses* 2.9.1.

8. Irenaeus of Lyons, *Adversus haereses* 4.6.4.

9. Irenaeus of Lyons, *Adversus haereses* 4.11.2.

10. Irenaeus of Lyons, *Adversus haereses* 4.11.2.

11. Irenaeus of Lyons, *Adversus haereses* 2.10.4.

12. F. R. M. Hitchcock, *Irenaeus of Lugdunum: A Study of His Teaching* (Cambridge: Cambridge University Press, 1914), 83.

13. Irenaeus of Lyons, *Adversus haereses* 4.20.1.

14. Joseph Ratzinger, *Introduction to Christianity*, rev. ed., trans. J. R. Foster (San Francisco: Ignatius, 2004), 178.

15. Ibid., 179.

16. Ibid.

17. Ibid.

18. Ibid., 180.

19. Ibid., 179.

20. Ibid., 182.

21. Ibid., 183.

22. Irenaeus of Lyons, *Adversus haereses* 4.14.2.

23. Irenaeus of Lyons, *Adversus haereses* 2.25.2.

24. See Matthew Levering, *Christ's Fulfillment of Torah and Temple: Salvation According to Thomas Aquinas* (Notre Dame, IN: University of Notre Dame Press, 2002).

25. Irenaeus of Lyons, *Adversus haereses* 4.6.6.

26. Irenaeus of Lyons, *Adversus haereses* 4.20.7.

Chapter 5 To See According to the Icon of Jesus Christ

1. Hans Urs von Balthasar, *Theo-Drama: Theological Dramatic Theory*, trans. Graham Harrison (San Francisco: Ignatius, 1990), 2:277.

Chapter 6 A Tale of Two Cardinals

1. Avery Dulles, *The Craft of Theology: From Symbol to System* (New York: Crossroad, 1992), 4.

2. Ibid., 5.

3. Ibid.

4. See Hans-Georg Gadamer, *Truth and Method* (New York: Continuum, 1990), 269–77.

5. See George Lindbeck, *The Nature of Doctrine: Theology in a Postliberal Age* (Philadelphia: Westminster, 1984), 34–35.

6. Dulles, *Craft of Theology*, 6.

7. Ibid.

8. Ibid.

9. Ibid.

10. Martha Nussbaum, *Upheavals of Thought: The Intelligence of Emotions* (Cambridge: Cambridge University Press, 2001), esp. 19–49.

11. See John Henry Newman, *An Essay in Aid of a Grammar of Assent* (Notre Dame, IN: University of Notre Dame Press, 1979), 136–37.

12. Ibid., 143.

13. Ibid., 230.

14. See Robert Barron, *The Priority of Christ: Toward a Postliberal Catholicism* (Grand Rapids: Brazos, 2007), 137.

15. Avery Dulles, *John Henry Newman* (New York: Continuum, 2002), 44.

16. Dulles, *Craft of Theology*, 6.

17. John Henry Newman, *An Essay on the Development of Christian Doctrine* (Westminster, MD: Christian Classics, 1968), 36.

18. Ibid., 40.

19. Ibid., 34.

20. Dulles, *Craft of Theology*, 106.

21. Ibid.

22. John Henry Newman, *Apologia pro vita sua* (New York: Doubleday, 1956), 323.

23. Dulles, *Craft of Theology*, 106.

24. Newman, *Apologia pro vita sua*, 328.

25. Ibid., 329.

26. Dulles, *Craft of Theology*, 106.

27. Newman, *Apologia pro vita sua*, 329.

28. Ibid., 340.

29. Dulles, *Craft of Theology*, 117.

30. Ibid.

31. Ibid.

32. Newman, *Apologia pro vita sua*, 340.

33. Dulles, *Craft of Theology*, 116.

34. Newman, *Apologia pro vita sua*, 339.

35. Dulles, *Craft of Theology*, 107.

36. Avery Dulles, *A Testimonial to Grace and Reflections on a Theological Journey* (Kansas City: Sheed and Ward, 1996), 36.

37. Ibid., 132.

Chapter 7 John Henry Newman among the Postmoderns

1. See Ian Ker, *John Henry Newman: A Biography* (Oxford: Oxford University Press, 1988), 721.

2. William Placher, *Unapologetic Theology: A Christian Voice in a Pluralistic Conversation* (Louisville: Westminster John Knox, 1989), 25–26.

3. Ibid., 34.

4. Ibid., 165–70.

5. John Henry Newman, *An Essay in Aid of a Grammar of Assent* (Notre Dame, IN: University of Notre Dame Press, 1979), 139.

6. Ibid.

7. Ibid., 228.

8. Robert Bolt, *A Man for All Seasons* (New York: Vintage, 1988), 99.

9. Newman, *Grammar of Assent*, 215.

10. Ibid, 227.

11. Ibid., 271.

12. John Milbank, *Theology and Social Theory: Beyond Secular Reason* (Oxford: Blackwell, 1990), vii.

13. Ibid., 1.

14. Ibid.

15. Ibid.

16. Ibid., 207.

17. Henri de Lubac, *The Mystery of the Supernatural*, trans. Rosemary Sheed (London: Geoffrey Chapman, 1967), 41.

18. Milbank, *Theology and Social Theory*, 222.

19. John Henry Newman, *The Idea of a University* (Notre Dame, IN: University of Notre Dame Press, 1982), 22.

20. Ibid., 19.

21. Ibid., 27.

22. Ibid., 55.

23. René Descartes, *Discourse on Method*, in *The Philosophical Works of Descartes*, trans. Elizabeth Haldane (Cambridge: Cambridge University Press, 1979), 87.

24. Bernard Lonergan, *Method in Theology* (Toronto: University of Toronto Press, 1971), 42–43.

25. See David Tracy, "The Uneasy Alliance Reconceived," in *Theology after Liberalism: A Reader* (Oxford: Blackwell, 2000), 349.

26. John Henry Newman, *An Essay on the Development of Christian Doctrine* (Westminster, MD: Christian Classics, 1968), 33.

27. Ibid., 34.

28. Ibid., 40.

29. Ibid.

30. John Henry Newman, *Apologia pro vita sua* (New York: Doubleday, 1956), 328.

31. Ibid., 329.

32. See John Caputo, "God and Anonymity," in *A Passion for the Impossible: John D. Caputo in Focus* (Albany: State University of New York Press, 2003), 7–8.

Chapter 8 Biblical Interpretation and Theology

1. Irenaeus of Lyons, *Adversus haereses* 1.10.1.

2. Ibid.

3. Ibid.

4. Ibid.

5. Ibid., 3.11.1.

6. James Kugel, *How to Read the Bible: A Guide to Scripture, Then and Now* (New York: Simon and Schuster, 2008), 14–16.

7. Ibid., 31.

8. Quoted in ibid., 31.

9. Ibid., 32.

10. Quoted in ibid., 34.

11. Jowett's 1860 essay, "On the Interpretation of Scripture," can be found in Josephine M. Guy, ed., *The Victorian Age: An Anthology of Sources and Documents* (New York: Routledge, 1998).

12. Friedrich D. E. Schleiermacher, *On the Glaubenslehre: Two Letters to Dr. Lücke*, trans. and annot. James Duke and Francis Fiorenza (Chico, CA: Scholars Press, 1981), 65.

13. Quoted in Francis Watson, *Text and Truth: Redefining Biblical Theology* (Grand Rapids, MI: Eerdmanns, 1997), 130.

14. Ibid., 130.

15. Schleiermacher, *Glaubenslehre*, 12, quoted in Watson, *Text and Truth*, 138.

16. Quoted in Watson, 141.

17. Ibid., 158–60.

18. Raymond Brown, *The Critical Meaning of the Bible: How a Modern Reading of the Bible Challenges Christians, the Church, and the Churches* (New York: Paulist, 1981), x.

19. Matthew Levering, *Participatory Biblical Exegesis: A Theology of Biblical Interpretation* (Notre Dome, IN: University of Notre Dame Press, 2008), 198.

20. Nicholas Lash, *Theology on the Way to Emmaus* (London: SCM, 1986), 81.

21. Brown, 1154.

22. Norman P. Tanner, ed., *Decrees of the Ecumenical Councils*, 2 vols. (Washington, DC: Georgetown University, 1990).

Chapter 9 The Eucharist as the *Telos* of the Law in the Writings of Thomas Aquinas

1. "Lex quaedam regula est et mensura actuum, secundum quam inducitur aliquis ad agendum vel ab agendo retrahitur." Aquinas, *Summa theologiae* Ia-IIae, q. 90.

2. "Definitio legis, quae nihil est aliud quam quaedam rationis ordinatio ad bonum commune, ab eo qui curam communitatis habet, promulgata." Aquinas, *Summa theologiae* Ia-IIae, q. 90, art. 4.

3. "Impossibile est esse amicitiam hominis ad Deum, qui est optimus, nisi homines bone efficantur; unde dicitur *sancti eritis, quoniam ego sanctus sum*." Aquinas, *Summa theologiae* Ia-IIae, q. 99, art. 2.

4. "Ceremonialia praecepta determinant praecepta moralia in ordine ad Deum."Aquinas, *Summa theologiae* Ia-IIae, q. 101, art. 1.

5. "In statu enim futurae beatitudinis, intellectus humanus ipsam divinam veritatem in seipsa intuebitur. Et ideo exterior cultus non consistet in aliqua figura, sed solum in laude Dei, quae procedit ex interiori cognitione et affectione." Aquinas, *Summa theologiae* Ia-IIae, q. 101, art. 2.

6. "Unde etiam praecepta de sacrificiis non fuerunt data populo Iudaeorum nisi postquam declinavit ad idolatriam, adorando vitulum conflatilem." Aquinas, *Summa theologiae* Ia-IIae, q. 102, art. 3.

7. "Et propter hoc omnia alia sacrificia offerebantur in veteri lege ut hoc unum singulare et praecipuum sacrificium figuraretur, tanquam perfectum per imperfectum." Aquinas, *Summa theologiae* Ia-IIae, q. 102, art. 3.

8. Aquinas, *Summa theologiae* IIIa, q. 48, art. 3.

9. "Et ideo principaliter lex nova est ipsa gratia Spiritus Sancti, quae datur Christi fidelibus." Aquinas, *Summa theologiae* Ia-IIae, q. 106, art. 1.

10. Jeremiah 31:31–33, cited in Aquinas, *Summa theologiae* Ia-IIae, q. 106, art. 1.

11. "Tertia ratio sumitur ex hoc quod lex nova est lex gratiae: et ideo primo opportuit quod homo relinqueretur sibi in statu veteris legis ut in peccando cadendo, suam infirmitatem cognoscens, recognosceret se gratia indigere." Aquinas, *Summa theologiae* Ia-IIae, q. 106, art. 3.

12. "Signum rei sacrae inquantum est sanctificans homines." Aquinas, *Summa theologiae* IIIa, q. 60, art. 2.

13. "Et hoc modo non potest causare gratiam nisi Deus: quia gratia nihil est aliud quam quaedam participata similitudo divinae naturae. . . . Causa vero instrumentalis non agit per virtutem suae formae, sed solum per motum quo movetur a principali agente. . . . Et hoc modo sacramenta novae legis gratiam causant." Aquinas, *Summa theologiae* IIIa, q. 62, art. 1.

14. "Et ideo opportuit ut aliquid plus haberet sacrificium novae legis a Christo institutum: ut scilicet contineret ipsum passum, non solum in significatione vel figura, sed etiam in rei veritate." Aquinas, *Summa theologiae* IIIa, q. 75, art. 1.

15. "In aliis sacramentis non est ipse Christus realiter, sicut in hoc sacramento. Et ideo in sacramentis aliis, manet substantia materiae, non autem in isto." Aquinas, *Summa theologiae* IIIa, q. 75, art. 2, ad. 2.

16. "Remoto enim priori, removetur posterius. Sed substantia est naturaliter prior accidente. . . . Cum ergo, facta consecratione, non remaneat substantia panis in hoc sacramento, videtur quod non possint remanere accidentia eius." Aquinas, *Summa theologiae* IIIa, q. 75, obj. 1.

17. "Et ideo virtute Dei, qui est causa prima omnium, fieri potest ut remaneant posteriora, sublatis prioribus." Aquinas, *Summa theologiae* IIIa, q. 75, ad. 1.

18. "Et ideo effectum quem passio Christi fecit in mundo, hoc sacramentum facit in homine." Aquinas, *Summa theologiae* IIIa, q. 79, art. 1.

19. "Quod scilicet sustentat, auget, reparat et delectat." Aquinas, *Summa theologiae* IIIa, q. 79, art. 1.

20. "Triplex est hominum status: primus quidem veteris legis; secundus novae legis; tertius status succedit non in hac vita, sed in patria. Sed sicut primus status est figuralis et imperfectus respectu status evangelici, ita hic status est figuralis et imperfectus respectu status patriae; quo veniente, iste status evacuatur." Aquinas, *Summa theologiae* Ia-IIae, q. 106, art. 4, ad. 1.

21. "In illo ergo statu, beatorum nihil erit figurale ad divinum cultum pertinens, sed solum gratiarum actio et vox laudis (Isa. 51:31). Et ideo dicitur *Apoc.* 21:22 de civitate beatorum: *Templum non vidi in ea, Dominus enim Deus omnipotens templum illius est, et Agnus.*" Aquinas, *Summa theologiae* Ia-IIae, q. 103, art. 3.

Chapter 10 The Liturgical Self

1. See Joseph Dunne, *Back to the Rough Ground: Practical Judgment and the Lure of Technique* (Notre Dame, IN: University of Notre Dame Press, 1993), esp. 64–65.

2. See Alasdair MacIntyre, *After Virtue* (Notre Dame, IN: University of Notre Dame Press, 1981).

3. *Sacrosanctum concilium* 10, in *The Documents of Vatican II*, ed. Walter M. Abbot, SJ (New York: Herder and Herder, 1966), 142.

4. Emmanuel Levinas, *Otherwise than Being: Or Beyond Essence*, trans. Alphonso Lingis (The Hague: Martinus Nijhoff, 1981), 141–52.

5. Casey v. Planned Parenthood of Southeastern Pennsylvania, 112 Sup. Ct. 2791 at 2807.

6. See Joseph Ratzinger, *Introduction to Christianity* (San Francisco: Ignatius, 1990), 129–32.

7. Plato, *The Republic* 7, in *The Collected Dialogues of Plato*, ed. Edith Hamilton (Princeton: Princeton University Press, 1961), 747–50.

8. See Aristotle, *The Nichomachean Ethics* 2, in *The Basic Works of Aristotle*, ed. Richard McKeon (New York: Random House, 1941), 952–64.

9. See especially Flannery O'Connor, "A Good Man Is Hard to Find," in *O'Connor: Collected Works* (New York: Library of America, 1988), 137–53.

10. See Robert Barron, *Bridging the Great Divide* (Lanham, MD: Rowman and Littlefield, 2004), 80.

11. Augustine, *The City of God against the Pagans* 3, ed. R. W. Dyson (Cambridge: Cambridge University Press, 1998), esp. 94–120.

12. See John Milbank, *Theology and Social Theory: Beyond Secular Reason* (Oxford: Blackwell, 1990), 390–92.

13. George Lindbeck, *The Nature of Doctrine: Theology in a Post-Liberal Age* (Philadelphia: Westminster, 1984), 31–41.

14. Ratzinger, *Introduction to Christianity*, 73–76.

15. *Sacrosanctum concilium* 7.

16. See Robert Sokolowski, *The God of Faith and Reason: Foundations of Christian Theology* (Notre Dame, IN: University of Notre Dame Press, 1982), 41–51.

17. Thomas Aquinas, *De potentia Dei*, q. 3, art. 3, ad 3, in *Quaestiones disputatae* (Turin: Marietti, 1965), 2:43.

18. See Jean-Luc Marion, *God without Being* (Chicago: University of Chicago Press, 1991), 95–99.

19. Hans Urs von Balthasar, *Theo-Drama: Theological Dramatic Theory*, vol. 3, *Dramatis Personae: Persons in Christ* (San Francisco: Ignatius, 1992), 152–62.

20. Ibid., 230–37.

Chapter 11 The Eucharist

1. N.T. Wright, "Jesus and the Identity of God," *Ex Audita* 14 (1990), 53.

2. Flannery O'Connor, *Collected Works* (New York: Library of America, 1988), 976–77.

3. See Joseph Ratzinger, "The Problem of Transubstantiation and the Question about the Meaning of the Eucharist," in *Collected Works of Joseph Ratzinger*, trans. Fr. Kenneth Baker, SJ, and Michael J. Miller (San Francisco: Ignatius Press, 2012), 11:25.

Chapter 12 Why Bernard Lonergan Matters for Pastoral People

1. See Bernard J. F. Lonergan, SJ, *Method in Theology* (New York: Herder and Herder, 1972), 363.

2. *Summa theologiae*, Ia, q. 8, art. 3.

Chapter 13 Announcing the Lordship of Jesus Christ

1. Edward Schillebeeckx, *Jesus: An Experiment in Christology*, trans. Hubert Hoskins (New York: Seabury, 1979), 346.

2. Roger Haight, *Jesus: Symbol of God* (Maryknoll, NY: Orbis, 2013), 145.

3. Ibid., 146.

4. See N.T. Wright, *The Resurrection of the Son of God* (Minneapolis: Fortress, 2003), 93ff.

5. See Servais Pinckaers, OP, *Morality: The Catholic View*, trans. Michael Sherwin (South Bend, IN: St. Augustine's Press, 2001).

6. Bruce Marshall, *Trinity and Truth* (Cambridge: Cambridge University Press, 2000).

7. John Henry Newman, *An Essay on the Development of Christian Doctrine* (Westminster, MD: Christian Classics, 1968), 185–89.

Chapter 14 From Correlation to Assimilation

1. John Milbank, *Theology and Social Theory: Beyond Secular Reason* (Oxford: Blackwell, 1990), 1.

2. See Karl Barth, *The Humanity of God* (Atlanta: John Knox, 1960), 23–24.

3. See Robert Barron, *Bridging the Great Divide: Musings of a Post-Liberal, Post-Conservative, Evangelical Catholic* (Lanham, MD: Rowman and Littlefield, 2004), 16–18.

4. Friedrich Schleiermacher, *The Christian Faith*, in *Friedrich Schleiermacher: Pioneer of Modern Theology* (Minneapolis: Fortress, 1991), 99–100.

5. See Rudolf Otto, *The Idea of the Holy*, trans. John W. Harvey (London: Oxford University Press, 1958); Paul Tillich, *Systematic Theology* (Chicago: University of Chicago Press, 1967), 1:8–12; Karl Rahner, *Foundations of Christian Faith: An Introduction to the Idea of Christianity* (New York: Crossroad, 1984), 44–50; David Tracy, *The Analogical Imagination: Christian Theology and the Culture of Pluralism* (New York: Crossroad, 1981), 160–61.

6. Bruce Marshall, *Trinity and Truth* (Cambridge: Cambridge University Press, 2000), 4–5.

7. Ibid., 108–9.

8. John Henry Newman, *Biglietto Speech*, as quoted in Ian Ker, *John Henry Newman: A Biography* (Oxford: Oxford University Press, 1988), 720.

9. John Henry Newman, *An Essay on the Development of Christian Doctrine* (Westminster, MD: Christian Classics, 1968), 185–89.

10. Barron, *Bridging the Great Divide*, 62.

11. Robert Kraynak, *Christian Faith and Modern Democracy: God and Politics in the Fallen World* (Notre Dame, IN: University of Notre Dame Press, 2001), 26–27.

12. Casey v. Planned Parenthood of Southeastern Pennsylvania, 112 Sup. Ct. 2791 at 2807.

13. Servais Pinckaers, *The Sources of Christian Ethics* (Washington, DC: Catholic University of America Press, 1995), 375.

14. See especially the encyclical letter *Veritatis splendor*.

15. Stanley Hauerwas, *After Christendom?* (Nashville: Abingdon, 1991), 70–88.

16. See Milbank, *Theology and Social Theory*, 380–92.

17. N. T. Wright, *Jesus and the Victory of God* (Minneapolis: Fortress, 1996), 203–4.

18. John Courtney Murray, *We Hold These Truths: Catholic Reflections on the American Proposition* (Kansas City: Sheed and Ward, 1960), 56–57.

19. Jeffrey Stout, *Democracy and Tradition* (Princeton: Princeton University Press, 2004), 129.

20. Ibid., 69–70.

21. Martin Luther King Jr., "Letter from Birmingham City Jail," in *A Testament of Hope: The Essential Writings of Martin Luther King Jr.* (New York: Harper & Row, 1986), 293.

Chapter 15 To Evangelize the Culture

1. See Søren Kierkegaard, *Purity of Heart Is to Will One Thing*, trans. George Pattison (San Francisco: HarperOne, 2008).

Index

Abel, 14–15
abortion, 183, 209
Abraham, 114, 123, 146, 157, 164
academic freedom, 76
accident, 9–10, 141–42, 170
accommodation, 13, 16, 97, 125
Adam, 59, 114, 115, 161, 193
aesthetics, 230
agency, 26–27
agnosticism, 20
Alison, James, 36
allegory, 115, 117, 122
Ambrose of Milan, 71–72, 168
American culture, 207–11
anakephalaiosis, 54–55, 114
analogy, 21, 36, 116, 179
Anderson, Gary, 109
"angelism," 82, 85, 99
animism, 225
Anselm of Canterbury, 10, 34, 39, 47, 66, 161
anthropology, 100–101, 147, 148–49, 191
anti-foundationalism, 96–99
anti-theism, xi
anti-traditionalism, 105
apologetics, 29, 92
Arianism, 65, 91, 124
Aristotle, 11, 24, 35, 48, 53, 148, 178, 184, 214
arts, 229–30
assent, 85, 92, 98
assimilation, 202, 207
astronomy, 226
Athanasius, 91
atheism, 17–29, 68, 230

atonement, 165
attentiveness, 176–77
Augustine
    vs. Arians, 8–12
    epistemology of, 37
    ethics of, 39–40
    on Eucharist, 168
    on God, 3, 46, 111, 114
    vs. Manichees and Platonists, 4–8
    vs. Romans, 12–16, 150, 211
    on tradition, 91
Austin, J. L., 171
authorial intention, 109, 113, 118, 120–21, 124–25
authoritarianism, 89
authority, 88–91, 106–7, 170, 228–29
autonomy, 41, 43, 67–68
Avicenna, 24

Balthasar, Hans Urs von, 32, 36, 51, 63, 81, 97, 126, 152, 157–58, 192, 201, 206, 207
baptism, 141
Barth, Karl, 81, 97, 151–52, 201, 203–4, 206
Bartimaeus, 147–48
Baxter, Michael, 15
beauty, x, 32, 92, 200, 221, 223, 229–30
"beige Catholicism," xv, 204–7
being, 15, 21–22
Benedict XVI. *See* Ratzinger, Joseph
Berakah prayer, 153, 154–55, 156
Berengarius of Tours, 169
Bernard of Clairvaux, 39
Bible. *See* Scripture

biblical criticism, 110
biblical theology, 110–15
Big Bang theory, 226
blasphemy, 218
blood, 141, 165
body, 141
Bonaventure, 39, 47, 76, 102, 177
Book of Kells, 31–32
Brahe, Tycho, 226
Brideshead Revisited, 32, 200
Brown, Raymond E., 120–22, 124, 126
Brueggemann, Walter, 109
Bruno, Giordano, 225
Bultmann, Rudolf, 118, 120
Burrell, David, 22, 34, 66, 175

Cain, 14–15
Calvin, John, 47, 116
Campbell, Joseph, 5
Caputo, John, 3, 107
Carroll, James, 187
Cartesianism, 184
Casey v. Planned Parenthood, 41, 146–47, 209
Catholicism, xiv, 4, 16, 28, 88, 106, 182, 197, 199
causality, 25, 26, 121
ceremonial laws, 135–36
chaos, 70–71
Chesterton, G. K., 22, 32, 214
Childs, Brevard, 109
choice, 209
Christology, 119, 191
Chrysostom, John, 168
church
    authority of, 88–91
    as indispensable, 196–200
City of God (Augustine), 12–13, 15–16, 150, 211
civil disobedience, 215
civil religion, 15
coinherence, 31–43, 71, 157, 226–27
commission, 157–58, 220
common good, 133, 209
common sense, 227
communio, 11, 14, 149–50, 157, 197
communion, 164–65
Communism, 16, 195
community, 103, 157
complacency, 149
condescension, 33, 47, 55
Confessions, The (Augustine), 4–5, 8, 200
Congar, Yves, 91
conquest, 13–14

conversation, 104
conversion, 176, 203
Copernicus, Nicolaus, 226
correlation, xiv, 12–13, 16, 201, 202, 205
corruption, 103, 197
Coumo, Mario, 214
Council of Chalcedon (451), 33, 65, 124, 140, 194, 224
Council of Constantinople (681), 41–42
Council of Ephesus (431), 192
Council of Nicaea (325), 8
Council of Trent (1545–63), 91, 170
covenant, 114, 164–65, 222
Coyne, George, 226
creation
    doctrine of, 111–12, 226
    and equality, 228
    from nothing, 22–24, 35–36, 48–50, 58, 69–71, 111, 229
    and sense of self, 153–54
    Thomas Aquinas on, 22–25
creativity, x–xi
Crossan, John Dominic, 191–92
crucifixion, 196
cultural-linguistic model, 151–52
culture, x, 29, 75, 207–11, 219
Curran, Charles, 87

Daniélou, Jean, 126
David, 114, 165
Dawkins, Richard, 18–19
Day, Dorothy, xiv, 183
Day of Atonement, 165
decision, 180–82
Declaration of Independence, 227–28
Dei filius, 122
Deism, 6–7, 15, 68, 116, 118, 228
Dei verbum, 122–26
de Lubac, Henri, xi, 100, 101, 126, 216
Dennett, Daniel, 18
Derrida, Jacques, 107
Descartes, René, 28, 38, 85, 86, 96, 97, 105, 184, 225, 226
desire, 42, 212
destabilization, 103
De Trinitate (Augustine), 8–9
devil, 72, 73
dialogue, 53
Dignitatis humanae, 213
dignity, xi, 77, 195, 212, 228
discernment, 179, 180–82
discipline, 148

diversity, 55, 90
divine agency, 27
divine otherness, 21, 24, 26, 34, 66, 111–12
divine providence, 50–52
divine simplicity, 9, 20–22, 23, 49
Divino afflante spiritu (Pius XII), 122
doctrine, 90–91, 151
Dominicans, 67
doubt, 38, 82, 85, 97
Dulles, Avery, 79–93
Duns Scotus, John, 15, 27–28, 40, 116, 208
Dupré, Louis, 36

Eagleton, Terry, 18
ecclesiology, 90, 197
Eckhart, Meister, 24
education, 148
ego, 146
Einstein, Albert, 70
election, 114
Elijah, 59, 155, 183
emotion, 83
Enlightenment, 77, 80, 195, 228
Enoch, 59
epistemology, 27, 37–39, 65, 80–86, 98, 184
equality, 227
eschaton, 188
essence, 21–22
eternal law, 133, 213, 215
ethics, 39–43
Eucharist, 131–32
    and evangelization, 199–200
    real presence of, 167–71
    as sacrament of New Law, 139–43
    as sacred banquet, 160–63
    sacrifice in, 136, 163–67
evangelization, 93, 185, 186, 199–200
Eve, 114, 161, 193
evidentialism, 99
evil, 4–8
excellence, 76, 194–95, 208, 209–10
exegesis, 109, 121, 125, 126
existence, 21–22, 36–37
existentialism, 194
ex nihilo, 22–24, 35–36, 48–50, 58, 69–71, 111, 154, 229
experience, 205, 206
exterior worship, 135

failure, x
fall, 210
false humility, 203, 211

fascism, 195
Feuerbach, Ludwig, xi, 17, 28, 40–41, 68
forgiveness, 166–67
formal inference, 98–99
Foucault, 81, 82
foundationalism, 83, 96–99
Francis of Assisi, 71
Franklin, Benjamin, 7
Franzelin, Johann Baptist, 91
freedom
    as choice, 194, 209
    cross as, 196
    divine vs. human, 42, 67–69
    vs. existence of God, 20, 40
    vs. truth, 164, 193, 194, 210
free will, 6, 27
Frei, Hans, 151
Freud, Sigmund, 68
friendship, 134, 139–40, 143, 149, 193
fruit of the Spirit, 181–82
fundamentalism, 225, 226

Gadamer, Hans-Georg, 76, 81, 104
Galileo, 226
garden of Eden, 193
Gilson, Etienne, 22
Girard, René, 73
Gloria in excelsis, 149–50, 162
glorification, 141
Gnosticism, 45, 46, 50, 51, 52, 111, 115
God
    accommodation of, 125
    as artist, 229
    being of, 220
    as creator, 102, 111
    existence of, 19, 47
    friendship with, 134
    godliness of, 7
    as love, 15, 147
    nature of, 222
    otherness of, 21, 24, 26, 34, 66, 111–12
    perfection of, 5–6
    personhood of, 56–57
    presence of, 177
    self-sufficiency of, 34, 45–46
    as truth, 221
    unity of, 152
"god of the gaps," 19, 27
goodness, 149, 221, 222–23
gospel, 137–39
Gould, Stephen Jay, 18–19
government, 12, 208, 215

grace, 43, 134, 138–39, 142, 156, 199
Gregory Thaumaturgus, 39, 198
Grisez, Germain, 141

Habermas, Jürgen, 104, 214
Hadot, Pierre, 198
Haight, Roger, 186
happiness, 133, 148, 196, 208, 212
harmony, 54, 223
Harnack, Adolf von, 118–19
Harris, Sam, 18
Hauerwas, Stanley, 15, 75, 210
heaven, ix, 143
Hegel, Georg Wilhelm Friedrich, 24, 114, 214
heresy, 8
hermeneutics, 221
heteronomy, 43
hierarchy, 198
historical criticism, 109, 120
history, 116, 123
Hitchens, Christopher, 18, 20
Hitler, Adolf, 195
Hobbes, Thomas, 12, 40, 149–50, 208–9, 212
Hodgson, Peter, 70, 225–26
holocaust, 137
Holy Spirit, 112, 118, 123, 137–38, 181
Hopkins, Gerard Manley, 35
Humanae vitae, 87
human freedom, 20, 27, 28, 41, 67–69
humanism, 37, 67–69, 193, 194
human nature, 124
human rights, 212
human weakness, 148
Hume, David, 80, 85, 96, 118
humility, 138
Husserl, Edmund, 86, 105
Hypatia, 225
hypotheses, 180

idolatry, 17–18, 136
Ignatius of Loyola, 176
"illative sense," 84, 92, 99
image of God, xi, 49
immanence, 7
immersion, 151, 179
immutability, 47
incarnation, x, 8, 32, 64–65, 112, 140, 194, 197
indifference, 69, 177, 194, 196, 209–10
individualism, 103, 209
infallibility, 89, 106
informal inference, 84, 98–99
injustice, 51

Inklings, 32
inspiration, 124, 134
intellect, 39
intelligence, 177–79
"intelligent design," 19, 70
intelligibility, 48–49
intentionality, 52, 115
interior worship, 135
interpretation, 116–22, 221
intertestamental period, 114
intimacy, 169
invisibility, 56–57
Irenaeus of Lyons, 28, 45–59, 69, 91, 110–15,
    161, 168
Isaac, 164
Isaiah, 66–67, 157, 162

Jaki, Stanley, 70
Jefferson, Thomas, 11–12, 28, 118, 191, 205,
    208, 212, 227–28
Jesuits, 67
Jesus Christ
    divinity of, 65, 124, 189–92, 218
    in the Eucharist, 139–43
    lordship of, 185, 195, 219
    ministry of, 162–63
    mission of, 72–75
    natures of, 194, 224
    as new Adam, 59, 114–15
    personhood of, 157–58
    resurrection of, 186–89
    sacrifice of, 166–67
    as truth, 221
    will of, 41–42, 67
Jesus Seminar, 191–92
John of the Cross, 18
John Paul II, x, 16, 43, 160, 161, 181, 195, 199,
    210, 212–13, 220
John XXIII, 90, 207
Jowett, Benjamin, 118
joy, 43
Joyce, James, 229
Judaism, 119
judgment, 181, 184
justice, 13, 134, 222–23, 227–29
Justin Martyr, 49, 57, 204

Kant, Immanuel, 11, 67–68, 76, 96, 103, 118,
    146, 191–92
Kepler, Johannes, 226
Kierkegaard, Søren, 114, 223, 224
King, Martin Luther, Jr., 16, 181, 213–14, 215

Kleutgen, Joseph, 91
knowing, 39, 85
Kraynak, Robert, 209
Kugel, James, 114, 117
Kyrie eleison, 147–49
Kyrios, 75, 218–19

Lainez, Diego, 91
Lamb, Matthew, 175
language, 151, 171
Laplace, Pierre-Simon, 18
Lash, Nicholas, 121–22
law
  as eternal, 133, 213, 215, 228
  and modernity, 43
  nature of, 132–34
  as New, 132, 137–39, 143
  as Old, 134–37, 139–40, 222
  of Rome, 13
  telos of, 142
laziness, 177
Leibniz, Gottfried Wilhelm von, 7, 11, 28
Lemaître, Georges, 226
Leo XIII, 122
Lessing, Gotthold Ephraim, 118
Levenson, Jon, 118
Levering, Matthew, 55, 121
Levinas, Emmanuel, 146
Lewis, C. S., 32, 190, 191, 218
liberalism, 87, 96, 118, 119, 151, 191–93, 201, 205
liberation theology, 101
liberty, 69, 138, 193, 196, 210
Lincoln, Abraham, 213–14
Lindbeck, George, 81, 82, 151
literalism, 168
literary analysis, 120
literary genre, 125
liturgy, xiv, 126–27, 145–58
Locke, John, 12, 40, 80, 83, 96, 149–50, 208, 212
Logos, 56–57, 65
Lonergan, Bernard, 38, 86, 104, 175–84, 222
love, 25, 35, 50, 71, 77, 147, 149, 157, 224
Lucas, George, 5
Luther, Martin, 86, 103, 105, 116, 140, 197, 204

MacIntyre, Alasdair, 36
magisterium, 86–91
Maher, Bill, 225
Manichaeism, 4–8, 198
Marcionism, 118–19, 120
Marion, Jean-Luc, 57

Maritain, Jacques, 82, 99, 103, 223
marriage, 222
Marshall, Bruce, 201
Martin, Francis, 109
martyrdom, 188
Marx, Karl, 40–41, 68, 214
Marxism, 195
Mary (mother of Jesus), 16
Maurin, Peter, xiv
McCabe, Herbert, 17, 28, 34
McCarthy, Mary, 167
meaning, 121
Mendel, Gregor, 226
Merton, Thomas, 22, 24, 36
metanarrative, 102
metaphysics, 11, 34–37, 53, 156
method, 176
Metz, Johann Baptist, 101
Milbank, John, 15, 24, 36, 99–103, 203
mind, 39, 176, 183
miracles, 120
mission, 157–58
modernity, 40, 43, 55, 69, 95, 126, 151, 195
modus significandi, 9, 20
monophysitism, 33, 124
monotheism, 152–53, 190
monothelitism, 67
Moses, 22, 66, 114, 123, 157, 164–65, 183
Moyers, Bill, 5
Murray, John Courtney, 91, 213
music, 11, 54, 113–14
mysticism, 116, 205, 225

Napoleon, 18
natural law, 133
natural reason, 37
neo-Kantianism, 191
neo-Marcionism, 118
neo-scholasticism, 100
Nestorianism, 33, 65, 124, 192
Neuhaus, Richard John, 210
New Age, 5
new atheism, 18–29
new covenant, 165, 167
New Law, 132, 137–39, 143
Newman, John Henry, 16, 38, 51, 76–77, 79–93, 197, 199, 202, 206–7, 211
Newton, Isaac, 7, 226
Nicene Creed, 152
Nicholas of Cusa, 8, 21, 34, 112, 154
Nietzsche, Friedrich, xi, 18, 40–41, 147
Noah, 230

nominalism, 116, 150, 208
noncompetitiveness, 25–26, 33–34, 65–67, 112–13
nonviolence, 14, 24, 36
Novak, Michael, 175
Nussbaum, Martha, 83

obligation, 43
O'Connor, Flannery, 148–49, 167
offertory, 153–55
Old Law, 134–37, 139–40
ontology, 11, 15, 116, 230
open table fellowship, 73, 163
opposition, 72–75, 106
opulence, 46
order, 208
Origen of Alexandria, 39, 91, 168, 198
original sin, 59, 162, 214–15
orthodoxy, 9
otherness, of God, 21, 24, 26, 34, 66, 111–12
Otto, Rudolf, 205
Oxford Movement, 199

paganism, 14
panentheism, 5
Pannenberg, Wolfhart, 189
pantheism, 117, 225
parable, 21, 155
paradox, 34, 65, 148, 194
participation, 113, 115, 116–17, 123, 172
Pascal, Blaise, 83, 85, 226
paschal mystery, 72–75
passivity, 146–47
Passover, 163, 169
patterns, 177–79
Paul, 7, 69, 75, 89, 135, 146, 183, 197, 219
peace, 14, 75, 167, 208
peace-offering, 137
penitence, 137
perfectibility, 148–49
perfection, 47–48
personhood, 10, 52–53, 56–57, 157–58
Peter, 219
philology, 120
Philo of Alexandria, 49, 111
philosophy, 198
physics, 226
Picasso, Pablo, 179
Pickstock, Catherine, 100
Pinckaers, Servais, 68–69, 76, 194, 209
Pius XII, 122
Placher, William, 96, 97
Plato, 24, 35, 38, 39, 48, 50, 52, 148, 214

Platonists, 6–8
Plotinus, 6, 7
pluralism, 213–14
plurality, 52
poetry, ix
Polanyi, Michael, 81, 82, 83
politics, 12
Polkinghorne, John, 38, 70, 226
Polycarp of Smyrna, 113
Pontifical Council for Culture, xi
Pontius Pilate, 74
Porphyry, 6
postmodernism, 95
postmodernity, 107
pragmatism, 16
prayer, 176–77
preexisting matter, 49, 154
prejudice, 81
presumptions, 85
privacy, 209
privatization, 210–11, 213, 231
problem of evil, 4–8
process theology, 51
property, 212
Protestantism, 79, 86, 87, 105, 197, 204
providence, 50–52, 113
Providentissimus Deus (Leo XII), 122
pseudo-Dionysius, 42

quantum theory, 226

radiance, 223
radical humanism, 67–69
Radical Orthodoxy, 36, 99–100
Rahner, Karl, 39, 91, 96, 100, 101, 119, 191, 192, 201, 205
rationalism, 80–81, 195
Ratzinger, Joseph, 11, 52–53, 70, 109, 110, 126, 153, 170, 207
Rawls, John, 214
reason, 37, 85, 92, 205
recapitulation, 54, 55, 114–15, 163
redaction criticism, 120
reductionism, 191
Reginald of Piperno, 131, 169
regula fidei, 110–15, 123
Reimarus, Hermann Samuel, 118
reincarnation, 187
relationality, 11, 53, 58–59, 71, 157
relativism, 88–89, 97, 209
relativity, 57–59
religion, 13

Remus, 13–14
responsibility, 182–84
res significata, 9, 20
ressourcement, 126
resurrection, 74–75, 77, 186–89, 217
revelation, 123
Ricoeur, Paul, 104
Rilke, Rainer Maria, ix
Roe v. Wade, 209
Romero, Oscar, 181
Romulus, 13–14
rule of faith, 110–15
Russell, Bertrand, 19

sacraments, 138–39, 199
sacrifice, 136, 139, 156, 163–67
Sacrosanctum concilium, xiv, 126
Salmeron, Alfonso, 91
salvation, 197
sanctification, 136
Sartre, Jean-Paul, 18, 20, 28, 41, 68, 146, 147, 194
scapegoating, 73–74
Schillebeeckx, Edward, 186
Schleiermacher, Friedrich, xv, 5, 96, 97, 100, 118, 120, 191, 193, 200–201, 203–4, 205
scholasticism, 81, 229
science, xi, 70, 76, 103, 225–26
Scripture, 87–88, 109–27
secondary causality, 121
sectarianism, 215–16
secularism, 7, 195
self, 152
    creation of, 59
    love of, 13
    nature of, 145
    preservation of, 208
sending, 157–58
sense experience, 96, 97, 98
September, 11, 29, 77, 204
shalom, 75, 77, 167
Shema, 152–53
Sheol, 187, 188
sign of the cross, 146–47
simplicity, of God, 9, 20–22, 23, 49
sin, 58–59, 148, 162, 196, 214–15
sin-offering, 137
skepticism, 82
Sokolowski, Robert, 111, 112, 225
sola scriptura, 87
soul, 188
space, 23
speculation, 88–89

speech, 53
Spinoza, Baruch, 5, 117–18, 125
spirituality, 63–64
Star Wars, 5
Stoicism, 5
Stout, Jeffrey, 213
Strauss, Leo, 118
subjectivity, 41, 86
substance, 9–10, 71, 141–42, 170
suffering, x, 4, 51
suffering servant, 165–67
Summa theologiae (Aquinas), 20, 40, 42, 115, 132–33, 169, 179
supernatural, 100–101, 191
"super-saint," 192
Syllabus of Errors, 80–81
syllogism, 83–84, 98–99
symbol, 167, 169
systematic doubt, 82, 85

Tanner, Kathryn, 21, 34, 66, 111–12
Tanner, Norman, 125
technology, xi
Teilhard de Chardin, Pierre, 114
telos, 142, 143
temple, 231
Tertullian, 91, 204
theology
    and exegesis, 121
    vs. magisterium, 86–91
    and spirituality, 63
    as university discipline, 76, 101–2
theonomy, 41
Thomas Aquinas, xi, xiv, 10
    on being of God, 15, 36, 66, 177
    on creation, 154
    creator God of, 22–25
    on epistemology, 37
    on Eucharist, 169–70
    on existence of God, 19
    on law, 132–39, 228
    on love, 35, 77
    opponents of, 211
    providential God of, 25–27
    on Scripture, 115
    simple God of, 20–22
Tillich, Paul, xiv, 41, 77, 96, 114, 119, 151, 191, 201, 205, 206, 221
time, 23, 55
Tolkien, J. R. R., 32
Torah, 218
totalitarianism, 20, 215, 228

Tracy, David, 89, 104, 105, 119, 175, 205
tradition, 103, 104, 179
transcendence, 7, 21, 34, 65–67, 220
transcendental anthropology, 100–101
transformation, 75, 170
transubstantiation, 141, 169
Trinity, Ratzinger on, 52–53
truth
  and authority, 90, 170
  conversational model of, 103–7
  vs. freedom, 193, 210
  God as, 176, 221
  in love, 77
  and revelation, 133, 134
  universality of, 97
typology, 117

unity, 52, 54, 55, 213
Urban IV, 131

Vatican I, 25, 35, 81, 91, 122, 160–61
Vatican II, xiv, 28, 91, 92–93, 145, 160, 179,
  185, 186, 202, 207, 213

Veritatis splendor, 161
violence, 13–14, 24, 70–71, 150, 196, 204
virtue, 138, 148
Vitruvius, 54
Voltaire, 118

Ward, Graham, 15, 100
Waugh, Evelyn, 32, 200
weakness, 148
Whitehead, Alfred North, 24, 34
wholeness, 223
Wilken, Robert Louis, 35, 109
will, 183, 193
William of Occam, 15, 27–28, 40, 68, 116, 208
Williams, Charles, 32, 71, 226
Williams, Rowan, 100
Wittgenstein, Ludwig, 64, 81, 82, 97, 145, 178,
  222
Wojtyla, Karol, 43. *See also* John Paul II
wonder, 184
words, 171
worship, 135, 143
Wright, N. T., 17, 74, 119, 162, 187, 212